THE ARCHAEOLOGY AND HI

ANCIENT DEAN

AND THE

WYE VALLEY

BRYAN WALTERS

Foreword by Dr. CYRIL HART OBE

For
Mr and Mrs H. Moore
with appreciation
for allowing so much
information about the
prehistory of the Bearse
to be discovered by

and Dean Archaeological Group.

February 1993!

THORNHILL PRESS
Publishers

About the author:
Bryan Walters' experience in archaeology extends
over twenty-five years. He has been a professional
writer for almost as long. He tutored part-time for
the Extra-Mural departments of Birmingham and
Aberystwyth Universities and taught for five years
at a teacher-training college in the West
Midlands. He still teaches archaeology locally.
His M.Phil. thesis researches into 'The Forest of
Dean Iron Industry – 1st to 4th Centuries AD'
have revealed essential new information about
Roman Dean, its iron industry and the
administration of the region.

First published by Thornhill Press (1992)
24, Moorend Road, Cheltenham, Gloucestershire

ISBN 0 946328 42 0

Printed in Great Britain by Ian Allan Printing Ltd,
Coombelands House, Addlestone, Surrey.

Foreword

by Dr.Cyril Hart OBE

My writing of *Archaeology in Dean* (1967) was simply a well-deserved tribute to the late Dr. C. Scott-Garrett: I am not an archaeologist! However, I have found this new book by Bryan Walters to be exceedingly interesting and informative – a well-timed and significant contribution to the archaeology of the region which, from the 11th century, has been known as the Forest of Dean; as well as of its complementary adjacent region, the Lower Wye Valley.

Bryan Walters is worthy of much credit and thanks for making available the enormous amount of relevant archaeological information – based largely on practical work – which has come to light in various ways during the last three decades.

Just a few of the author's assumptions and interpretations may attract some constructive thought-provoking questions – what sound book does not? – but this in no way detracts from a well researched, ably written, and appropriately illustrated treatise. For many years ahead it will be the standard source for study of the archaeology of the two regions. I am pleased to welcome it, and to recommend it to a wide readership.

Chenies,
Coleford,
Gloucestershire.
1 October 1992.

Cyril Hart
HM Senior Verderer of the
Forest of Dean,
President of the Forest of Dean
Local History Society

Author's Notes

My brief from the publishers was to produce a book that covered, as comprehensively as possible, the prehistory and history of Dean and the Wye Valley as revealed by archaeological discoveries and primary historical sources. It had to be written in an approachable and accessible style that would appeal to a wide readership, including local residents and visitors alike, who had an interest or curiosity in the distant past of this unique borders' region. At the same time it must be acceptable to serious researchers: students, historians and archaeologists who would require detailed references of source material. Finally, it must provide a guide for those who would like to explore more intimately, and experience the atmosphere of some of the ancient sites that do not appear in any tourist brochures and yet reward the walker of public footpaths and quiet trackways with breathtaking views, enchanting horizons and haunting groves that excite the imagination.

The lower Wye Valley is not easy to geographically define. For the purpose of this book I have included some relevant archaeological and historical sites that are up to 10km (6 miles) west of the Wye in south Herefordshire and Gwent, and a few miles upstream of Ross-on-Wye.

Again, for the purposes of this book, Dean should be taken to include the whole of west Gloucestershire although parts of it never came within the ancient bounds of the Forest of Dean while parts of south Herefordshire did.

Dates are given in calendar years to avoid confusion. Most dates, especially for the pre-Roman period are prefixed with a c. *(circa)*, implying 'around' or an approximate date.

I have adhered to the traditional terminology of Mesolithic and Neolithic when referring to the hunter/gatherer and early agricultural eras simply because they will be familiar to most readers. Likewise to the Bronze and Iron Ages. No changes in the prehistoric periods were instant. The climatic warming was gradual after the last Ice Age ended some 12,000 years or so ago. Possibly for hundreds of years after agriculture and livestock farming were introduced into Britain many inhabitants would have preferred the semi-nomadic hunter/gatherer lifestyle. Several centuries elapsed before copper-alloy tools and weapons displaced the use of flint and other stone artefacts. Even though the technology that was necessary for the smelting and forging of iron was known, and the resources were certainly available locally, there is as yet no evidence that iron artefacts were common-place in the Dean region until the first century BC.

Although many locally-discovered artefacts are illustrated in this book, it should never be forgotten that archaeology is essentially about revealing the past of people; those who lived and died in Dean and the Wye Valley; people who desired the same basic needs as we do like shelter, warmth, food, drink, clothing, company, care and love. Whoever finds a tiny flint implement on the surface of a field is almost certainly the first person to have touched it in four thousand years, or more. What closer link could there now be with the person who mined the nodule of flint; the people who transported it a hundred miles or so to this side of the Severn; the person who exchanged goods for the flint; the person who used a bone or stone tool to fashion the implement, and the person who used it and finally lost or discarded it? All were temporary possessors, in one form or another, of that tiny artefact. So too is the present-day finder. In reality it rightfully belongs in this region as part of its past. Only the past is certain. Only the past is secure. We have but little time to learn about it.

Bryan Walters,
Forest of Dean, Gloucestershire. 1992.

Acknowledgements

My first acknowledgement must be to my son, Mark who, while at University studying for a B.A.(Hons.) degree in Archaeology, helped to stimulate the revival of interest in local archaeology that has largely filled this book. He is now a widely experienced archaeologist whose frequent companionship on field surveys and excavations has been much appreciated. He has also been a constant source of information. His aerial survey initiative in the drought years of 1989 and 1990 has massively illuminated the past of this region, and all aerial photographs included in this book were taken by Mark.

The unbounded enthusiasm for fieldwalking of Norman Webley and his wife Elsie has revealed scores of important new prehistoric sites north of the A40. Terry James has been a stalwart for many years. His skills have been applied on the south side of the Forest and his contribution to our knowledge of the past there has been considerable. David Hancocks' assiduous researches into early Christian church sites in the lower Monnow Valley have been invaluable. David has generously supplied information and comprehension on the post-Roman period and has allowed me ready access to his extensive library, even permitting me to borrow new books before he himself had read them. Elizabeth Taylor has kept me constantly informed on south Herefordshire sites and has provided essential documentary sources of information. Stephen Clarke, the doyen of Monmouth Archaeology, has never been less than generous with his time, extensive knowledge and archaeological expertise. His friendship is highly valued. Alan Saville, of the Artefact Research Unit, Royal Museum of Scotland, Edinburgh, has patiently viewed, identified and reported on many thousands of prehistoric flints from Dean. His association with Dean Archaeological Group (DAG) is deeply appreciated. Dr.Graham Webster OBE is the President of DAG. His interest in, and frequent visits to this area have stimulated

much research on the Roman period. The time he has generously spent in researching and reporting on some of our Roman finds is gratefully acknowledged. Dr.Cyril Hart OBE is the Dean historian par excellence. For a quarter of a century his 'Archaeology in Dean' (1967) has been a standard reference work. His meticulous and perceptive documentary research is exemplary. I am most grateful to him for reading and commenting on the part of my draft relevant to his expertise and for sharing his vast experience as an author.

Many other people have made important, individual contributions to the compilation of this book. I gratefully acknowledge the assistance of Jill David and Shaaron Robbins in gathering information; Alf Webb, DAG's over-worked secretary, who made available to me his word-processor and who has undertaken extra DAG duties which have provided me with more time for my research; Donald Macer-Wright, Dave Pritchard, Alan Probert, Felicity Taylor, Julia Wilson, John and Joyce Pullinger, Dave Allen, Rocky Price, Mike Hill, Martin Sterry, Keith Burge, Nick Butt, John Bryant, Tony Gill, Richard Jones and his father, Martin Pollard, Gary and Averil Collier, Phil Catherall, Richard Eggl, Brian Johns, Mike Lewis, Tony Liddiart, Robin Malim, Geoff Sindrey, Audrey and Fred Carman, Merle and Leigh Marsden, Brian Milford, Roger Wilkins, Bill and Sheila Williams, Merwyn and Virginia Morgan, Gordon Clissold, and Brian Cave. All, in varied ways, have made significant contributions. The foundation archaeological work of Dr.C.Scott-Garrett and his colleagues in the earlier decades of this century should never be forgotten.

By far the majority of the artefact drawings have been undertaken by Andy Stait, Dave Watkins, Dave Thomas and Carolyn Mortimer. Dave Thomas also produced for me his artistic impression of the High Nash, Coleford Roman temple site. Eric J.Rice, former Principal of Lydney School of Art, went out of his way to produce masterly depictions of difficult-to-photograph sites at very short notice. I am deeply grateful.

My thanks are due to Malcolm Watkins of Gloucester City Museum for his co-operation and for permission to reproduce artefact drawings by Phil Moss and Wayne Laughlin. Acknowledgement is also made to Susan Banks whose drawing of a flint axe from Dean first appeared in the Transactions of the Bristol and Gloucestershire Archaeological Society. My thanks to A.P.Garrod for permission to reproduce his photograph of the Roman road at Mitcheldean. Andrew Helme of Monmouth Museum, and Keith Kissack, its former curator, have always been extremely helpful. Malcolm Atkins, of Gloucester Excavation Unit, for information on recent excavations in Gloucester. Professor Peter Salway and Dr.Henry Cleere proffered valued advice on my M.Phil. thesis concerning iron-working in Dean and the Wye Valley in the Roman period which I have drawn upon considerably for the section of this book relating to the 1st to 4th centuries AD.

Particular mention must be made of the excellent and prompt service provided by the Gloucestershire County Library in obtaining research material, and my specific thanks go to the staff of Lydney and Coleford libraries. My thanks also to the staff of the Wilderness Field Study Centre, Mitcheldean, for access to their library.

Due recognition and sincere thanks are acknowledged to all the many helpful landowners who have allowed local archaeologists access to their lands, and sometimes to conduct an excavation. Without their co-operation this would have been a very slim volume.

Finally I must thank my publishers for commissioning this book, and John Pemberthy in particular for his enthusiastic interest in the archaeology of this region and for his guidance and patience while I was writing this book.

Bryan Walters

Abbreviations

ARCH	Archaeological	MA	'Monmouth Archaeology' (Occ. pub. of MAS)
AS Chron	Anglo-Saxon Chronicles		
BAR	British Archaeological Reports (Oxford)	MAS	Monmouth Archaeological Society
		MS/S	Manuscript/s
BGAS	Bristol and Gloucestershire Arch. Society	NR	'The New Regard' (J. FoD LHS)
		Occ	Occasional
CADW	Welsh Historic Monuments	OE	Old English
Ch	Chapter	op. cit	A further reference to a work already cited
DA	'Dean Archaeology' (Annual publication of DAG)		
		Pers.Comm	Personal Communication (usually written)
DAG	Dean Archaeological Group		
Ed	Edited by	p/pp	Page/pages
FoD	Forest of Dean	PRO	Public Record Office (London)
GADARG	Gloucester & District Arch. Research Group	Proc	Proceedings
		Pub	Publication
GRO	Gloucestershire Record Office	Ref	Reference
HAN	'Herefordshire Archaeological News' (WNFC)	SMR	Sites and Monuments Record
		Soc	Society
HMSO	Her Majesty's Stationery Office	Trans	Transactions
ibid	Another ref. to the previously mentioned authority	Univ	University
		WNFC	Woolhope Naturalists Field Club (Herefs.)
J	Journal of		
LHS	Local History Society of the FoD		

Contents

Part One

Prehistoric Dean and the Wye Valley

The End of the Last Ice Age

Any human who stood on the summit of May Hill around 15,000 years ago, and then cast his eyes northwards through the crystal air and the faceting arctic winds, may just have been able to see far distant peaks standing up like bezels on the rings of shadowy glacial remains.

Beneath his feet icy probes were at work expanding the cracks and fissures of the Silurian coarse sandstone and conglomeratic pebble deposits. Below, the Herefordshire Plain was white with permafrost. To the east many river channels trickled through what is now the Severn Valley. Westwards into Wales, the Black Mountains were glazed white with snow. No trees cast their shadows across the landscape. In fact, our hypothetical human would not have stood there, for there was nothing to hunt; no immediate cave in which he could shelter; no wood with which to fuel a warming fire.

During the next 3,000 years the very earliest precursors of the Forest of Dean gradually emerged, probably in the form of dwarf birch and arctic willow; woody species, but very much a tundra-type flora. Their presence marked the end of the late-glacial period, about 10,000 BC in the chronological record. Yet, insignificant as they were, among mosses and lichens, they represented the return of life to a long-barren region. As the permafrosted ground thawed so rodents and insects returned; so did the birds of prey, the fish-feeding birds, the grazing animals, followed by carnivorous animals, then, inevitably, by man the hunter of them all; the gatherer of the fruits of the renewing earth; the only creature needing fire for warmth, for cooking food and to melt the fat of animals to protect his own vulnerable skin; the only creature that needed to kill to clothe himself (1),(2).

The first hunters of the late-glacial period, made use of the naturally formed caves and rock shelters which are found in the limestone rocks in and around Dean. They belonged to the period referred to by archaeologists as the Late Upper Palaeolithic (the last period of the Old Stone Age). They arrived here by simply following the herds of grazing beasts who moved ever farther northwards as the icy grip relaxed, the days warmed, and the wildwoods spread. They had no need for boats: Britain was not yet an island; just the western tip of the great European continent and still connected to parts of Scandinavia by low-lying plains.

'King Arthur's Cave'

Notable evidence for the earliest hunters was found by the excavators of the so-called 'King Arthur's Cave' on the lower slopes of the Doward, above the 'Seven Sisters Rocks' (3). As with most cave dwellers they occupied the cave entrance and here they constructed their fire hearths. The lower deposits revealed the earliest man-made flint artefacts. It was called the 'Mammoth Layer' by the excavators because in it were found the remains of mammoth, woolly rhino, hyaena, wild ox, giant deer, horse and hare mixed with charcoal fragments from a nearby hearth. They represent the first known animals to have occupied this region in unfossilised form, however, before long, as on the rest of the continent, the mammoth, hyaena and rhinoceros were to become extinct. Not all of the bones were derived from successful human hunting expeditions; the teeth marks of hyaenas are very visible on some of the bones and must

Left:
Frontispiece **Plate 1:** *Excavation at 'King Arthur's Cave' on the Little Doward in the 1870s.*

Plate 2. *Excavation at 'King Arthur's Cave' 1870/71.*

represent their own hunting successes and intermittent solitary occupation of the cave.

Some archaeologists have placed the 'Mammoth Layer' in the Earlier Upper Palaeolithic, not later than 18,000 BC (4), however, immediately above, and overlapping it, according to the excavators, was an occupation layer that was full of charcoal and wood ash and very rich in animal bones, most of the long ones being split lengthways probably for the extraction of the marrow. The faunal remains were now limited to those of horse, deer, ox and hare. Flint implements, although not plentiful, were more diversified and included knife-like blades, scrapers, notched blades and shaped artefacts useful as borers, gravers, awls and chisels.

It was probably during this period of occupation that the Upper Palaeolithic began to merge into what archaeologists term the early Mesolithic (the beginning of the Middle Stone Age). Britain was by then ice-free due to the continued warming. Recognisable trees, such as the pine and birch, featured prominently in the greening landscape. The sea level, although slowly rising, was still low and people were able to walk across, on dry land, what is now the North Sea and the English Channel.

The Boreal Period

By c.8,000 BC Britain was entering what is termed the Boreal period, that is, a climate of warm and dry summers with cold winters. The Severn estuary began to broaden as the seas gradually rose. Marshy areas and water channels formed to the south and east of Britain. Mixed oak woodlands, interspersed with hazel, joined the already-established pine and birch to form, in places, denser woodlands.

During this early Mesolithic period the hunter/gatherers, no longer cave-based except in the colder winters, moved throughout the hills and valleys between the Severn and the Wye, probably in small, family groups, in search of food. Here and there they left clues of their temporary presence which have only been recognised in very recent years due to extensive field-work by members of the Dean Archaeological Group (DAG) and the Monmouth Archaeological Society (MAS).

The surviving evidence is in the form of the flint and chert implements which they used for hunting, timber gathering, and animal and bone preparation. These implements were manufactured from durable stone and are still in excellent condition when ploughed up by modern farming methods. They used other tools and weapons: simple spears of sharpened wooden shafts, and more sophisticated weapons of bone and antler, with neatly cut barbs, suitable as spears or

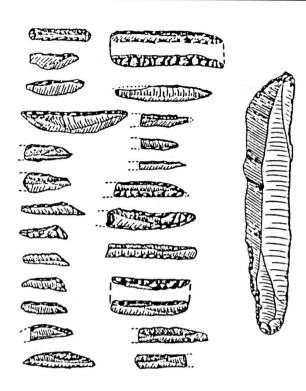

Figure 1. *A selection of flint artefacts retrieved from 'King Arthur's Cave'.*

harpoons, but bone, wood and antler only survive under certain conditions that are rare around Dean, such as peat layers, waterlogged ground, and caves.

Acquisition Of Flint

Here it should be observed that the finding of any flint implements in Dean and the Wye Valley is testimony to ancient trading or exchange. Apart from the yellowed and smoothed, glacially deposited flint pebbles, which are quite common, but found mainly on the river terraces above the Severn, flint-stones are not a natural resource of this area. High quality, easily-worked flint is found in the chalk well east of Dean, more than a hundred miles in fact, yet implements made from quality flint were present in 'King Arthur's Cave' and are to be found on most local, ploughed fields. This flint can only have been traded or bartered into Dean. It is quite possible that the earliest hunters brought flint with them, or else a goodly store of ready-made, or partly-worked artefacts. Loss and breakages would have made eventual replacement a necessity, possibly requiring regular, seasonal, long-distance journeys by some members of the family groups, or maybe trading with other family groups who hunted

closer to the flint sources. Initially, partly-worked nodules may have been easier to transport, or even finished artefacts. One thing is certain: as the hunting groups increased so did the trade in flint. The evidence is to be found on field surfaces where considerable quantities of flint debris are to be found. Here flint nodules were worked on the spot with stone and bone hammers, and the chips, flakes and rejected cores of flint were discarded nearby: proof that flint was being imported in nodular form.

Early Mesolithic Sites c.8000 to c.6000 BC

Not far from the village of Woolaston, and within a few metres of the Severn estuary, a superb example of an early Mesolithic flint core was found in 1988. It measures 10cm (4 inches) long and is around 5cm (2 inches) thick. From it had been extracted eight, long, broad blades for fashioning into artefacts, most of them as long as the core. The flint was of the highest quality. The core was by no means exhausted and therefore must have been lost rather than discarded. So far no other flints have been found in the area as old as the core, so it might reasonably be assumed that it was accidentally lost from a hunter's pack while in transit alongside the Severn. One must remember that the river estuary would not have been as wide as it is today and it was probably lost during the period when Britain was still joined to the continent. This also implies that there ought to be other very early sites which were later engulfed by the rising and tidal waters of the estuary.

6km due north of Woolaston, alongside a stream south west of Bream, a small Mesolithic flint axe/pick, 56mm (2¼ inches) long, was discovered in the same year which may date from the early Mesolithic period. It is worthy of note that the stream flows southwards through the Western Valley to join the Severn between Woolaston and Lydney.

Another stream-side Mesolithic find occurred near Littledean. The stream enters the Severn at Broadoak. This fine core tool, 8cm (3¼ inches) long, was reported on by Alan Saville (5) in 1986. Although possibly of the early Mesolithic period, the implement could not be fully classified due to partial reflaking in antiquity which had obscured any working edge, however it was probably used as an axe-type, heavy woodworking tool which had been hafted in a sleeve of bone, antler or wood.

Both of these 'axes' are of a type that was also used in the later Mesolithic period.

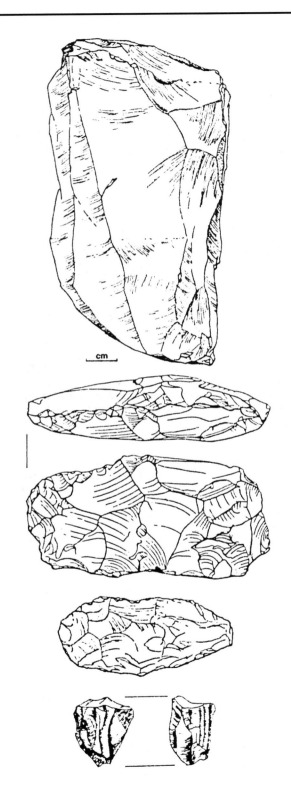

Figure 2. From top: *Early Mesolithic broad-blade flint core from the Severn estuary, Woolaston. Drawn by D.Watkins. Courtesy of T.James. Mesolithic flint axe from near Littledean. Drawn by S.Banks. Courtesy of A.Saville and BGAS. Mesolithic flint axe/pick from near Bream. Drawn by D.Watkins. Courtesy of T.James. Bottom: Compare this tiny late-Mesolithic, narrow-blade flint core from Blaisdon with the earlier one from Woolaston above. Drawn by A.Stait.* Courtesy of N.Webley.

The Oldest Camp-Site In Dean

By far the most important early Mesolithic site to be found in recent years was identified in 1990. It lies in Taynton parish alongside a stream that emanates from the lower slopes of May Hill, just over 2km to the south west, then continues past the site for 5km until it flows into the River Leadon and thence to the Severn near Gloucester. It is at a height of only 40m above OD which means that its flow eastwards is slow, meandering, and fed by several other springs en route.

Around five hundred flints have been gathered from the stream-side area mainly of the earlier Mesolithic, but including some later Mesolithic narrow-blade cores. In all twenty-seven cores and core fragments have come to light along with numerous core rejuvenation flakes. The worked flint must have been obtained from several sources. It included good quality imported flint, flint of a poorer quality of which a number of chunks had been rejected due to internal faults, and glacially-deposited pebbles which had been utilised. One exceptionally rare blade had what is known as a 'Creswellian-type' point which may even pre-date the Mesolithic period. Other artefacts included a selection of scraping, piercing and cutting tools. This is the only known site in west Gloucestershire that is exclusively Mesolithic.

Some time later, perhaps soon after 6000 BC, and probably due to flooding, the later Mesolithic settlers preferred the more elevated position (100m above OD) of Irelands Hill, 750m to the south west, as did subsequent settlers.

Two kilometres south, at the northern tip of Huntley parish, another broad blade core was found along with early Mesolithic broad blade debris, but no worked early implements. The site was still favoured in the later Mesolithic judging by the 750 flints recovered which included narrow blade cores and similar artefacts. It lies alongside a stream on the 60m contour not far from a spring area where the stream originates. It, too, flows eastwards into the Leadon.

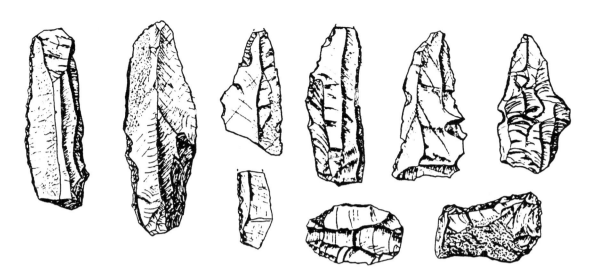

Figure 3. *Early Mesolithic flint and chert implements from a stream-side camp-site near Taynton.* Drawn by A.Stait. Courtesy of N.Webley.

Three kilometres north of the Taynton site there is further evidence for a possible early Mesolithic presence just south of Newent, on Common Fields. Close on 400 flints have been retrieved from the field surface and included over 30 Mesolithic cores, one a broad blade type, broad blade debris, and a very fine point which was used as an arrow-tip. The fields lie 40m above OD and the area must have been visited by hunters on occasions throughout the whole of the Mesolithic period, benefiting from the abundance of streams and springs. More fields to the west of Common Fields contain similar material. One field provided the rare 'pen-knife' point which is illustrated.

A solitary find, almost certainly early Mesolithic, is a retouched broad blade found in Morse Lane, Drybrook. This important implement has, to my knowledge, never been published together with an illustration. At the time of writing it is on loan to the Dean Heritage Museum from Mr. and Mrs.J.Welsh, on whose property it was found.

West of the Wye, near Llanishen in Monmouthshire, there was another isolated find, in 1989, of a 6cm long, broad, pointed blade, retouched along its curved back to blunt it. Similar implements have been found in the Mendip caves, of the late Upper Palaeolithic or early Mesolithic periods. Once again one has to report a nearby stream. The blade is now on display in the National Museum of Wales, Cardiff.

Also west of the Wye isolated finds of probable early Mesolithic flint artefacts have been found by MAS members at Skenfrith, Hadnock and Dixton, the latter two being in easy hunting reach of 'King Arthur's Cave'.

The above find locations represent all that is currently known about the movements of the early Mesolithic hunters during the 4000 year period up to c.6000 BC. It still doesn't amount

Figure 4. Left: *Creswell-type blade from Taynton. Centre: 'Penknife' type point from Newent, both drawn by A.Stait, courtesy of N.Webley. Right: Cheddar-type point from Llanishen. Drawn by A.Saville.* Courtesy of J.Wilson.

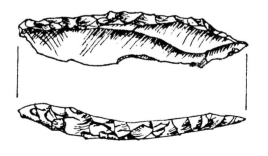

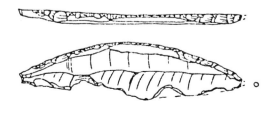

to much, however, it must be borne in mind that until 1986 the only known site was 'King Arthur's Cave'. All the others are open-air sites and have been identified by members of DAG who have walked more than four hundred well-washed ploughed fields since that date, over 90% of which have produced prehistoric flint material, but only 2% of these have so far included flint finds of the early Mesolithic.

Site Identification Problems

There were, logically, fewer hunters around in the early Mesolithic than during the 2000 years of the later Mesolithic. There is, however, another factor to be considered. Much of the debris left by the later hunters was still in the top-soil when the agriculturists took over. Land cultivation may therefore have kept it in the top-soil until modern times. The flint debris of the early hunters may well have been covered with alluvium, humus or wind-blown deposits to a depth that left them secure from early shallow ploughing. Even the deep ploughing that is common nowadays would not reach these deposits unless they lay on shallow bed-rock just 30cm or so below the present ground surface. All the flints retrieved were from thin top-soil where bed-rock fragments are to be observed on the field surface. It may therefore be reasonably conjectured that many temporary, open-air camp-sites of the early Mesolithic are still securely buried. One further factor to be considered is that much of Dean and the Wye Valley is pasture land and woodland, therefore rarely ploughed or disturbed. Such areas are beyond the scope of detection by the usual methods employed in field survey.

Later Mesolithic People c.6000 to c.4000 BC

The Atlantic Epoch

The later Mesolithic period, as it is termed by archaeologists, is distinguished by climatic, vegetational and human artefact developments.

Britain gradually entered the Atlantic epoch characterised by optimum warmth, ultimately two or three degrees C. warmer than it is in Britain now, with plentiful rain. The affect on the landscape was dramatic. The rising seas breached the low-lying land between Britain and the continent making it impossible for hunters to cross without water transport. Likewise, the animals that were here, remained here; some to be hunted to extinction. Woodland proliferated. Elm, lime and alder thrived in the warm, moist

conditions and the Dean woodlands became as dense as they were ever to be, impenetrable in places. Towards the end of the period ash and yew became established (6). Marshy areas became common-place and, in other parts of Britain, peat bogs began to form.

The water barrier of the rising sea and the loss of low-lying hunting grounds probably caused population pressures along the new coast-lines, especially along the Severn estuary in this region. Each family hunting group would have valued a section of the estuary for fishing and the gathering of shell-fish. An area of woodland and scrubland, penetrated by streams, would also have been considered highly desirable. Such prime locations are clearly limited and serious disputes over ancestral hunting 'rights' no doubt occurred with increased frequency, although there is as yet no proof of this in the archaeological record. Expanding family units would have split up, possibly sub-dividing hunting grounds at first, then, later, being obliged to move ever north and west in quest of new, unoccupied, higher ground.

Figure 5. *Later Mesolithic microliths, scrapers and core fragments from Newent. Drawn by A. Stait.* Courtesy of N. Webley.

The great migrating herds of herbivorous mammals, the key to survival for the earliest post-glacial hunters, were no more. Reindeer, and later, elk disappeared from the faunal record. Timid red deer, roe deer and aurochs (wild oxen) grazed woodland glades. Beavers and otters frequented the streams and rivers, red squirrel, marten and polecat welcomed the luxuriant tree cover.

New Hunting Techniques

The hunting groups needed to adapt to these environmental developments. The bow took on a new importance; long bows made from elm and yew with bow-strings of animal sinew. Cores of flint were worked until only 2-3cm (1-1½ inches) remained before they were discarded. The blades extracted were now very narrow, frequently only

Figure 6. *A selection of late Mesolithic microliths and scrapers from Blaisdon, Taynton and Newent. Drawn by A. Stait.* Courtesy of N. Webley.

5mm wide or less, a considerable contrast to the broader 10-15mm wide blades that the early Mesolithic hunters worked into tools. From these short, narrow blades, new shapes were crafted; scalene triangles (tiny triangles of unequal sides), crescent shapes, trapezoids (having four sides but only two of them parallel); slim, rod-like shapes up to 15mm long, and tiny cores which were frequently adapted as scrapers.

Narrow blades, used to tip arrows, were blunted to a point on one end, the opposite end slotting into the arrow shaft to which it was tied and glued with tree resin. One side of the blade was left razor sharp. Triangular shapes were slotted below the tip to act as barbs. Arrows were usually fletched. Plant poisons may well have been used; crushed in a small hollowed stone or perhaps an empty shell, then poured into a slot in the arrow shaft a few centimetres below the tip, sealed in with wax and a trapezoid shaped flint which was knocked away as the arrow entered the large animal, allowing the warmth to melt the wax and release the poison. The poison would work slowly. The hunters would need to follow the weakening animal until it sank to its knees when the final kill would come from spears or axe blows.

The larger animals were never easy to kill. One elk, preserved in a waterlogged pool in Lancashire, had escaped its pursuers even though it carried seventeen wounds inflicted by flint-tipped arrows and axe blows and with a barbed bone point still lodged in the left hind foot (6a).

In the denser forests of the later Mesolithic the problems facing the hunters were much greater; the quarry more easily lost. Among the steep-sided, rocky-sloped, tree-dense valleys of Dean and the Wye Valley the hunted held the advantage.

To increase their chances of success local hunters may well have cleared trees around watering places. This would stimulate the growth of grasses and encourage grazing animals. It would also supply the bow-men with an uninterrupted line of vision. Tree clearance is well attested during Mesolithic times in some parts of Britain through palaeo-botanical analysis of virtually indestructible pollens from moist deposits. No such analyses have yet been made in Dean so we lack the confirmatory evidence.

Open-Air Camp Sites

One thing we can now be certain of is that later Mesolithic communities populated virtually the whole of our region. It was as recent as 1985 before the first camp-site was located near St. Briavels. When Alan Saville edited '*Archaeology in Gloucestershire*', which was published in 1984, he found it impossible to cite any definite Mesolithic finds from Gloucestershire west of the Severn. In 1986, after commenting on the St. Briavels flints, he concluded: 'The above finds now allow the quite categorical assertion that Mesolithic settlement activity did take place, at least in the later Mesolithic, in the Forest of Dean region...' (7). Since then more than fifty sites have been located in west Gloucestershire

Figure 7. *Mesolithic-type long bow.* Artist's impression by D. Watkins.

and across the close borders of south Hereford-shire and Monmouthshire, including the already listed early Mesolithic ones. Not all of these sites can be described as camp-sites. Frequently they are only isolated finds of lost arrow-tips which may have been carried for miles by an injured animal, or may represent a 'miss' by a nomadic hunter.

West of the Wye later Mesolithic finds have been made at Hygga, Llanishen, Troy, Mon-mouth, and Monkton near St.Weonards (8).

East of the Wye, near Ross, single, isolated microliths have been found on Chase Hill, near Brampton Abbotts and at Lea. Further north, at Gamage Farm, Much Marcle, several Mesolithic flints were found in a collection of mainly Neolithic material (9). All of the known major settlement sites, except for 'King Arthur's Cave', are in Dean and west Gloucestershire.

A selection of Mesolithic artefacts is illustrated herein. Their find-sites can be located by con-sulting the distribution map:

Significant Mesolithic Concentrations

Site 1 is 'King Arthur's Cave' on the Doward. The Mesolithic layer is described as 'represent-ing a far more extensive occupation'. This is borne out by both the artefacts and the faunal remains which indicate occupation at times throughout the whole of the period down to c.4000 BC. Giant red deer and reindeer occur only rarely and at the base of the layer, the earli-est of its formative horizons. The later Mesolithic is represented by the remains of: Deer (*cervus elaphus*); pig (*sus scrofa*); horse (*equus caballus*); ox (*bos spp.*); beaver (*castor fiber*); brown bear (*ursus arctos*); wildcat, marten and hedgehog. Domestic animal remains are absent. It should be observed here that hunting dogs were employed by later Mesolithic hunters and the absence of their remains in the Doward cave should not be taken to imply that dogs were not used for hunting around Dean. Most dog remains have occurred on open-air sites else-where in Britain. It has not yet been possible to excavate on any of these sites in Dean.

Site 2 is Nedge Cop, St.Briavels. It is situated on the 600 feet (185m) contour on limestone, immediately north of the steeply sloping gorge through which the Slade Brook flows to the Wye. The gorge is still thickly wooded with stunted sessile oaks through which ancient trackways zig-zag down the precipitous sides to the brook. Sev-eral holes surround the site down which water flows to subterranean passages. They are known locally as 'swallow' or 'swallet' holes. The Mesolithic camp-site lies below the highest point of the field, thus affording protection from west-erly winds. Frequent field surface survey has revealed that it was also popular during subse-quent archaeological periods, for distinctive flint implements of the Neolithic and the Bronze Age are very common. Roman pottery has also been found.

Site 3 is 2km east of Nedge Cop within an area of major importance in all of the prehistoric peri-ods from the later Mesolithic to the later Bronze Age. The fields lie within a triangular area known as The Bearse. Again the underlying geology is limestone with swallow holes and filled-in wet areas. The fields now form an agricultural plateau up to which valleys penetrate in a south-north direction from the Severn estuary. Isolated Mesolithic finds, usually arrow-tips, suggest that these same valleys were the routes followed by the hunters. These, usually singular finds, have been collected from north of Stroat close to the Piccadilly Brook, at Clanna, and north of Alving-ton near Colliers Brook; also in the valleys that run north west from Lydney towards Bream.

Site 4 is on the 350 feet (115m) contour above Plummers Brook, near Oldcroft, north of Lyd-ney. Here the brook flows down a narrow valley towards the Severn. The hunters chose to set up their camp-site on gently sloping ground over-looking the brook and in a position that was well sheltered from winds. Most of the flints recov-ered were of Mesolithic type but some suggested a later presence as well.

The following major sites are either on the north or north east side of the now main area of the Forest of Dean:

Site 5 is on the summit of Huntsham Hill at 472 feet (144m) above OD. The views are impres-sive, overlooking the large loop of the Wye around the Huntsham peninsula and close to Symonds Yat rock. The geology is Upper Old Red Sandstone of the Tintern group. Although there was a strong later Mesolithic presence the site really came into its own in the Neolithic and Bronze Age periods when there was a succession of occupations.

Site 6 is 3km east of Site 5 and is really a series of fields extending northwards from the summit of Hangerbury Hill. To the east the hill falls steeply into the Lydbrook Valley. To the west, where the camp-sites are just below the summit ridge, the land slopes gently down to the Brooks Edge Grove where a stream flows, with intermit-tent descents into swallow holes in the limestone, towards the Wye. From the summit ridge there are extensive views westwards towards the Black

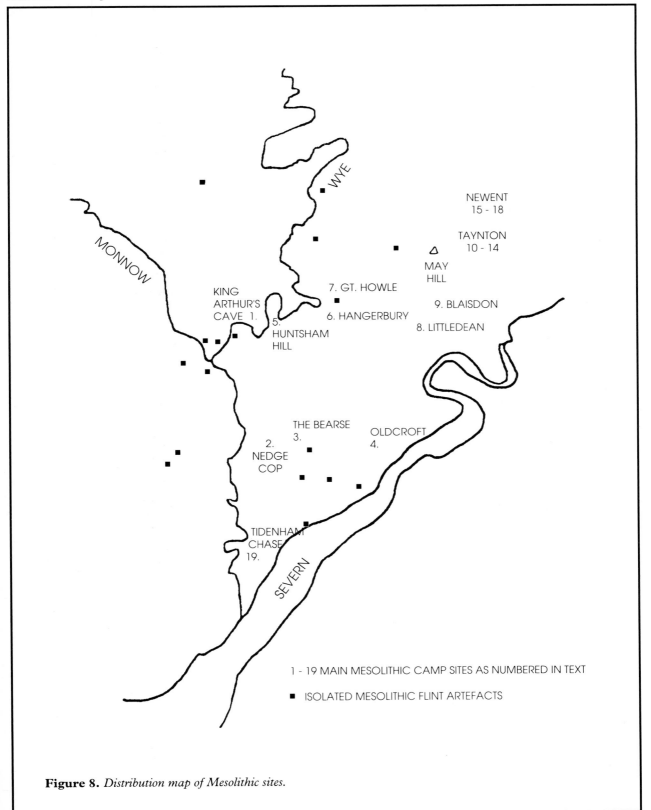

Figure 8. *Distribution map of Mesolithic sites.*

Mountains, and eastwards across a spread of dense woodland. These were important summer camp-sites; too exposed during the winter. They were also favoured during succeeding archaeological periods, in fact the area has received intensive environmental survey and some excavation which has proved human habitation for much of the last 7000 years. There are two distinctly different sites, the one below the summit displaying use of pebble flint while the other, below the ridge and three fields north, has produced evidence for the use of better quality flint and a wider range of tools.

Site 7 is a further 3km north east of Hangerbury Hill and can be seen from its summit. The site, at Great Howle, is around 500 feet (153m) above OD and most of the Mesolithic material is to be found on the Lower Limestones, close to a spring area which feeds the Lodge Grove Brook, which runs east to west, immediately below the site, and from thence into the Wye near Bishopswood. Once again the location was later selected by the Neolithic and Bronze Age peoples, and, in the 1st century AD by a family involved with iron-working.

Site 8 covers a wider area which includes the grounds of Dean Hall, Littledean, Chestnuts Hill to the north, the stream area that proceeds from Chestnuts Hill to the Severn, and St.Anthony's Well which is one of the spring sources for the Westbury Brook. Later Mesolithic microliths and unretouched narrow flint blades, retrieved during excavations on the Dean Hall Roman temple site, confirmed a hunter-gatherer presence there. All of the other nearby locations have produced distinctively Mesolithic material. It is very doubtful that the implements were produced and used by the same family group because we are dealing with a long time span, however, it can be asserted that the spring area at Dean Hall, overlooking a loop of the Severn, was a camp-site and that the surrounding area was hunted. The hill-top is around the 600 feet (183m) contour.

Site 9 is slightly over 3km north east of Dean Hall, at Blaisdon. The Longhope Brook passes the site on its way to the Severn. It is not an elevated site, being only 165 feet (50m) above OD, but it is alongside a logical route from the Severn leading up the Longhope Valley to May Hill. It

Plates 3 and 4. *Rock shelters such as these near Symonds Yat were probably temporary homes for Mesolithic hunters.* Photographs courtesy of M.J.Walters.

was a major camp-site from which were retrieved twelve Mesolithic flint cores, four of them being from glacially deposited flint pebbles, ten flint arrow-tips, and three tiny scraping tools. It was clearly well chosen for its location and resources because, over the next two milennia, the later Neolithic peoples left behind ample evidence of their presence among the more than 800 flints so far discovered.

Sites 10-14 all lie within three square kilometres to the north of Taynton parish, the south of Newent parish and the northern tip of Huntley parish. They include the aforementioned early Mesolithic sites and Irelands Hill could be considered the central point. Within this area forty six fields have so far been surveyed, seven of which have produced flint debris and artefacts of the later Mesolithic period. All lie to the east or south east of Newent Wood and May Hill, and within 3km of both. Discarded flint cores have been found on all seven sites, proof of on-the-spot artefact production. The flint quality is variable. Sometimes the hunters had managed to obtain a goodly supply of quality flint. At other times they had to make-do with more local, poor-quality flint pebbles. Worthy of note here is the occurrence on some of these sites of chunks of tabular chert which was formed in thin layers in certain limestone beds, the nearest, of which I am aware, being some 60km (37 miles) west of Dean, just south of the Brecon Beacons (10). Implements and rejected chunks of Greensand chert, possibly of Somerset origin, have also been found. Chert was recorded during the excavations at 'King Arthur's Cave'.

It is not surprising that the fields south and south west of Newent, which is within 3 km of the above sites, should also have attracted the hunters. To the east and west of, and on Common Fields, there are four definite later Mesolithic flint-knapping sites identified by the discarded narrow-blade-removed cores. Also present are several microlithic arrow-points and barbs as well as the necessary, all-purpose tool, the scraper. One large, angular piece of flint had been used as a strike-a-light, as archaeologists call it. When struck against hard stone or iron pyrites it produced the sparks required to ignite dried twigs and leaves to start a fire. These, usually square-ended, and durable flint implements are often encountered around Dean and easily noticed because of their generous proportions. The four fields may be identified as **Sites 15-18**.

Site 19 is on Tidenham Chase. The Mesolithic evidence came from the earthen material which covered a Bronze Age barrow excavated in 1951

under Dr.C.Scott-Garrett. The soil cover had been gathered from nearby and re-deposited over a stone cairn. The flint material contained five Mesolithic cores, retouched microliths, scrapers and flint debris. Flints collected from the adjacent fields also contained typically Mesolithic material (11 & 12)).

Camp-Fire Talk

The above locations all represent notable Mesolithic encampments where the hunters and their families gathered in the open around fires, prepared their meals, exchanged stories about the ones that got away, exaggerated their size, weight and ferocity, bemoaned the unretrieved favourite arrow, the bow that split, the torn animal skin jacket, sore feet, the inflamed thumb due to a misdirected stone hammer blow, insect bites, and herbal remedies. The women complained about the incessant rain and drying clothes, the wet and smoky firewood, the constant stitching together of skins, the increasing distance they had to travel for berries and hazel nuts. They discussed the merits of various bone needles, pins and combs, and argued over who should have the next boar's teeth. They compared the colours of their shell-beads; why some shell-fish they found, far from rivers, had turned to stone, and the easiest way to pierce them for suspension. They talked about childbirth, worried over ailing infants, explained away the fears of their daughters approaching puberty, initiation, and the strange family of which they would soon be a part. The older men, who had survived thirty winters, recounted the histories of their ancestors, the ways they had travelled, and their heroic exploits in quest of the great beasts that roamed on frozen waters. They talked about the spirits, both good and bad, which to respect; which to fear. They also created new legends about the great flood of water that had separated them from the lands of their forefathers, covering hills and filling valleys, making seas out of pools, channels out of streams and islands out of mountains.

It is not only their indestructible artefacts that remain today. To the truth of their tales was added the embellishments, elaborations, exaggerations and experiences of their future generations. Their descendents were to mix, inter-mix, conquer, be conquered, but the very essence of their existence survived until it could eventually be recorded in writing. Some of our folk lore must have originated with the Mesolithic hunters and their families.

European Innovations

Isolated, as they had now become, the later Mesolithic peoples in Britain were unaware of the revolutionary developments that were slowly spreading across the European continent from east to west. There widespread hunting and gathering for survival on the richer and more fertile lands was, for most, a thing of the past. Territorial boundaries were jealously guarded and fought over as people cultivated cleared land, sowed wheat and barley and enclosed sheep and cattle. They made pottery vessels from which to eat, drink, cook and store their food; made bread from the grain; wove garments from the long hair of the sheep; constructed permanent dwellings and developed new stone tools better suited to the environment in which they now lived. Sometime around 4,500 BC these innovations reached the shores facing southern Britain. It was inevitable that they would eventually be introduced to these islands, but how did it happen and what was to be the effect on the people and the landscape? What is the evidence for change in Dean and the Wye Valley?

Neolithic Farming and Agriculture c.4000 to c.2000 BC

The name Neolithic, meaning The New Stone Age, has been used by archaeologists to define the developments in stone tools that occurred during this period which saw the introduction of deep flint mining, long, slim polished flint axes, axes of polished igneous and metamorphic rocks, and new flaking techniques for a wider range of more generously proportioned artefacts which included flint sickle blades and the much preferred leaf-shaped arrow-head.

Many of these developments were due to the extension of trading and communication networks and the gradual adaptation to a new, more settled community existence based on an agricultural and farming economy which was to support British society for the succeeding five milennia. The period may be identified with a major social transformation in our islands.

It was a very slow but inexorable transformation. Hunter-gatherer communities probably survived for centuries in many parts of Britain, although they may have been obliged to herd deer and cattle with the assistance of neighbouring groups.

Some changes were monumental. By c.4000 BC the first megalithic (large stone) tombs had been constructed in Britain and by c.3600 BC a new, distinctive enclosure form was prevalent in parts of the south, the causewayed enclosure, as it is known to archaeologists, due to the many causewayed entrances between the ditches and banks which surrounded the central, roughly circular area.

In parts of the south, and along the eastern side of England, long, parallel ditches were dug and the soil was thrown up between them to form earthen long barrows under which some of the dead were laid to rest.

Trading Or Colonisation?

Many writers have proposed colonisation of coastline and estuarine lands by continental settlers who brought with them boat-loads of trussed-up animals and sacks of grain, however, caution obliges one to consider other, and perhaps more logical possibilities.

It is probable that before c.4000 BC, some continental farmers' flocks and herds had multiplied to such an extent that they exceeded the grazing capacity. Likewise, grain production might have eventually exceeded personal needs. Continental outlets for surplus livestock and grain may well have been limited. The exchange rate would decrease. Such a situation would encourage the opening up of export markets to a population that lacked their resources and would therefore be willing to offer a higher goods exchange rate for their surplus produce. The nearest such market was only twenty or so miles away across the English Channel from which point a whole, new coastline population was accessible. Boats would be necessary.

Such boats were available to the earliest European and Scandinavian traders. Made from skins on timber frames, they are well attested (13). It has been suggested that one of these open boats, around 9m (30 feet) long, could have carried a total cargo of about 3 tons, equal to a crew of eight, one steersman and three to four cattle (the earliest domestic cattle were smaller than the wild oxen). Alternately the cargo could have been 15 pigs or 25 sheep or goats.

It is hard to believe that colonisation preceded trading. A small group of primary colonists with their small number of sheep or cattle landing in the territory of a hunter/gatherer community with limited resources would just as likely have had their possessions confiscated and their lives taken.

Much more likely is it that continental traders first of all introduced to the coastal people of Britain their sheep and goat-skins, woven garments, pottery, products made from ewe's milk, goat's milk and cow's milk, grain produce or flour, and superior, choice stone tools such as jadeite axes, polished flint tools and beads of colourful pebbles unavailable in Britain. Eventually the richer communities would acquire their own livestock and grain. Grassland would be at a

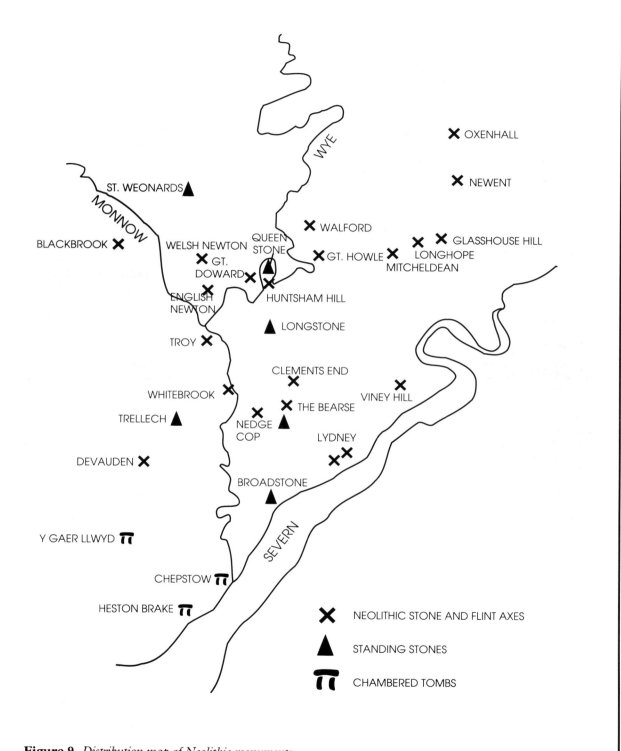

Figure 9. *Distribution map of Neolithic monuments and stone axes.*

Plate 5. *The Longstone alongside the road from Staunton to Berry Hill.* Photograph by M.J.Walters.

premium for grazing. Woodland clearance would be necessary to increase land suitable for cereal production. When these communities produced surplus to their needs, they too would have been in a position to trade on at a high exchange rate, thus becoming wealthier. So, through foreign trading, then internal trading over several centuries, much of Britain, especially where fertile soils were to be found, slowly grew into a society of land-owning families with cultivated and grazed field systems. There is some evidence, as we shall see later, that larger groups of colonists did settle here and may even have introduced the Indo-European language that would eventually be spoken by all people of these islands in one of its several forms.

The Evidence for Neolithic Settlement in Dean and the Wye Valley

Prior to 1985 there was no firm evidence whatsoever for even one single settlement site in this region although there had been a number of isolated finds of leaf-shape arrow-heads and axes of flint and polished stone, all typically Neolithic. Since then the very extensive survey of ploughed fields has produced a mass of concentrated flint debris and artefacts that suggests it will now be hard to find an area of agricultural land around Dean that was not occupied during this period.

It must be stated at the outset that the current evidence is based almost entirely on groups of artefact finds. No excavation has yet taken place on any of these potential settlement sites. Neither can we look to the siting of megalithic long-barrows and chambered tombs as indicators of Neolithic community centres. None have yet been confirmed between the Severn and the Wye, in Dean, although they are common to the east in the Cotswolds, and to the west in South Wales. They are also to be found along the Black Mountains and the Herefordshire borders.

Chambered Tombs And Megaliths

Until 1990 the nearest chambered tomb, which might just be considered as a Wye Valley site, lay 3 miles (5km) south west of Chepstow at Heston Brake, near Portskewett. Little remains of the covering, beneath which is a 4.5 metre long stone passageway which leads into a terminal chamber measuring 3m by 1.5m.

Nine miles (15km) west of Chepstow there are the remains of another ruined megalithic tomb, Y Gaer Llwyd, at Wentwood.

In 1990, right at the foot of the Wye Valley, close to where the Wye enters the Severn estuary and only 1½ miles (2.4km) south of Chepstow two burial mounds were located. The older was a Neolithic chambered tomb with human remains from at least four people and pottery sherds of the late Neolithic period. Next to the main chamber two secondary burials had been inserted at a later date in stone-lined cists, probably during the early Bronze Age around 2,000 BC. One contained skeletons of two adult males in crouched positions, one above the other. Grave goods included a Bronze Age type flint arrow-head with tang and barbs and an all-over corded pottery beaker. The second mound was a typical Bronze Age round barrow type (14).

The fact that these tombs, close to the Wye and the Severn and on the very borders of Dean, had remained unrecognised by archaeologists for so long due to the erosion or removal of their distinctive covering shapes, offers some optimism that Neolithic barrows were constructed within Dean. If so, then the stone chambers lie buried without any visible above-ground features. The places to look for them are where large concentrations of Neolithic artefacts have been recovered, and they are many.

Single monoliths, known as standing stones, have survived somewhat better within and around Dean, east of the Wye. Four are known; only three remain. They are accepted by most archaeologists as belonging to the Neolithic period although they are notoriously difficult to date.

On the present available evidence the local stones seem to have marked trading centres which, at certain times of the year, were probably the focus of ceremonies and festivals.

The 'Broadstone' is close to the Severn estuary in the parish of Tidenham, 750m south east of Stroat. It stands just inside an ancient land boundary. An aerial photograph, taken by Mark Walters for Dean Archaeological Group in September 1989, shows that in the early medieval period the land within the boundary was cultivated as broad ridge and furrow, however, the existence of the stone was respected and the ridges go close to, but not beyond it (15). It is perfectly positioned for a riverside trading point with the adjacent Horse Pill as a landing/mooring place. Surrounding fields have not been ploughed in recent years so it has not been possible to retrieve flint debris.

Between Stroat and Madgett an ancient row of stones used to exist which passed close by the Tidenham Bronze Age barrow, and can still be identified in sections north west of Stroat. The row of stones was later incorporated into the defined boundary of Tidenham and were named in a charter of AD 956 (16). This boundary ended at Horse Pill (17). Although these stones cannot as yet be dated to a specific prehistoric period, or any period earlier than Saxon, it is pertinent to point out here that DAG's aerial photographic survey of 1989 also located below-ground features as crop marks only 175m from the stone row near Sheepcot, which may well represent the robbed stones of a chambered tomb with a passageway leading to the entrance

Figure 10. *The Broadstone by the Severn near Stroat. Artist's impression of the prehistoric setting by Eric. J. Rice.*

Figure 11. *The Queen Stone in the loop of the Wye below Huntsham Hill.* Drawn by Eric J.Rice.

which had two, large, vertically set stones either side of it, also robbed. Nothing is now visible above ground and the site has not yet been excavated, but it is less than one kilometre north of the barrow excavated by Scott-Garrett which was of a type that post-dated Neolithic chambered tombs.

The second standing stone used to stand in 'Longstone Field', part of Closeturf Farm, and 2.5km east of St.Briavels. It was destroyed in 1875/76 by the then tenant farmer as it was considered to be a hindrance to the cultivation of the field (18). This stone stood almost 8km (4⅛ miles) due north of the 'Broadstone' and precisely the same distance from the third standing stone, the Staunton 'Longstone', which is 1km south east of Staunton alongside the Monmouth to Gloucester road. Whereas the Broadstone stands among uncultivated meadows and the Staunton Longstone is surrounded by woodlands, the demolished Longstone was in the midst of regularly ploughed farmland which, with the kind permission of the landowners, has been regularly and thoroughly walked over after

prolonged washing by heavy rain. This fieldwalking has produced convincing evidence that many hundreds of acres surrounding the stone were part of an extensive Neolithic settlement and activity area.

The fourth standing stone is on low-lying ground within a loop of the Wye, below Huntsham Hill, which is adjacent to Symonds Yat Rock. It is known as the 'Queen Stone'. It stands within an agricultural area but accumulated alluvium from flooding means that the plough does not reach the prehistoric levels so no flint material is to be found on the field surface. However, looming over the Huntsham peninsula is the 472 feet (144m) summit of Huntsham Hill which has produced an abundance of evidence for a strong Neolithic presence in the form of a wide variety of artefacts.

Four kilometres west of the Wye, at Trellech, is a group of three stones known as 'Harold's Stones'. Coincidentally they are also 8km due west of the Closeturf 'Longstone' site, but only as a bird could fly for the steep gorge of the Wye intervenes. So does Beacon Hill, one kilometre east of 'Harold's Stones' and 100m higher at 300m (close on 1000 feet) above OD. Members of the Monmouth Archaeological Society have extensively walked the ploughed fields around Trellech and Hygga for many years and have come up with an impressive amount of distinctively Neolithic flint material which dominates an all-period prehistoric assemblage.

Half a mile (750m) south of St.Weonards alongside the Hereford to Monmouth road there is a small monolith in a hedgerow. Only the top one metre of the stone is visible above the accumulated hedgerow soil. It is 29cm (11 inches thick) and two cup-like hollows can be seen on its facing surface just above the soil level.

There is a 'Longstone Field' just south of Monmouth at Troy, but there is no longer a standing stone there. 'Langstone', near Llangarron, may indicate the presence of a standing stone there in former times.

Tools and Trading

Settlement, agriculture and stock-rearing, even in the formative years, meant a need for new tool forms. Grazing and arable land required tracts to be cleared of woodland and scrub. Felled timber would be utilised for homesteads and enclosure fencing. Strong axes became a necessity.

Flint Axes

Axes shaped from flint were not new. As we have seen the hunter/gatherers had used them for thousands of years, however, Neolithic innovations made them much more effective. The shape changed. The preference was for longer, slimmer axes that could be hafted, with a ground and polished chopping edge. The quality of the flint was also consistently better due to the opening of flint mines in the south and south east of England. Shafts were sunk up to 15m (close on 50 feet) deep in order to mine the floorstones which were, potentially, flaw-free and once shaped, less likely to fracture under impact.

The finest example of a polished flint axe from this region was found in 1989 between Bream and St.Briavels only 600 metres from the site of the demolished 'Longstone' on the Bearse, and close to a spring. It survived intact, which is rare, and suggests that it may have been ritually deposited in an ancient pool and was not disturbed by ploughing until the year that it was found. It had originally been all-over polished, but, at some time before deposition had been partly flaked to make it more suitable for hafting. The axe is now regularly exhibited locally by Dean Archaeological Group. This locality, on

present evidence, must be considered the focus of Neolithic religious and trading activity in the Dean uplands. Many thousands of broken and partly-worked flint tools along with flint-knappers' debris have been found on numerous fields. There are many springs, and swallow holes where streams go subterranean in the limestone. It is a well-watered, well-drained agricultural area and is still favoured for cereal crops.

Other complete polished flint axes have been found in the past at Mitcheldean (now in Gloucester City Museum (A.3074), and at

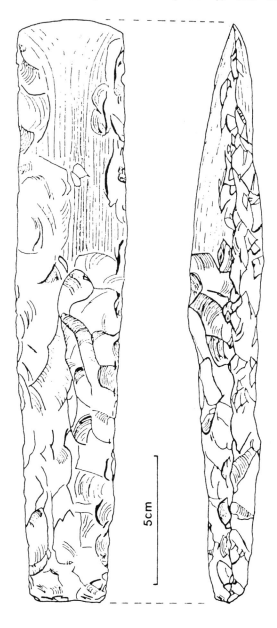

Figure 12. *Neolithic polished flint axe from the Bearse. Drawn by A.Stait.* Courtesy of H.Morse and B.Skidmore.

Figure 13. *Butt of finely flaked Neolithic flint axe from Blackbrook, Monnow Valley. Drawn by T.Darvill.* Courtesy of MAS.

Polished Stone Axes

Flint was not the only stone that was shaped and polished into axes.

More than thirty axe 'factories' are now known, mostly down the western side of Britain where hard, igneous and metamorphic rocks abound. The utilised rocks are generally to be found high on the crags from which they were hewn, then roughly shaped close by, however stones were also selected from scree slopes. Grinding and polishing probably took place elsewhere. These stone axes were traded or gift-exchanged over hundreds of miles. The ones found in Dean and the Wye valley were mostly formed from stone which originated as far apart as the Cornish peninsula and the Langdale hills of the Lake District. The grey stone axes of Graig Llwyd, near Penmaenmawr in North Wales, are often found on the opposite side of Britain along the Yorkshire coast, and in east Anglia. One exceptional, polished stone axe 18cm (7½ inches) long was found on the Great Doward hill just west of the Wye in 1969. Petrological analysis indicated that the nearest source of the stone was Scandinavia. How it got here is unfathomable (20). A Cornish green-stone axe was found at Welsh Newton in 1973 and a grey-stone axe at Tor-y-Mynydd, Devauden in 1968. A Cumbrian stone axe was actually found during excavations of a medieval house on English Newton Common in 1978. It had probably been found locally and placed within the house as protection against the powerful forces of nature, possibly lightning. From

Newent (Gloucester City Museum A.2993). In more recent years members of DAG have found fragments of polished flint axes on field surfaces at Huntsham Hill, Great Howle, Glasshouse Hill on the northern boundary of Huntley parish, Nedge Cop (Bearse Farm), at The Holmes, Lydney and at Park Farm, Lydney. The latter was a large, slim, oval section of axe that had been re-worked round the edges and used later as a knife. The fragments may reasonably be viewed as evidence for tree-felling and timber working close to where they were found and the result of impact damage to the axe.

West of the Wye, and in the Wye valley, field-walking by members of Monmouth Archaeological Society has produced comparable evidence for the use of polished flint axes. The butt end of a broken axe was found at Welsh Newton in 1972. Close to the Wye at Whitebrook a 12cm long axe was found in the same year. Another sizeable fragment of polished axe that had been re-worked was found on Troy Meadow in 1983. Along the Monnow valley a finely-flaked butt (6cm long) of a flint axe was discovered at Blackbrook, Skenfrith, in the same year (19).

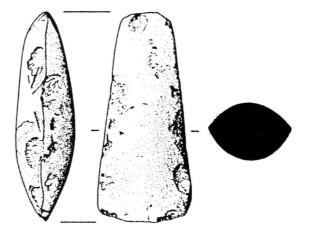

Figure 14. *Neolithic polished stone axe from Oxenhall. Actual size 13.5cm (5¼ inches). Drawn by S.Banks.* Courtesy of A.Saville, D.Bick and GADARG.

Garway came a polished stone adze which could have been used equally well as a carpenter's tool or in agriculture (21).

Within Dean complete polished stone axes have been found at Clements End, Viney Hill, Longhope and Oxenhall, just north of Newent. The former three are now in Gloucester City Museum. The Clements End axe, found in 1952, was of polished green-stone, possibly Cornish. The Viney Hill axe, found in 1955, was given a petrological examination and proved to be another from Cumbria. The Oxenhall axe, which did not derive from a known axe-factory, is 13.5cm long and was found in 1980 (22). Large fragments of polished stone axes have also been found on Huntsham Hill and Glasshouse Hill, both locations also producing fragments of polished flint axes. The most recent find was in

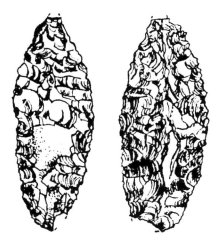

Figure 15. *Finely-worked Neolithic leaf-shaped flint arrowhead from Penallt.* Courtesy of S.Parkinson and MAS.

December 1991 when a polished grey stone axe/adze was discovered on Bulls Hill, Walford. It was 9.7cm long and was found a few paces from a flint knife, although the two may not originally have been associated.

The twenty one find-spots for Neolithic axes in Dean and the Wye valley may not seem many, but they are widespread throughout the region. It must also be borne in mind that most of them were found on ploughed fields and that only around 5% of the land is ploughed regularly within the area under survey, the rest is woodland and pastureland. Perhaps only half of the regularly ploughed areas have so far been walked,

and on these it is only possible to retrieve what is visible on the surface. It has therefore only been possible to investigate about 2% of all the potential find-spots which means that around 1,000 flint and igneous stone axe-using sites may still remain undiscovered.

Fashion Change In Flint Arrow-Heads

By far the commonest of the distinctively Neolithic artefacts to be found in Dean and the Wye valley are flint arrow-heads. Of these the leaf-shaped ones are predominant. Most are up to 2cm (less than one inch) long, finely flaked on both sides and very slim. They bear no resemblance to the pointed arrow-tips preferred in the Mesolithic period, or to the later arrow-shaped ones of the Bronze Age. The leaf-shaped ones have no barbs and rarely a trace of a tang.

Thanks to the widespread field surveys of recent years it can now be said that these arrow-heads are ubiquitous in this region, although thirty years ago only three had been recorded as isolated finds. A field-walker may expect to find either a complete or a broken one on a ploughed field surface just about anywhere. Most are not isolated finds which may have been lost on a hunting expedition but part of an assemblage which includes other artefacts and flint debris of the period. One exceptionally long (5.7cm) and superbly worked example was found at Penallt in 1982. It was intact, which is rare except when deposited in a grave.

Two less common types of Neolithic arrow-heads are also to be found within Wye/Dean. The first is identified by archaeologists as an 'oblique' type. They are usually much larger than the leaf-shaped ones, roughly triangular in shape with one side being longer, acting as a kind of single barb. East of the Wye they have been found at Ruardean, Clanna, Joyford and between Bream and St.Briavels. West of the Wye good examples have been found at Great Crumbland, near Trellech and at Perthyr, Rockfield. Oblique arrow-heads are associated more with the latest phase of the Neolithic period. The other type is termed 'tranchet' which simply means that it has a cutting or chisel-shaped leading edge. It was shot with the flat, sharp edge forwards and is believed to have been specifically used for shooting down birds. This type has only so far been identified in Dean at Blaisdon and on Irelands Hill, Taynton. A selection of locally found Neolithic arrow-heads are illustrated (overleaf).

In summary it may safely be asserted that, by the later Neolithic period between c.3000 and c.2000 BC settlements had gradually evolved and spread throughout Dean and the Wye valley. The focal point of at least the uplands zone appears to have been between

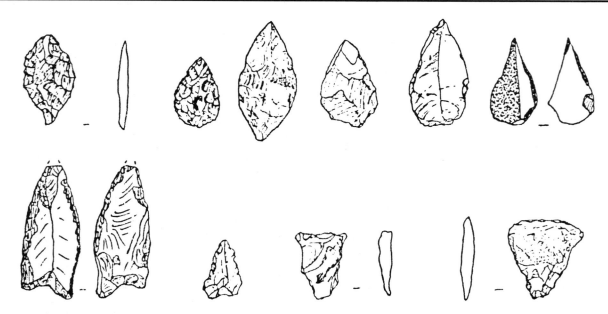

Figure 16. *A selection of Neolithic flint arrowheads from Dean. Top: Leaf-shapes. Bottom left: Oblique arrowhead. Bottom right: 'Tranchet' or chisel-head arrows.* Courtesy of G.Walters, T.James and N.Webley.

Bream and St.Briavels where hundreds of acres are strewn with flint debris. Other very important occupation locations may be found on Huntsham Hill, at Blaisdon, around Littledean, and either side of the ridgeway route between Lydney and Symonds Yat, and the route between Berry Hill and the Wye near Lydbrook which passes through Joyford and English Bicknor. North of the Dean uplands extensive occupation areas are to be found between Huntley and Newent, to the east of May Hill. To the north of Mitcheldean, Far Hill, Linton and Lea have produced a considerable amount of distinctively Neolithic material. In the late 1960s tree clearance, land levelling and subsequent ploughing within the hill fort on Chase Hill, Penyard near Ross, revealed what was described as 'a considerable flint industry. The implements are Neolithic in character and include scrapers, blades, burins and a lozenge (diamond) shaped arrow-head' (23). The large expanse of agricultural land eastwards from Newent towards the Severn is now slowly being surveyed and can be expected to produce a similar pattern of occupation.

Manufacture And Distribution Of Stone Axes

In an area that is devoid of high quality flint one might reasonably ask in what form this flint was traded, and by what means were some stone axes distributed from their source. It has proved easier to determine the origin of some of the rocks from which stone axes were shaped than it has been to identify the specific flint source from which flint artefacts were made.

A distribution study of stone axes was undertaken by W.A.Cummins of the Department of Geology, the University of Nottingham, and was published in 1980 (24). Cummins observed that six distinct petrology groups accounted for almost half of the axes examined. In every part of the country one or other of these six is the most abundant individual group and the distribution pattern suggested three major provincial distribution areas.

Cummins asserted that northern and central parts of England were supplied with axes whose stone originated mainly from Cumbrian 'factories' but which appear to have been distributed from at least one secondary centre on Humberside which is on the opposite side of England. Wales and the border counties formed another province which was dominated by Welsh axes, some originating in north Wales and some from the south west of Wales. Southern England was dominated by Cornish green-stone axes. Dean and the Wye valley lie on the overlapping boundary of these three provinces which is possibly reflected in the variety of petrological sources for the axes found here.

Cummins further observed that the three major axe groups were produced in factories whose output vastly exceeded the local demand. He also pointed out that the largest concentrations of find spots for their axes were far away from the factories: '...the broad distribution of stone axes seems to represent a genuine Neolithic distribution pattern.' There would appear to be principal consumer areas for each group: 'It seems probable that each of the three big factories owed its growth and development to direct contact and bulk 'trade' with major centres of population at a considerable distance from them.'

One interesting fact to emerge from the study was that, although the Penmaenmawr, North Wales factory axes dominated in Wales and the border counties, there were also, apparently, direct trade links to the Derbyshire Peak District. Cummins proposed a coastal and riverine link to this central area. Rivers could certainly provide important links between some population centres. Long-distance trackways could have been necessary links between others, however, the likely use of coastal seaways ought not be underestimated. Great hoards of Danish flint axes have been found in northern Sweden over 1,000km (more than 600 miles) from their source, presumed lost during shipment in the seas which then covered the coastal region where they were found. Stone axes found in Dean and the Wye valley may well have been shipped along coastal routes and up the Bristol Channel from all three major axe factory groups. Some could have been slowly dispersed by means of gift exchange through neighbouring communities.

It should be noted here that there is ongoing research into the manufacture and distribution/dispersion of stone axes, and especially the origins of the stone from which they were shaped. Not all are agreed that they were traded over great distances. As C.Stephen Briggs recently pointed out (25) erratic boulders of Cumbrian stone are to be found in many of the distribution provinces proposed by Cummins and axes could have been shaped from these as well as geologically similar beach pebbles. This may well be a possibility, however, the chippings and other stone-working debris which is abundant around known Cumbrian manufacturing sites has not yet been identified in areas where the erratic boulders occur. As far as Dean and the Wye valley axes are concerned the stone sources are several which suggests distribution and trade rather than local utilisation of erratic boulders. It should also be added that the first thing DAG fieldwalkers are told to familiarise themselves with before walking over a field is the geology. Any stone observed, that geologically should not be there, is retrieved for examination. Had working of 'foreign' stone, other than flint, have taken place on any of the more than four hundred known sites of prehistoric activity then it would surely have been evident by now.

It is thought that some stone axes were roughly shaped before transit, with finishing and polishing taking place elsewhere, but it should not be assumed that this was the usual practice. Polished, partly polished and unpolished axes are known. It has likewise been proposed that flint was moved from the mines as trimmed and prepared nodules, thus reducing weight during transportation. This may well have been the practice in some instances, however, virtually all Dean flint collections contain an enormous amount of worked and unworked flints with the cortex (chalky white external layer) intact. They clearly had not had this layer trimmed away before transit. What might have been removed in order to lessen weight are the lean, mis-shapen ends which often form on flint-stones. A few of these have been found as trimmed-off pieces in Dean, but they are rare. Removing them at source would not only lessen weight but would also reveal the quality and colour of the essential flint. A very fine example, weighing 2kg, of a trimmed nodule was found south of Stonebury Wood, Lydney. Six flint-lean protrusions had been removed, revealing good quality flint and leaving a neat nodule ready for working with much of its cortex intact. An excellent example of a large trimmed-off piece of flint, heavily cortexed, came from Irelands Hill, Taynton, where some flint, at least, was acquired as intact nodules. Such pieces are uncommon.

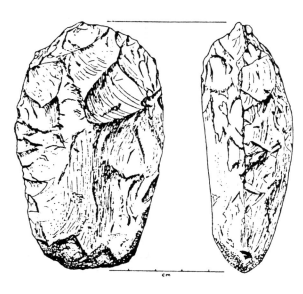

Figure 17. *A polished stone axe from Bull's Hill, Walford. Drawn by A.Stait.* Courtesy of M and V Morgan.

Local Trade Routes

The present local evidence strongly suggests that both flint, in nodular form, and axes of hard stone foreign to Dean were traded in, and that these trade links were established at least five thousand years ago.

Much more research needs to be undertaken before one could propose long-distance trade routes to Dean. Coastal and river routes appear obvious but are still conjectural. Within Dean there is evidence for a ridgeway route from the Severn, near Lydney to the Symonds Yat area. East to west there appears to have been a route which followed ridges and crossed valleys from Mitcheldean via Drybrook, Ruardean, Lower Lydbrook, English Bicknor and Staunton to Monmouth. Sections of this were upgraded by paving in the Roman period. Another followed the ridgeway from Drybrook, past Great Howle towards Ross-on-Wye. Much of the Roman-paved Dean Road may well have served as a pre-historic unpaved trackway. Ancient hollow-ways ascend from the Severn towards the Bearse. The stone row, previously mentioned, if prehistoric, is more likely to have been an ancient boundary than a trade route. It runs from near the Severn towards the Wye near Brockweir. As the Wye was tidal to this point it would be easier to ship upstream on the tide than to trek overland from the Severn. The Broadstone remains the obvious landing place on the Severn shore. Easily identifiable with sheltered, accessible mooring nearby it would have been a logical primary trading post upstream of Chepstow and the Wye.

Downstream of Chepstow and west of the Wye a long-distance trackway has been proposed by David Hancocks from the Severn estuary in the Sudbrook-Portskewett locality running northwards to Monmouth and beyond (pers. comm. with author). It would certainly pass by, or close to, many known sites of Neolithic and Bronze Age activity. It is unthinkable that so many known prehistoric settlements did not have their own communication and trade links. They would have been well-worn, adequately marked trackways, not paved roads, and some of these should still exist as such. Identifying them takes much dedicated research and field survey; a very slow process.

Local Farming And Agriculture

There is at present a disappointingly small amount of excavated archaeological evidence to confirm the extent of farming and agriculture in Dean and the Wye valley. This is entirely due to a general lack of excavation on prehistoric sites, especially in recent years when, due to vastly improved excavation techniques and scientific analysis of remains, much more information would have been retrieved. The excavations at 'King Arthur's Cave' on the Doward revealed sheep bones for the first time in the Neolithic layers, accompanied by a leaf-shape arrow-head. In fact the most abundant faunal remains were the bones of sheep followed by those of pig, deer and ox. An ox bone was recovered from the Heston Brake long barrow. From beneath the Tidenham Bronze Age round barrow, excavated by C.Scott-Garrett (26), portions of the fruits from white-charlock were found, a flower which thrives among corn crops. This may indicate cereal farming either before, or soon after 2,000 BC on Tidenham Chase. Not far away, at Crickley Hill on top of the Cotswold scarp that faces Dean, analysis of carbonised seeds of grain confirm the growing of wheat and barley there during the Neolithic occupation. Quern stones for grinding it into flour were also found during excavations (27). The climate, being warm and stable, throughout most of the Neolithic period would have favoured local farmers.

Much more information may derive from excavations planned by Dean Archaeological Group on suspected prehistoric sites over the next few years.

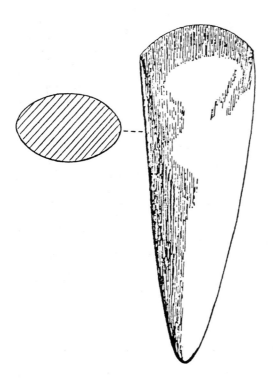

Figure 18. *A polished stone axe from Clement's End. Actual length 24.3cm (10 inches). Drawn by M.D.Craster.* Courtesy of BGAS.

Plate 6. *The Bearse looking north from Roads Farm. This great agricultural expanse was probably first cleared for farming over 5,000 years ago.*

Late Neolithic Developments

Late in the Neolithic period, from c.2500 BC, archaeological evidence from elsewhere in Britain indicates a period of change and development.

Round barrows began to replace the long barrows. Long barrows were sealed up. New pottery styles were preferred culminating in the ubiquitous beaker. Flint arrow-heads with barbs and a tang eventually replaced the leaf-shaped ones and copper artefacts were introduced to Britain. Independent stone circles dotted the landscape and, at the end of the millenium the superhenges dominated parts of southern England, to be abandoned within a century or two until Stonehenge was left as the sole ceremonial centre in Wessex from c.2000 BC.

It is appropriate to observe here that the discovery of 'Iceman', frozen in a 10,000 feet (3,048m) high Alpine glacier, in September 1991 along with his hunting equipment, bow, quiver, arrows, flint knife and a hafted copper axe caused a considerable stir among archaeologists. This was not solely because of the remarkable preservation of body, clothing and artefacts, but because of the several independently undertaken Carbon-14 tests which agreed that the hunter

died c.3300 BC. This indicates a use of copper quite early in the European Neolithic period; much earlier than had previously been postulated. It must now be considered a possibility that some of the copper axes in Britain's museums are maybe centuries older than their labels indicate, and the use of alloys to produce bronze may yet push the beginnings of the Bronze Age back towards the middle of the third millenium BC.

Continuity And Contrast

The family settlements of the earlier Neolithic period apparently became part of larger tribal areas. The earlier authority of lineage may well have been overthrown by the landowners who had developed greater wealth and power and who now ruled by reason of it. This certainly appears to be the pattern in parts of southern England, but what of Dean and the Wye valley?

It has to be said that, on present evidence, the visible developments that took place on Salisbury Plain, throughout Wessex and, for that matter, on the Cotswolds made little impact, if any, on what was taking place in and around Dean. No henge monuments are known here; no large stone circles were constructed. There is not a shred of evidence for the domination of a rich and powerful landowning elite, in fact the opposite appears to be the case. Bronze Age flints are found on all Neolithic flint sites. There seems to be uninterrupted continuity. The only changes apparent are ones of fashion and not politics. Beaker-shaped vessels succeeded later Neolithic types. Barbed and tanged arrow-heads were accepted as the preferred shape. A few round barrows were constructed over an unidentifiable minority while many were laid to rest in simple, stone-lined, unmarked graves. As elsewhere throughout Britain some of the population were not slow to acquire the revolutionary new metal artefacts of, first copper, and later, bronze.

The Bronze Age from c.2000 BC to the 7th Century BC

Death And Burial Customs

Around the middle of the second millenium BC, in the early autumn following a warm dry summer, and the harvest gathered in, a young lady of high status was cremated with her infant child and laid to rest in a stone-lined grave which was sealed in with red clay and capped with flat stones. Another adult, who had also been cremated, was placed nearby in a smaller, separate grave, unsealed but for a lesser cap-stone.

Beside the young mother lay a bronze knife-dagger with two rivet holes to which had been attached a wooden or bone handle, since decayed. Alongside were a bronze pin, a shale pendant with a suspension loop, and three beads made from the fossil stems of sea-lilies, all representative of her status and personal possessions.

Above her grave was placed a 6-feet high cairn of stones. Around this was a circle of random stones and over-all was a bowl-shaped mound of earth and small stones.

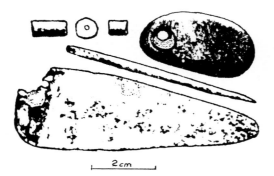

|_____ 2cm _____|

Figure 19. *A young mother's grave goods from Tidenham Chase barrow: Three fossil beads, a shale pendant, a bronze pin and a bronze knife/dagger.* Courtesy of BGAS.

Mixed in with the cremated bones were fragments of the funerary pyre including the fruits of white charlock which grew amongst corn whose straw stubble was probably used to light the pyre of sessile oak wood.

This early Bronze Age round barrow, which was excavated under the direction of Dr.C.Scott-Garrett in 1951/52 (28), was erected high on Tidenham Chase, 1km from the Wye and 2km from the Severn. Some 300m to the south, in dense woodland, are the eroded remains of two more round barrows, of identical dimensions. They are mis-identified on some ordnance survey maps as 'hut circles'. Another possible round barrow lies to the west near Offa's Dyke.

From the earthen cover of the mound and from nearby fields ample evidence was found for occupation during the early and middle periods of the Bronze Age in the form of a pottery fragment from a collared urn (29) and several barbed and tanged flint arrowheads.

Probably the earliest metal artefact from Dean was found on the lower slopes of Irelands Hill in Taynton parish. It is a copper knife, 6.5cm long, which was attached by three rivets to a bone or antler handle. It may just pre-date 2,000 BC. Similar knives are usually associated with burials accompanied by a beaker-shaped pottery vessel and this knife could have been deposited in a grave which was disturbed by recent ploughing (29a).

At Beachley, in Tidenham parish, a probable beaker-period burial was identified in 1964. Within a slab-lined grave was the crouched inhumation of a tall young man. Although no grave goods were found to confirm the dating, the burial is typical of the 'beaker' period in that the knees were drawn up to the chin in a foetal position and the corpse was placed, below ground, in a stone-lined cist (30). No mound or permanent marker covered these graves so there are no visible remains at ground level. The original pit that was dug, before the stone lining was inserted, need only have been around 5 feet (1.5m) square. Unless there were a whole cemetery of these pits they would go un-noticed as crop marks on aerial photographs. It seems likely that countless such burials await discovery close to where surface finds of late Neolithic and early Bronze Age artefacts are recorded, especially groups of barbed and tanged flint arrow-heads and flint knives.

At Coombs Park, Coleford, on the site of a 1980s housing development, a group of two flint knives and a barbed and tanged arrow-head were found by the Hiley family in their garden, which slopes down towards the Thurston Brook. Such a grouping again suggests a disturbed burial of the early Bronze Age.

Figure 20. *Barb and tang arrowheads from Tidenham Chase.*

Another possible site of an eroded round barrow cairn is at Hewelsfield. In his report on the Tidenham Chase barrow excavation Scott-Garrett observed: 'On the north side of the Carpenters' Arms Inn Hewelsfield, close beside the main roadway, is an elevated corner of a field which when ploughed over shows an unusual scatter of stones, roughly circular, which may very well indicate the disseminated cairn of a former barrow...'

Near Eastbach Court, in the parish of English Bicknor, two similar spreads of stone are noticeable from aerial photographs and on the ground. The stones have been re-deposited and include ones not from the immediate vicinity. The same field has produced late Neolithic and early Bronze Age flints including a leaf-shape arrowhead and flints with barbs and tangs. Much Bronze Age flint material is spread over the field, and especially around the suspected barrows.

Near Blakeney, in the parish of Awre, two round barrows, mostly ploughed out, were detected during the 1989 DAG aerial survey by reason of shadow marks from the low, evening sun. The Parish Tithe map of 1840 names neighbouring fields as 'Barrow' fields. Another 'Barrow' field was recorded just north of Blakeney but there are no visible remains in the field. Just south of St.Briavels there is a 'Barrow Hill', again with no visible remains. Neither of these latter two areas are presently ploughed so it is not possible to detect concentrations of stone which may indicate where a burial mound once stood.

During 1990 Brian Johns discovered a low, circular mound partly surrounded by a skirting of stones, set upright, in the Blakeney Hill woodlands. A flint flake was found among the stones. The mound is situated just below the summit ridge with views over the Severn. It is unexcavated and could be another round barrow (31).

For close on 1,000 years in southern Britain round barrows, in their several forms, were favoured as visible markers of where the elite dead were laid to rest. From c.1500 BC their construction began to decline and existing barrows were utilised for secondary burials in the covering mound. By c.1200 BC construction of round barrows had virtually ceased and between c.1100 BC and c.600 BC, during the later Bronze Age, there is little archaeological evidence to indicate how and where the dead were disposed of.

West of the Wye, in south Herefordshire, there are round barrows in the parish of Tretire with Michaelchurch, 7km west of Ross-on-Wye. Close to the parish church of St.Weonards there is another round barrow which was opened in 1855 and revealed two cremations. On the Little Doward in Ganarew, 3km north west of Monmouth and overlooking the Wye, there are remains of three, possibly four round barrows which now lie within a hill-fort and are presumed to be of the early Bronze Age. The first, when recorded, was only 9 inches (22cm) high with a diameter of 21 feet (6.4m). The second was 42 feet (13m) in diameter and 4 feet (1.2m) high with traces of a surrounding ditch. A third was 34 feet (10m) in diameter and 4½ feet (1.4m) high with traces of a surrounding ditch. More recent observation of this barrow has noted a central excavation crater of which nothing is known. A fourth was originally recorded as being

Figure 21. *Barb and tang arrowheads from Great Howle, Eastbach, Newent, Ruardean, the Bearse and Joyford.* Courtesy of N.Webley, T.James and A.Stait.

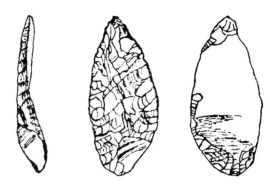

Figure 22. *Bronze Age plano-convex flint knife from Crick barrow.* Courtesy of Arch. Camb.

33 feet by 27 feet and 2½ feet high with traces of a surrounding ditch. This has since been levelled. A fallen tree just within the southern rampart of the fort revealed two skeletons, a male of about 25 years and a female between 18 and 25 years. It was suggested that the rampart construction may have damaged another barrow which at one time would have covered the human remains (32).

A plough-damaged round barrow is recorded at Middle Hendre, Llangattock-Vibon-Avel, the remains of which are 4 feet (1.5m) high, with a diameter of 70 feet (18m) (32a).

Lower down the Wye, near Tintern, three round barrows are recorded in Lower Hale Wood. Two are large, one 50 feet (15.2m) in diameter, the other 80 feet (24.4m) in diameter but very heavily robbed. Both stand 4-5 feet high. The third was recorded as being only 18 inches (44cm) high with a diameter of 30 feet (9m). They are on rising ground 200 feet (61m) above OD (33).

A bell-type round barrow at Crick, close to the Caerwent-Chepstow road was excavated by H.N.Savory (34). It was surrounded by a ring of stones two of which had cup marks on them. The primary burial, at the centre, was possibly that of a young woman. There was a secondary burial of a bundle of cremated bones in a pit that had been dug down through the mound. A flint knife was the only buried possession. The barrow probably dates to around the mid-2nd millenium BC.

The last round barrow to fall within the Wye Valley region is the one already mentioned, 1½ miles (2.4km) south of Chepstow, close to the confluence of the Wye and the Severn. It is unexcavated but lies near to the late Neolithic tomb that was excavated by Joyce Pullinger in 1990 and should therefore date to around 2,000 BC. It is worth recalling that the excavated barrow contained two secondary burials, one of them with two adult males in the typical crouched position, as well as an all-over corded pottery beaker and a barbed and tanged arrow-head.

Cup-Shape Hollows In Stones

The reference to cup marks on two stones which were incorporated into the ring of stones surrounding the Crick barrow deserves further comment and elaboration.

These usually shallow, circular, cup-shaped, man-made hollows in rock are commonly found in the north of England, Scotland and Ireland, although examples are known in south Wales and south-west England, especially Cornwall. They range from simple cups through cups surrounded by carved rings and spirals to cups associated with complex designs. Most are on horizontal surfaces but many were shaped on vertical surfaces. Some are associated with Neolithic burial chambers, some incorporated into the cairn stones and ring stones of later round barrows. Other examples are in stone circles while

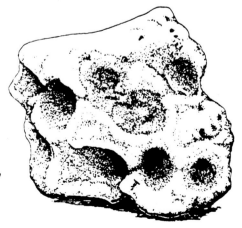

Figure 23. *'Cup-stones' from Blakeney Hill Woods.* By kind permission of B.Johns.

some are apparently away from known human settlements. They are enigmatic and their significance remains inscrutable to modern man although countless postulations have been made. Some sceptics have suggested that they could have been added to prehistoric monument stones in relatively recent years, however some are found inside tombs that have been sealed for more than 3,000 years until recently excavated. A frequently proposed theory is that they served as 'mortars' for crushing seeds, nuts or colouring materials, however this would not account for those found on vertical surfaces, even cliff faces. If they were mystical symbols then their symbolism is still a mystery to us (35).

Recent field work by Brian Johns has identified several cup-marked and incised groove stones in Dean. The first to be found were in Blakeney Hill woods where one had been incorporated into a later stone structure while two others lay nearby. Three more were found on Broom Hill near an ancient trackway and not far from the 'Drummer Boy Stone', itself hollowed out. Other rocks with incised grooves were found near the above sites. Examples are now in the Dean Heritage Museum. A further cup-stone was noted by Toby Groves in a field near Abbot's Mill, Brockweir, although it was more bowl than cup-shaped being 18cm in diameter and over 7cm deep (36). As previously mentioned, the small standing stone south of St.Weonards has two shallow cup marks on its vertical surface. It is not known whether the buried, lower part of the stone carries similar shapes.

Earlier, in 1985, a utilised bowl in a large limestone boulder was recorded alongside a trackway on Tidenham Chase, not far from the early Bronze Age barrow. The bowl was 24.5 cm in diameter and was 15cm deep (37).

Early Bronze Age Flint and Stone Artefacts

Flint, by now an easily obtained and 'cheap' commodity continued to be used well on into the metalworking period. Typical of the flint artefacts are: barbed and tanged arrow-heads, thumb-nail size scrapers, and stubby (5-6cm long) very broad-bladed knives usually displaying the percussion bulb where struck from the core, and with one side left smooth (plano), while the other is convex and retouched around the cutting edges.

Figure 24. *Bronze Age flint knife from Joyford.* Courtesy of A.Stait.

On present evidence these seem to group around ten distinct areas of Dean and south Herefordshire, east of the Wye. They are:

1. Tidenham Chase.
2. Lydney.
3. Within the Bream/St.Briavels triangle.
4. Around Coleford.
5. Symonds Yat/Huntsham Hill.
6. The Joyford/English Bicknor/Eastbach/Hangerbury valley sides.
7. Ruardean to Great Howle.
8. Edge Hills to Flaxley Woods north of Littledean.

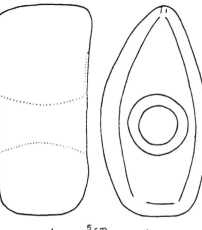

5 cm

Figure 25. Left: *Sandstone spindle-whorl from Nedge Cop. Drawn by D.Watkins.* **Right:** *Quartz Dolerite battle-axe from the Bearse.* Courtesy of A.Saville, F.Roe, Cheltenham Museum and BGAS.

9. Taynton and Newent areas.
10. The higher ground north west of May Hill including Aston Ingham and Linton.

West of the Wye there are clear groupings around:

11. Welsh Newton.
12. Monmouth, Dixton and Little Wonastow.
13. The Doward hills.
14. Just inland of the Severn estuary between Chepstow and Caldicot.

Much of this region is hilly and therefore unploughed pasture-land which limits field-walking and the retrieval of artefacts. Several other groupings ought to be evident between Monmouth and Chepstow.

Battle-Axe

The only stone artefact finds are rare indeed. The first is a stone battle-axe found during ploughing in 1978 at Roads Farm between Bream and St.Briavels. It is typical of the early Bronze Age in Britain. The axe was given a petrological examination and proved to be of Group XVIII quartz dolerite from Whin Sill, Northumberland (38). The second is a sandstone spindle whorl retrieved from among late Neolithic/early Bronze Age flint debris at Nedge Cop, St.Briavels. It had been 'drilled' from each side but the centering was imperfect producing an 'hour-glass' effect. It would have been used with a wooden spindle for spinning wool or flax (39). Both of these finds fall within the Group 3 East of Wye sites above. The third find could belong to any period from the later Neolithic to the later Iron Age. It is a splendid saddle-type quern stone that was found in the Clawdd-du ditch in Overmonnow, Monmouth. It measures 51cm by 29cm and is undamaged. It can be viewed in the Nelson Museum, Monmouth, and its effectiveness for grinding corn is frequently demonstrated to visitors.

Bronze Age Metalwork

Metalwork finds in Dean and the Wye valley are now considerable. Before discussing them a brief summary of the technology involved will perhaps enable the reader more fully to appreciate the organisation, skills, communications and developments during the thousand years or so following emergence from the 'stone age'.

Raw Materials And Manufacturing Methods

Bronze is an alloy of copper with about 10% of tin. In the later Bronze Age lead was used

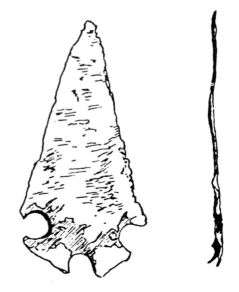

Figure 26. *Late Neolithic/early Bronze Age knife/dagger from Taynton. Drawn by C.Mortimer.* Courtesy of N.Webley.

instead of tin to facilitate casting. Prior to c.2000 BC the first copper and bronze artefacts, axes, daggers and knives, may well have been imported from abroad. The only copper object so far found in Dean is the knife from Irelands Hill, Taynton. Artefacts of gold are numerous in other parts of Britain but none have been found yet in Dean.

It would appear that during the early Bronze Age, defined here as before c.1400 BC, production was at regional centres. During the middle Bronze Age, c.1400-c.1000 BC, it has been suggested that regional production by specialist craftsmen was concentrated on weapons while local, community craftsmen produced tools and ornaments (40). In the later Bronze Age, between c.1000 and c.600 BC, weapons, tools, horse harness trappings and personal items were made everywhere by local smiths or bronze founders, including within Dean.

Copper ore deposits were to be mined in Devon, Cornwall, central and north Wales, western Scotland and in the south west of Ireland. The largest north Atlantic deposits of tin are in south-western Britain but small amounts are also found in Scotland and Ireland. Lead may be found in most parts of Wales, the nearest known deposits occurring just 10km west of Newport, Gwent. South east of Dean lead was available from the Mendips.

Recent archaeological work in Wales has proved copper mining during the early and middle Bronze Age periods at Nantyreira and Cwm Ystwyth, mid-Wales, on Parys Mountain, Anglesey and on the Great Orme, Llandudno where stone-hammers and bone tools were found up to 40m (130 feet) deep in galleries, with other underground workings noted at a vertical depth of 70m (230 feet) and which extend, laterally, for 250m (820 feet), a staggering mining achievement of some 4,000 years ago (41,42,43). There is now a splendid visitor centre on the Great Orme which is open to the public from April to October while excavations continue.

A temperature of at least 1150 C. was required to melt and pour pure copper. Adding 10% tin would lower this to around 1000 C.. An induced draught would be necessary to achieve these temperatures probably using bellows (44).

Clay was the commonest material used for making artefact moulds although the earliest flat axes were cast in open moulds carved into stone, usually sandstone. Later two half moulds were used into which the molten copper-alloy was poured. Another method was to fashion the object in beeswax which was then covered with clay and baked. The beeswax melted and was poured out leaving a ceramic mould into which the bronze was poured. All methods required a final smoothing and polishing. Moulds made from bronze were also used but there was always the possibility of the molten bronze fusing to the mould.

Damaged or scrap bronze items were recycled into new artefacts. Hoards of buried scrap are quite common and have been found in Dean. Bronze workshops should be identifiable by the fragments of copper and copper-alloy slags, the waste material from the smelting and casting process, which should be found in abundance nearby. Where these slag fragments are absent the hoard may indicate that a Bronze Age 'tinker' had buried his accumulated scrap while on a journey and had failed to retrieve it.

Early Bronze Age Metalwork Finds Pre-2000 BC to c.1400 BC

There have been eight finds that fall within this period including the copper knife/dagger from Irelands Hill and the knife/dagger and bronze awl from the Tidenham round barrow. The other five bronze objects are axes: A low-flanged axe from High Nash, Coleford with a crescent-shaped cutting edge (45); a flanged axe with a

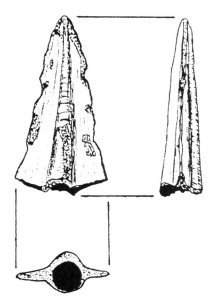

Figure 27. *Middle Bronze-Age spear-tip from Boughspring. Drawn by A.Stait.* Courtesy of L.Smith.

low stop-ridge and a crescent-shaped cutting edge from Staunton, Coleford; a flanged axe without a stop ridge from Viney Hill in Awre parish and a flat axe, decorated with incised lines in a chevron design from Kilcot Wood, 3km west of Newent (46). A further flanged axe was found at Aston Ingham (47).

Copper-Alloy Finds c.1400 to c.1000 BC

During this period new weapon forms are to be found in this region for the first time; bronze spear heads and a rapier, all of them from east of the Wye. The rapier and one spear-head were found at Aston Ingham just north of Dean (48,49). A spear-head with two basal loops was found in Kilcot Wood near Newent in 1854 (50) and a similar one was found in 1988 by Mr.C.Smith of Coleford who was using a metal detector on farmland within 1km, and just north, of Mitcheldean (51). Another spear-tip of similar style and date has recently been found in a garden at Boughspring, Tidenham and was illustrated in the 1991 edition of Dean Archaeology.

All of the other metalwork finds demonstrate an advancement in technology and fall into the axe category, although they are termed palstaves by archaeologists. The palstave is designed to

Figure 28. *Middle Bronze Age spear-head from near Mitcheldean.* Courtesy of C.Smith.

low-flanged palstave was found at Newent in 1961 (56), and another at Lydney in 1890. Further evidence for a settlement site at Lydney during these centuries was the discovery of a funerary urn in Grove Road (57). An unpublished 'shield pattern' palstave, now in the National Museum of Wales, was found at Tidenham (58). One further axe is probably from this period. Described as middle or late Bronze Age it was found in a quarry at Lydbrook in 1890. Its present whereabouts are unknown but it was reported on, and given a metallurgical analysis which indicated that the alloy was 87% copper and 13% tin (59).

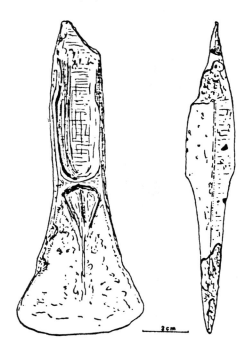

Figure 29. *Bronze palstave from Newent. Drawn by R.D.Abbott.* Courtesy of Gloucester City Museum.

slip in between the split end of a wooden handle and is held in position by side flanges and a stop-ridge that prevents the axe from splitting the handle when in use. Some palstaves were also fitted with a loop that enabled it to be tied to the handle thus preventing it from slipping out.

To the immediate north of Dean, in south Herefordshire, palstaves have been found at Aston Ingham, Weston-under-Penyard, and near Ross-on-Wye. An urn cremation was also found in the parish of Weston, at Pontshill, but without any grave goods (52). In 1989 the Aston Ingham unlooped palstave was retrieved from a field surface next to a spring from which a channel had recently been excavated out and in which water pipes had been laid. It had almost certainly been deposited in the spring area during the middle Bronze Age (53). The palstave from near Ross was of the looped type (54). Within the Forest of Dean another palstave was extracted from clay beds near a pool edge at Steam Mills, Cinderford, in 1974. It was an unlooped, high-flanged type with a V-shape pattern on the blade (55). A

Two and a half miles (4km) north of Ross-on-Wye, just east of the river, in Foy parish, a hoard of what was described as 'Bronze Age celts' was found c.1791 on rising ground between Hole-in-the-Wall and Old Gore. The term 'celts' is now an obsolete word but was used, archaeologically, to describe either stone or bronze axes. In this instance it is likely to have been referring to axes made from bronze (59a).

There appear to be no other recorded finds of bronze metalwork in the immediate Wye Valley that date to the four centuries prior to the beginning of the last millenium BC. The nearest is

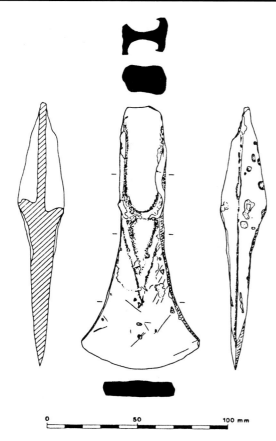

Figure 30. *Bronze palstave from Steam Mills, Cinderford. Drawn by A.Saville.* Courtesy of C.E.Hart and BGAS.

habitable land, the sea has risen leaving the whole area waterlogged, an ideal condition for the preservation of otherwise destructible artefacts such as wood, bone and leather. Excavations by the Glamorgan-Gwent Archaeological Trust began in 1988. An early find, which is relevant to the present discussion of metalwork, was a bronze chape from a sword scabbard of c.1000 to c.900 BC. A timber trackway probably dates to the same period. Pottery remains of the preceding centuries suggest that there may also be evidence, yet to be discovered, of domestic activity in the middle Bronze Age. Most important of the discoveries to date were the stitched-oak-plank remains of a boat around 15.5m (50 feet) long. The evidence so far revealed implied to the excavators that Caldicot could have been a focal point for maritime and wetland orientated activities during the later Bronze Age (61,62).

North of Chepstow, at Liveoaks Farm, St.Arvans a hoard of seven socketed axes with loops were found in 1926 (63). The socketed axe was radically different to those that preceded it. It was cast with a hollow socket into which a carefully shaped and tight-fitting wooden handle was inserted. The loops were for tying it to the shaft. Less than 4km north of St.Arvans, at Chapel Hill, Tintern, two other loop and socket

from Caldicot where a palstave without loops was found (60). During the ensuing centuries, in the later Bronze Age period, there is a remarkable reversal of this trend.

Copper Alloy Finds c.1000 to c.600 BC

All but two of the late Bronze Age find-spots for this region are in the Wye Valley and immediately west of the Wye.

A Late Bronze Age Boat

Since the spring of 1988 there have been a series of spectacular finds in the Caldicot Castle Country Park as a result of work to construct an artificial lake at the bottom of the Nedern Valley. Since the Bronze Age when an earlier channel of the river formed a creek, either side of which was

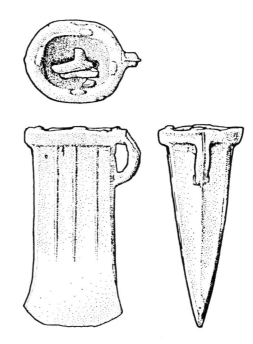

Figure 31. *Late Bronze Age 'loop and socket axe', possibly part of a bronze founder's hoard from Sling, near Coleford. Drawn by P.A.Moss.* Courtesy of M.J.Watkins, Gloucester City Museum.

axes were found as part of a hoard, one a Breton type (64). Socketed axes have also been found at Trellech, 6km north of Tintern (65). In 1962 a socketed spear-head was found on the Great Doward, now in Monmouth Museum (66), while from 'Merlin's Cave' came a bronze maple-leaf shape, tanged razor (67). Another socketed spear-head with a peg-hole was found in Coughton Marsh, below Chase Hill fort, near Ross (68).

Bronze Founding At Sling?

The only late Bronze Age metalwork find spot in the Forest of Dean is at Sling, near Coleford. Here, on the Common in 1956, a South Wales type socketed axe with a loop was found. In 1989 two more were located while digging out the foundations of a house nearby, one of the axes containing fragments of scrap bronze inside the socket while the other held a fragment of a broken blade, possibly from a sword. Since then two more loop and socket axes have been disclosed which were found in the 1970s when a greenhouse foundation was being dug in a neighbouring garden (69,70). Although it has not yet been possible to excavate on the private properties in order to confirm the presence of bronze-smelting and casting debris, the three separate, but adjacent locations for these finds strongly suggests that a bronze founder was working in the vicinity and was burying his collected scrap and out-of-date artefacts in anticipation of recovering them for melting down and re-working.

Continuity Of Settlement

Possible continuity of settlement from early to mid-Bronze Age may be inferred where copper-alloy objects have been found close to typical flint artefact groupings. Groups, as previously referred to, which contain both flint and metalwork finds east of the Wye are:

1. The parish of Tidenham
2. Lydney area
4. Around Coleford
6. Lydbrook/Hangerbury
9. Taynton/Newent
10. Aston Ingham, Weston-under-Penyard

West of the Wye just two of the four groups contain both flint and metalwork finds:

13. The Doward hills
14. Caldicot

Thus eight of the fourteen groups may well have had continuity of settlement during the second millenium BC. One should not conclude, however, from negative evidence that the others did not. For example, Tintern has both early Bronze Age round barrows and late Bronze Age socketed axes. Virtually the whole area is densely forested with no opportunity to survey ploughed fields for flint material. Coughton Marsh is now drained, levelled and regularly ploughed but only recent artefacts are to be found on present field surfaces. All earlier material is well buried below plough level. Much flint debris is being recovered from fields around Viney Hill but nothing, as yet, has been found that can be said to be distinctively from the Bronze Age. There are no fields to walk around the palstave find-spot at Cinderford. The area is either woodland or a levelled opencast-mined coal area. Most of the Group 8 area, Littledean, Edge Hills and Flaxley is Forestry land and few fields are ploughed. By far the majority of the flint finds that have been made came from the excavation of a Roman site at Dean Hall. Welsh Newton is so close to the Doward hills in the neighbouring parish of Ganarew that the two might be considered as one group in which case nine groups could be said to demonstrate continuity of activity. St.Arvans may well have developed as a late Bronze Age site but more field-walking in the area would be necessary before this could be confirmed. The apparent dearth of Bronze Age flint material around Trellech is enigmatic as is the absence of Bronze Age metalwork from the Monmouth district. Group 3, the Bearse, between Bream and St.Briavels may yet reveal ritual deposits of metalwork.

No less than eleven of the fourteen Bronze Age groups under review have produced positive evidence for occupation in at least the later years of the Iron Age while all of them show evidence for sustained occupation during the Roman period, as we shall see in succeeding chapters.

People, Settlement and Customs in the Later Bronze Age

With a respectable amount of artefactual and monumental evidence for the presence of settlements throughout the Bronze Age period in Dean and the Wye valley it must now be admitted that nothing is known about how the local population managed their economy, what their dwellings looked like, how many people lived within each settlement, what they wore and what their relationship was to neighbouring groups of people. Apart from the Tidenham barrow there has been a total lack of excavation on any potential Bronze Age site. Neither can one conjecture

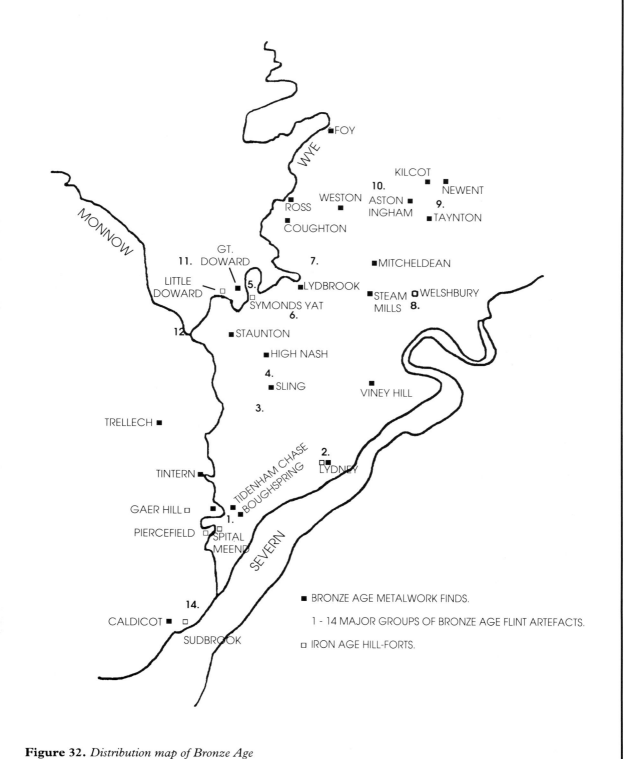

Figure 32. *Distribution map of Bronze Age metalwork finds and Iron Age hill-forts.*

with any assurance that what is known about excavated Bronze Age settlements in parts of southern England, Devon, Cornwall and Wales applies here.

Geographically, the Dean uplands have always been remote with the natural access being from the Severn estuary. This also applies to the Wye valley and the upland areas immediately west of the Wye. North of Dean the natural access is from the Severn and along the vale of the Leadon. There may well have been contact, along with trading, but the proof of the extent is lacking. One may reasonably conjecture that their dwellings were circular, of timber and with conical thatched roofs, as elsewhere. The concentrations of artefacts suggests small groups of homesteads, possibly as part of larger territorial groups with an essentially agricultural economy but supplemented by food that was hunted. The wide dispersal of isolated flint arrow-head finds suggests the latter coupled with their manufacture debris on settlement sites.

It is also quite possible that some of the fortified hill sites that surround Dean and occur in the Wye valley, west of the Wye, also originated in the late Bronze Age. On Nottingham Hill, near Cheltenham, a very important hoard of early to mid-1st milennium BC metalwork was discovered in 1972 within the hill-fort ramparts. Elsewhere in southern Britain many, of what were thought to be Iron-Age hill-forts, have proved to have earlier origins (71).

Deteriorating Climate

One known factor for the late Bronze Age, which would have affected communities here, but to what extent is not yet known, is the deteriorating climate; cooler and much wetter. The deterioration was evident prior to 1000 BC and continued for perhaps five or six centuries.

The people farming the upland and highland areas of Britain were the first to be affected. Because of the relative warmth and dryness during most of the second milennium BC it had been possible to arable farm as well as graze livestock on much of the higher ground, in fact it would appear that some areas were over-farmed. A considerable proportion of the population was able to live above the 1000 feet (300m) contours.

The unpredictable shorter growing season and probable soil exhaustion meant that many upland zones became untenable. Fields were abandoned. Waste land abounded and, in places, peat bogs began to form. The movement of upland farmers seeking pastures in the lower lands would put substantial pressure on the communities who already lived there. It is around this time that many of the Welsh borderland hill-forts were probably constructed and the events

may well be connected. The other development which may have been triggered by the deterioration in the climate was the gradual change to iron artefacts where bronze had sufficed for many centuries. Copper, especially, had to be mined from the igneous rocks of the highland zones, areas of diminishing population. Iron is found in greatest quantity in the sedimentary rocks of lowland regions. It could be that the essential ingredients for bronze working were harder to obtain, or that trade links were disrupted. Whatever, iron gradually replaced bronze as the preferred metal with which to manufacture weaponry and agricultural equipment although bronze continued to be preferred for decorative and personal adornment (72,73).

Ritual Deposits In Water

One custom, which is very well attested, grew in popularity during the closing centuries of the second millenium BC until it was common after 1000 BC and well into the Iron Age. It was the ritual of casting weapons and ornaments, of bronze especially, into lakes, rivers, pools, springs and wetland areas such as bogs and marshes. The practice was widespread in most parts of Britain and in Ireland. Many of the arte-

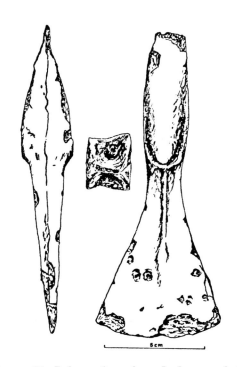

Figure 33. *Palstave from Aston Ingham, probably a ritual water deposit. Drawn by C.Mortimer.* Courtesy of D.Allen.

facts deposited were deliberately bent or broken, rendering them of no further practical use. The ritual purpose may have been to release the 'spirit' of the object, or the person to whom it had belonged, to the safe-keeping of the water spirit. The custom may explain why cemeteries are so rare during these centuries; perhaps the cremated ashes or the picked bones were cast into watery graves, in which case many of the deposits may represent grave goods. Whether this was so, or whether they were simply sacrificial items eludes us at present. Certainly not all artefacts committed to water were valuable, personal possessions. Some were miniature replicas, perhaps symbolic; maybe the sacrifices of the less-well-off (74,75).

There are several examples of probable ritual deposits on the Gloucester side of the Severn including a late Bronze Age socketed spearhead from Abbeydale, near Gloucester, which was found in a waterlogged area. At Wainlode a palstave was retrieved from the River Severn. Numerous collections have come from bogs and old river beds in the upper Severn Valley (76). West of the Severn there are four possible ritual deposits of bronze metalwork. The palstave from Aston Ingham seems to have been deposited in a spring from which it was dredged on to the field surface. The other palstave from Steam Mills, Cinderford was found in a clay-based wet area into which springs still flow. Just north of Mitcheldean, the spearhead was detected from a hollow which used to be a pool. The spearhead from Coughton Marsh is a clear case of a wetland deposit.

The Bearse, previously referred to, must be considered as an area for potential metalwork depositions although none have yet been located. The splendid flint axe of the late Neolithic was ploughed out of a very wet area not far from a spring. From the spring itself a Roman altar was dredged out from where it had been cast probably in the 5th century AD by local Britons (now in the Dean Heritage Museum: 77). The whole area abounds with springs, streams, filled-in pools and swallow holes where streams drop suddenly into subterranean passages. It is most unlikely that metalwork cast into one of these holes would ever be recovered.

In summary it can be said that during the first 1500 years or so of metal use artefacts evolved from the scarce and prestigious copper and bronze knife/daggers used by the few, to a very varied and plentiful supply of metal artefacts used by many in the late Bronze Age. Hand to hand fighting with swords and long knives became a feature of warfare. Bronze cauldrons adorned the hearths; bronze pins and brooches the people. Timber succumbed more easily to the hard axe blade. Bronze arrow-heads are extremely rare and it would seem that, following the demise of the flint arrow-head, sling-stones were preferred as long-distance missiles.

Despite the revolution in metal-working and the lesser use of stone, it is perhaps startling to realise that, if it had been possible to have transported a group of late Bronze Age peoples forward in time 2,000 years to the 14th century AD, it would probably have been the massive architectural stone cathedrals and castles that would have amazed them most and not the further advances in metalwork.

The Age of Iron c.7th Century BC to AD 43

The British Iron Age is often cited in books on prehistory as beginning in the 7th century BC. Other academics would point to the 5th century BC as a preferred date for the generalised use of iron in Britain. It all depends on how one defines 'Iron Age'. Iron objects were certainly to be found in Britain by the 7th century BC but some propose that these may have been forged from imported iron or else the tools themselves were imported. There is little evidence as yet to indicate the generalised use of iron before the 5th century BC and it was some time later before it became commonplace (77a).

In his *'The Prehistory of Metallurgy in the British Isles'* (78) Professor R.F.Tylecote tabled forty seven British sites offering evidence for pre-Roman iron-working. Only one of these, at Huckhoe in Northumberland, was proposed as

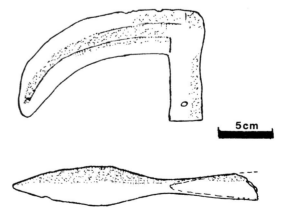

Figure 34. *Iron sickle and iron spear-head from the Llyn Fawr hoard.*

functioning in the 7th-6th centuries BC. Sixteen sites produced dates between the 5th and 3rd centuries BC, seven dated to the 2nd century BC while no less than twenty two fell into the late Iron Age period from the 1st century BC up to the Roman invasion of AD 43. The table was fairly up-to-date when published (1986) but was not comprehensive. On only sixteen of the forty seven sites was there clear evidence for furnaces and smelting. The others produced iron-working debris suggesting smelting or smithing on site, but without locating the actual furnaces or smithing hearths.

Llyn Fawr Bronze And Iron Hoard

One of the most important hoards of prehistoric metalwork ever found in Britain came from the bottom of a lake less than forty miles west of Dean. The lake, Llyn Fawr, to the north of the Rhondda Valley in Glamorgan, was drained in 1911. In the peat deposits at the bottom of the lake were found a remarkable hoard of bronze and iron artefacts including a sheet bronze cauldron, cast bronze socketed axes, cast bronze sickle blades, bronze horse harness discs and other harness fittings, bronze socketed gouges and a bronze razor. The special significance of the hoard, which was dated to around 600 BC, was the association with iron artefacts: a wrought iron sickle blade, a wrought iron spear-head and the hilt and part of the blade of an iron sword. The style of some of the artefacts reflects a popular central European trend possibly derived from metalworking at Halstatt, Austria. Some writers view them as 'British' regional variants, rather than imports, forming part of a continuous tradition of adopting and copying European fashions in bronze and iron. The bronze loop and socket axes and the iron sickle were more definitely proposed as of local derivation (79).

Whether or not the iron objects were of British manufacture, their presence in Llyn Fawr indicates that at least some people in this region were aware of iron and its potential at this early date.

Midsummer Hill

Even closer is the early Iron Age hill-fort of Midsummer Hill, just fourteen miles north of Dean on the southern edge of the Malvern Hills. It was part excavated under S.C.Stanford between 1965 and 1970. Iron ores, smelting slags and parts of iron blooms were identified and dated from the founding of the settlement in the 5th century BC. The fort of Croft Ambrey, six miles north west of Leominster, was also excavated by Stanford. It produced similar evidence and a similar foundation date.

An examination of the ores which were found resulted in the following extract from the report made by Eric.L.Crooks: 'Evidence for identifying positively the prehistoric ore source is slight but the suggestion of the Forest of Dean haematite is probably justified analytically and geographically for Midsummer Hill. A more local source such as the Clee Hills seems possible for Croft Ambrey' (80).

In summary, although the ore source of Dean cannot be accepted as proven, the fact that iron was being smelted during the 5th century BC only fourteen miles from Dean is beyond doubt. Because no hill-fort has yet been extensively and meticulously excavated in Dean or the Wye Valley the proof is lacking for ore extraction and smelting as early as even the 5th century BC, although few will doubt that it was.

Lydney Park Hill-Fort

The only hill-fort to receive excavation of any substance in Dean was at Lydney Park where Sir Mortimer and Lady Wheeler (as they were to be known) excavated the later Roman temple complex which lay within the fort. The latter part of that sentence says it all; most of the fort interior was destroyed by Roman period activity within it, ranging from ore mining to the construction of a temple, a mansio (guest house), a large baths' house, a long building of uncertain use, a water tank, an aqueduct and a substantial precinct wall surrounding all but the water tank. The fact that the Iron Age fort earthworks were also reinforced and heightened during the Roman and post-Roman periods meant that there was very little of

Figure 35. *Lydney Park hill-fort defences, the northern rampart: Period 1: Iron Age. Period 2: Fourth century AD. Period 3: Fifth century AD 'Arthurian' (after REM Wheeler.*

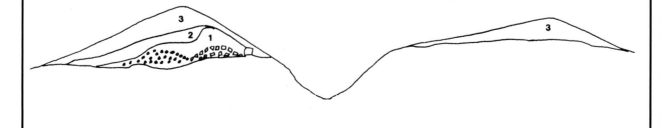

the pre-Roman period undisturbed when Wheeler and his team got to grips with it in 1928 (81).

As Wheeler plaintively summarised the situation: 'The interior of the camp was extensively trenched in the hope of finding traces of the hutments of its prehistoric inhabitants. Two factors

militated against our success. In the first place, the natural rock lies very close to the surface and almost the whole of the superincumbent soil in the southern half of the area had been thoroughly disturbed by the Roman builders. In the second place, the whole of the northern half is pockmarked with the filled-up adits of iron-mines cut by Roman or later miners. The only evidences of a prehistoric structure, and they are slight enough, occurred under the foundations of the temple .... For the rest, the only tangible evidence consists of the few pieces of burnt daub found within the prehistoric rampart' (82).

The hill-fort ramparts were sectioned in three places to a width of about 7 feet. The Iron Age rampart was 5 feet (2.13m) in height and was originally about 20 feet (6m) in width. The earthen rampart had probably been revetted internally by means of a timber stockade. There had been a rampart-walk, about 5 feet wide which had been roughly paved with broken stone. Except where the steep slopes formed natural defences there were single rock-cut ditches. The main, southern entrance had in-turned flanks. The prehistoric finds were mainly of bead-rimmed pots typical of the 1st century BC to the mid-1st century AD and included a few sherds of 'Glastonbury'-type ware, an upper quern stone of local conglomerate grit and of bee-hive form, and food bones of ox, pig and sheep or goats (83).

Excavations elsewhere on the site produced a few other very interesting finds including an iron spear-head which could have been of any date within the last three or four centuries BC, a small iron bowl adorned with bulls' heads of 1st century BC/AD date, a La Tène II one-piece brooch (c.150 BC to mid-1st century AD) and a 'Langton Down' type brooch (c.AD 25-50). It is interesting to note that, in 1991, identical examples of these brooches were found on the Bury Hill late Iron-Age iron-working settlement near Weston-under-Penyard, which, about AD 50 became the Roman iron-working site of Ariconium (84).

In short, the evidence points to occupation from at least the 1st century BC and probably up to the time when the Roman military entered Dean c.AD 50.

Welshbury Hill-Fort is on the western perimeter of Blaisdon parish, 2km north of Littledean. It is impressive but not large, enclosing a little over 3 acres (1.3 ha) of land. It has triple ramparts and ditches on its south and west sides and a single bank and ditch on its north and east sides. The conformation of the sinuous entrance at its south-east corner is somewhat obscured by recent trackways. It is on Forestry land and is still heavily wooded, although accessible.

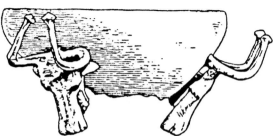

Figure 36. Bottom: *Iron bowl decorated with bulls' heads. Top: Iron Age spear-head. Both items from hill-fort, Lydney Park.*

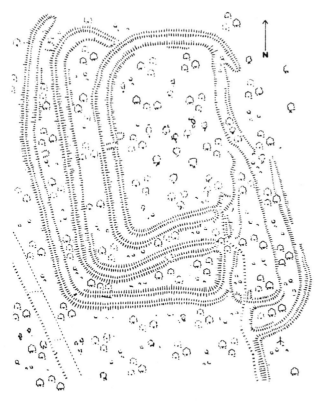

Figure 37. *Plan of Welshbury hill-fort (after the 25-inch O.S. map of 1878).*

Welshbury fort has never been excavated but has received damage from forestry operations over the years. In 1987 an iron spear-head was retrieved from ground disturbance within the ramparts. It was of a type used by the Roman military and similar to one found at Ariconium, during excavations in 1989, which had probably been manufactured there by local Britons on behalf of the Romans (85,86,87). It suggests a Roman military presence but much more evidence would be required before an attack could be implied. The Roman military road from Ariconium to the Severn is only 1km west of the fort.

An extremely rare and important coin find was made recently in a field at the foot of Welshbury Hill, 450m from the fort. The electrum coin, 11mm in diameter, is known as a 'bullet' type due to the thick, 3mm, convex shape of its reverse side. The obverse side depicts a stag or horse leaping left. The coin is Celtic and of the late Iron Age. Its proximity to the hill-fort suggests an association between the two (87a).

Symonds Yat Hill-Fort encloses about 6 acres (2.5 ha) and occupies an imposing position on a promontory at the northern gateway to the lower Wye valley. It is triangular in plan, its northern tip being close to the famous Symonds Yat Rock viewpoint. Its vulnerable south side is protected by a series of five banks and ditches. The other two sides have natural, precipitous defences. In the past it has been heavily damaged by the Forestry Commission. Two separate trackways have been cut through all five ramparts. There has been a car park in the interior and various buildings and signs have been erected for visitor convenience. In the more distant past the interior was also quarried.

During the violent storms of January 1990 several very mature trees were blown down within the central fort area. One of these lifted a three-metre long section to bed-rock which revealed iron-smelting slag and sherds of local, early-Roman pottery. Later in 1990 and early in 1991 a Gloucestershire County Council Archaeological team carried out small-scale excavations in advance of further Forestry Commission visitor facilities. These revealed iron slag and early-

Plate 7. *Unique Celtic electrum coin from near Welshbury hill-fort. Photograph by B. Walters.* Courtesy of M. Hill.

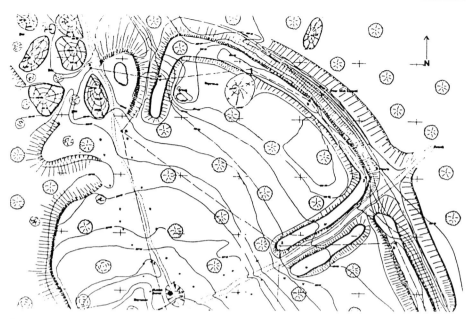

Figure 38. *Survey plan of the Buckholt earthworks near Monmouth.* Courtesy of Woolwich College and MAS.

Roman pottery plus local black, bead-rimmed native pottery, some of similar form to what Wheeler located at Lydney hill-fort and also similar to pottery from the mid-1st century AD site at Ariconium. It would appear that the natives were also smelting iron during the period immediately following the Roman invasion of Dean (88,89).

Spital Meend (Hospice Hill) fort, in Tidenham parish, is finely positioned at the neck of the loop in the Wye above Lancaut. It is similar in size and shape to the Symonds Yat fort and is protected by sheer cliffs on its north and south side. There are at least two ramparts and ditches along its east side. The fort also has the advantage of good landing places on the peninsula to the west with a tidal flow on the Wye at this point. Aerial photographs taken in the summer of 1989 revealed no internal features and no finds are recorded from the site.

Chase Hill Fort is 1½ miles (2km) south of Ross-on-Wye and occupies a commanding position 650 feet (200m) high with extensive views in most directions. In its final form it enclosed around 19 acres (7.7 ha) with steep slopes protecting its northern side. In 1968 tree clearance and subsequent ploughing revealed a considerable amount of archaeological material from within the fort including Neolithic-type flints and possible late Iron Age pottery. A larger quantity of pre-Roman pottery was found on a ploughed area immediately west of and outside the defences (90). Unfortunately the agricultural

developments meant that yet another Dean hill-fort received irreparable damage.

Soudley Camp is very small, enclosing less than one-eigth of an acre with a single bank and ditch. It was constructed with a natural steep escarpment on the south side and its entrance on the north side fronting the Dean Road. It is situated on a cross-roads at the head of the valley that runs down to the Severn through Blakeney. There is no dating evidence apart from a few sherds of Roman pottery, bloomery slag, iron ore fragments and a flint flake, all brought to the surface by moles from the interior (91). Dr.Hart placed it as possibly Norman and compared it with a similar earthwork at Stow (92). Alan Saville recently included it in a list of Iron Age forts in Gloucestershire (93). Until such time as there is a very meticulous excavation of the interior its origins must remain extremely doubtful. It is very possible that it was used in pre-Roman, Roman and medieval times for it is located alongside a probable prehistoric trackway that was paved in the early Roman period and was still in use following the Norman Conquest.

WEST OF THE WYE the nearest major hill-fort to the Forest of Dean is on the **Little Doward** in Ganarew parish. It is on the summit just 750m north west of 'King Arthur's Cave' and at the head of a steep slope overlooking the Wye. The fort consists of an oval enclosure of about 12 acres (5ha) most of which is surrounded by a double bank with a medial ditch. On the south east side is a rectangular annexe defended by a natural outcrop of rock on three sides. Sections of the rampart were damaged in the 19th century when the owner cut paths through them, and an outer rampart on the north west side was levelled. There is a filled-in well at the southern end of the oval enclosure.

The Buckholt is two miles (3.5km) west of the Little Doward and 3km north of Monmouth. Its summit, at 738 feet (225m), is surmounted by what appears to be an unfinished univallate earthwork with an inturned entrance on its north side. What is strange is that the rampart does not continue to the edge of the steep drop on the south side thus making it an incomplete enclosure. A section of the rampart also appears to have been 'bulldozed' through at one point to admit a track. Without excavation it is not possible to determine whether there was a second ancient entrance at this point. But for the inturned entrance, which gives it a distinctly Iron Age fort look, it could easily be viewed as a causewayed, or interrupted ditch enclosure.

Trellech Gaer is just short of 2km south west of Trellech and about 600m east of Hygga. It is a small, almost circular earthwork on a moderately steep promontory at 220m (720 feet) above OD. From the immediate area a number of 1st century BC/AD finds have been made by members of the Monmouth Archaeological Society including an 'Oldbury' type glass bead of dark blue with marvered, opaque white spirals, and black, bead-rimmed pottery from the late Iron Age tradition. Later 1st century early Roman pottery has also been found along with much iron-working debris. The present evidence strongly suggests a British community, probably engaging in iron-

Figure 39. *'Oldbury' type glass bead from Trellech Gaer. It is dark blue with opaque white spirals. 1st century BC/AD.* Courtesy of MAS.

working in the pre-Roman period and certainly doing so in the early Roman period up to around c.AD 85 (94).

Just north of St.Arvans is **Gaer Hill** on the top of which is a small defended settlement enclosed by two banks and ditches. One kilometre north east is another small enclosed settlement on the promontory of **Black Cliff**, while a fort occupies a strong cliff-top position at **Piercefield** with double ramparts protecting the neck of the peninsula.

More is known about **Sudbrook Camp** near Portskewett. Sudbrook is 6km south west of Chepstow and the camp is on the cliffs of the Severn estuary which has severely eroded the southern area of the camp including the entrance or entrance-ways. The triple banks and ditches of the remainder are well preserved on the west side but only the main inner rampart is intact on the eastern side.

The fort was strategically placed, commanding the most ancient route from England into Wales, the crossing from Aust to Portskewett (Porth

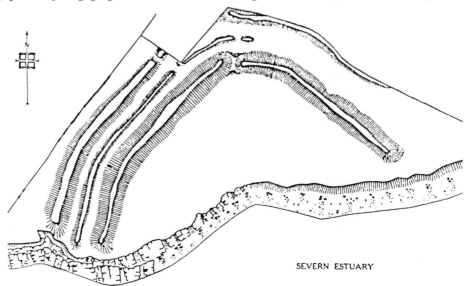

Figure 40. *Plan of Sudbrook fort after V.E.Nash-Williams 1936.*

SEVERN ESTUARY

Iscoed), which is less than 2 miles (3km) wide at this point.

The camp was part excavated under V.E.Nash-Williams in 1934 revealing two prehistoric hut-sites. Of even greater importance was the evidence, from imported Gaulish samian pottery and Roman coin finds, that the camp was used by the Roman invaders from c.AD 50 as a landing and supply base. It continued as such for most of the second half of the first century AD. The late Iron Age pottery and bronze brooch finds suggested that it had been occupied from the 1st century BC until c.AD 50 by Britons before being commandeered by the Romans. There was evidence for industrial activity in the form of waste slags from bronze, iron and glass-working (95).

IRON AGE SETTLEMENTS, other than the more distinguishable hill-forts, must have existed in Dean and immediately west of the Wye. Perhaps the more visibly enclosed forts should be viewed as tribal centres where 'Council' meetings were held. There is evidence elsewhere in Britain that some were also religious centres and incorporated a shrine. For certain they would have been used for safe storage of produce, some with above-ground covered granaries, some possibly containing clay-sealed storage pits. Farm-steads and small settlements should have abounded. They are difficult to identify for the timber-constructed houses would have left no visible surface features. Some of these settlements were surrounded by a simple ditch with perhaps a stockade fence. Aerial photography during a period of summer drought may reveal the moisture-retaining ditched enclosures. Several such potentially Iron Age enclosures were identified during the years 1989 and 1990 by Mark Walters who took over seven hundred aerial photographs in and around Dean on behalf of Dean Archaeological Group.

With no positive proof yet for the manufacture of iron artefacts in this region before the 1st century BC, it may well be that the so-called late Bronze Age loop and socket axes and bronze spear-heads continued to be used here until quite late on into the Iron Age period in which case their find-spots could indicate occupation post 5th century BC.

Place-Names And Iron-Age Sites

Another clue to pre-Roman settlements is to be found in the *-bury* suffix of many places named during the Saxon period, and where there were still-visible remains. In every instance locally where it has been possible to archaeologically investigate sites with the *-bury* suffix, late Iron Age or early Roman remains have been con-

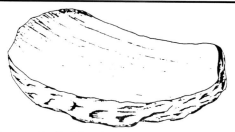

Figure 41. *Prehistoric saddle-type quern stone from Clawdd Du, Overmonnow. Actual length 51cm (21 inches).* Drawn by A.Stait. Courtesy of MAS and Monmouth Museum.

firmed. Examples are Bury Hill at Weston-under-Penyard and Hangerbury Hill near Lydbrook. North of the Forest in Herefordshire there are Ledbury and Aconbury hill-forts among many more. East of the Severn Towbury, Beckbury, Salmonsbury, Norbury, Pinbury. Ranbury, Trewsbury, Brackenbury and Uley Bury are all Iron Age hill-fort sites.

The earthworks of four probable pre-Roman settlements were recorded by past local historians on the south side of the Forest close to the Severn and the Wye. Plans of all of them are included in Dr.Cyril Hart's *'Archaeology in Dean'* which was published in 1967.

The first is at Tallard's Marsh, 1km south of the old Chepstow bridge on the Dean side of the Wye and on the cliff edge. Traces of a partially levelled rampart and ditch are still visible to the north while the cliff edge is the natural boundary on the west and south side (96).

Coombesbury is 500m south west of Tidenham Church alongside the A48 road but is very heavily quarried. Dr.G.Ormerod sketched the outlines of two camps in 1842 but little remains visible today (97,98.99).

Oldbury Camp is another earthwork sketched by Ormerod and published in 1861 (100,101). It lies in fields off Rosemary Lane, Garston near Stroat, again close to the A48 and the aforementioned Stone Row. The *Gar-* prefix is from the ancient British (Welsh) *caer*, *gaer* (fort, settlement), or *caered* (enclosure, wall). Recent observation confirmed Dr.Hart's view that the earthworks are now ploughed out and almost impossible to define.

Edge Farm Camp lies a little over 1km (less than a mile) north east of the Oldbury camp, near High Woolaston. A reasonably well-defined bank and ditch encloses a small area of level ground. It was originally recorded by Dr.C.Scott-Garrett and Frank Harris in the mid-20th century. Like the other enclosures noted above it is typical of what one might expect of small, perhaps later Iron Age, local family settlements (102).

The following place names east of the Wye could indicate pre-Roman settlement sites which have not yet been confirmed by archaeological finds.

STONEBURY Within 1km of Lydney to the west of the Bream road.

HIGHBURY Within 1km of Lydney to the east of the Bream road.

HIGHBURY Just south west of Bream with development planned.

HIGHBURY Above steep slopes just south of Lower Redbrook.

COXBURY 2km south of Lower Redbrook, above the Wye.

SEDBURY South of Tidenham. Roman period site confirmed.

WILLSBURY Between Bream and St.Briavels. Some Roman pottery.

BOSTONBURY 1km west of Parkend. Heavily quarried hill.

GLASTONBURY 1km south of Soudley camp.

GLASTONBURY 1km south west of Cliffords Mesne.

BERRY HILL North of Coleford.

TOWBURY 1.5km north west of Blakeney in woodlands.

ACONBURY Great Berry, Brierley. Traces of enclosure.

PRESTBURY On the southern edge of Taynton parish.

PRESTBERRY Hartpury parish.

CATSBURY Hartpury parish.

LIMBURY Hartpury parish. Aerial photos show enclosure ditches.

CINDERBURY Great Howle. Nearby 1st century AD iron-working site.

CINDERBURY Field name on Tithe map. Now beneath Tutnalls, Lydney.

CARSWALLS Between Newent and Upleadon. Also near Madgetts.

Two Celtic elements, *din-* (*dinas*: fortified place) and *gaer* may be incorporated into Dinnegar which Dr.Hart draws to our attention as a field name located north of Stroat Farm (103). There are no visible ground level remains. The name Duncastle is also recorded in Alvington which is deserving of further investigation. Another Forest place-name which may have ancient British origins is Ruardean, with the elements *rhiw* (hill, ascent or sloping hill) and *-din*, combining to suggest a fortified hill. Medieval spellings of the name usually give *-din* or *-dyn*, never *-dean*. There is an important 1st century AD iron-working site in Ruardean but as yet there is no confirmation of one pre-dating the Roman invasion. Earlier earthworks are visible, from the air, beneath the old manor remains.

Outside of Dean there is a Caerswall Farm near Much Marcle, just over a kilometre north of the Oldbury fort. West of the Wye in south Herefordshire there is Pengaer on Orcop Hill. 1km south of St.Weonards the Tithe map shows a Bury Hill and a Bury field. An 1828 survey map of Monmouth, now in the British Library, names Bury Farm, Upper Bury Wood and Lower Bury 500m north west of Little Garth Farm on the Wonastow Road. Near St.Owens Cross in Hentland parish there are the ploughed-out remnants of Gaer Cop (104).

The above list of place-names is a guide to potential sites with Iron Age origins, but, without excavation they are going to be difficult to prove.

The commonest kind of artefactual evidence is pottery. Earlier hand-made and even later wheel-thrown Iron Age pottery is usually of a soft fabric, fired at a low temperature and subject to disintegration once disturbed by the plough. Even when found in-situ, pottery inclusions of limestone may have leached out over the centuries leaving the fabric vesicular (full of hollows) and liable to fragment when washed. Clay with natural organic inclusions was frequently used around Dean. These inclusions burned away during firing but did not usually show on the surfaces of the pot during use, however, once it was broken and disposed of, water and hard frosts soon caused decomposition. Iron artefacts also corrode and mineralise requiring X-rays to reveal what is left of their original form. Bronze artefacts survive better as do glass beads. Both were made locally and were also traded in during the first centuries BC and AD, however, they were also fashion-durable so that many manufactured before the Roman invasion were still in use in the later 1st century AD making dating of the site where they are found subject to doubt. Securing indisputable evidence for pre-Roman settlements is not going to be easy.

Due east of Lydney, on the other side of the Severn at Frocester Court, extensive excavation by Eddie Price has revealed a nucleated settlement comprising six round houses within a ditched enclosure dating to the 2nd century BC. Iron-working and bronze-working took place on the site and the Forest of Dean would be the logical source of the iron ore. There were no visible, above ground indications that the site existed and its discovery was due entirely to the large area excavations conducted over several decades by Eddie Price.

NATIVE-WARE POTTERY from the Iron Age tradition has been found at a number of locations east and west of the Wye in recent years. The pottery is usually bead-rimmed and black, but there are variations in rim form,

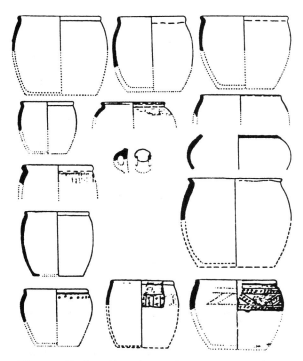

Figure 42. *Late Iron Age native-ware pottery from Lydney Park hill-fort (after REM Wheeler).*

colouring and fabric, however the pot-sherds are very distinctive. It should be borne in mind, when considering the sites, that like brooches and beads the native pottery was still in use for a while after c.AD 50 when the Romans entered Dean. It should, in most instances, indicate a pre-Roman settlement perhaps continuing into the Roman period. The places listed below are in addition to the ones already mentioned where native-ware pottery has been noted:

EAST OF WYE: Round Hill, Huntley, just to the north of the Gloucester to Mitcheldean Roman road, is an elevated position on which was located a small industrial settlement, the evidence for which is iron bloomery slag and baked clay fragments. Most of the pottery slots into the post AD 50 period but some black, limestone-tempered native-wares were present. Aerial photographs show a number of filled-in clay extraction pits one of which was excavated by DAG in 1989 and produced some of the above finds (105).

Limestone tempered native-ware pottery was also found in a small excavation on an enclosed settlement at Lower Lydbrook not far from Hangerbury Hill. The settlement, on present evidence, had a long occupation from the late pre-

Roman period to the end of the Roman period, possibly into the 5th century. It is situated on a promontory overlooking the Wye and served by a cross-Forest prehistoric trackway, in use during the Roman period and still used in sections (106).

A number of ditched enclosures were revealed by the DAG aerial survey on the Huntsham peninsula close to the later Roman villa site. Excavations by N.P.Bridgewater in the 1960s on a section of the largest enclosure ditch produced only native-ware pottery and iron-working debris suggesting a pre-Roman settlement succeeded by a Roman villa (107).

Similar artefacts were excavated from and near the Hadnock villa site which is close to the Little Doward hill-fort but on the east side of the Wye. The native pottery collection included both local and Malvernian wares (108).

During excavations of the High Nash temple site at Coleford a few rims and sherds of late Iron Age pottery were encountered. The importance of this pre-Roman and Roman-period site is discussed more fully below.

On the Severn cliffs, south of the Woolaston Roman villa and just north of Horse Pill, a small excavation by DAG, on a site discovered in 1989, revealed sherds of native-ware pottery and early Roman pottery (109).

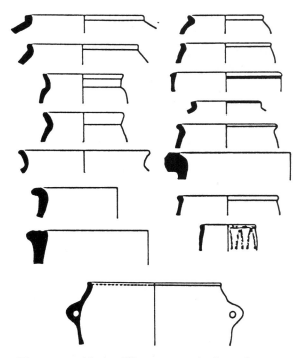

Figure 43. *Native-Ware pottery rim forms from Bury Hill, 'Ariconium', Weston-under-Penyard.*

Native-ware pottery along with Belgic-type pottery is present among a large collection of Flavian-period (later 1st century) ceramics on the site of a an early Roman high-status building at Blakeney which is currently being excavated by DAG (110).

The largest collection of native-ware pottery has come from excavations and field survey on the Bury Hill and Roman military sites at Ariconium, Weston-under-Penyard. The native settlement here was producing iron artefacts before the advent of the Romans and will be fully discussed below.

WEST OF THE WYE: Excavations in Monmouth indicate a late Iron Age presence with native-ware pottery finds on the site of the Glendower Street school and the adjacent Spencer's Yard. The saddle-type quern stone from Clawdd-du could also have been used during the Iron-Age (111).

At Lords Wood on the Wye-facing lower slope of the Great Doward there is a bank and ditch enclosed settlement from which A.L.Sockett excavated native-ware pottery and early Roman material (112).

Native, bead-rimmed pottery was also excavated from the Claudio-Neronian Roman military fort site at Castlefield in the Monnow Valley but this may have been brought in by the soldiers from elsewhere (113).

GLASS BEADS from the Iron Age tradition have been found on a few sites apart from the Trellech Gaer one already mentioned. A blue glass bead was found near Chase Hill fort similar in form to ones excavated by Stanford in the Iron Age hill-fort at Croft Ambrey in Herefordshire

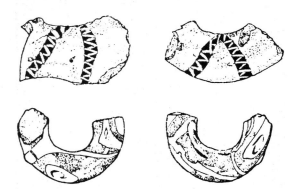

Figure 44. Top: *Amber glass bead with blue and white cables from Great Howle, 1st century AD. Bottom: Glass bead with yellow and white swirls from Hangerbury, 1st century AD. Courtesy of D.Knight.*

(114). A clear glass annular bead decorated with swirls of white and yellow was found on Barnfield, below Hangerbury Hill (115), and an amber glass bead with blue and white cables was discovered within an enclosed settlement in cleared woodland at Great Howle (116). Both are of 1st century form and late Iron Age types. Several late Iron Age glass beads, decorated and plain, have been found at the Bury Hill settlement, Weston-under-Penyard.

BRONZE ARTEFACTS of the late Iron Age, mostly brooches, may also indicate pre-Roman activity close to their find-spots. Recent fieldwork produced a 'Colchester' type brooch from The Moors area between Littledean and Newnham and another early 1st century AD British brooch from fields near Elton. An early 'Dolphin' type brooch was found on Chestnuts Hill, Littledean (117). Several definite pre-Roman brooches have been found at Bury Hill since 1989.

West of the Wye a most remarkable and extremely rare continental bow- type, heavy bronze brooch with an almost circular boss and three protruding knobs was found during excavations at Tregate Castle, Llanrothal. It probably dates from the 1st century BC. As far as is known, only two identical brooches have been found in Britain, at Dorchester and Barrow-on-Soar, Leicestershire (118).

'Celtic' Ritual Sites and Objects

The placing of inverted commas around Celtic requires explanation. It has become commonplace to refer to the pre-Roman peoples who lived in our islands as Celts. People with long Welsh, Cornish, Scottish Gaelic and Irish ancestry are still referred to as being of Celtic origin. It has for long been accepted by many that the Celts were an expanding, warrior-dominated people who spread through Europe during the first millenium BC in successive waves, conquering and settling, moving relentlessly westwards until their influence changed the religion, politics, culture and language of the indigenous British and Irish peoples. However, as Dr.Anne Ross admitted: 'We cannot, in all truth, know when, or even where, the people whom we recognise as Celtic originated' (119).

In recent decades many have questioned the 'invasion' theory and have proposed that the inhabitants of these islands slowly imported and absorbed the cultural traits, fashions, beliefs and customs of the Celts and, no doubt, many immigrants (120,121).

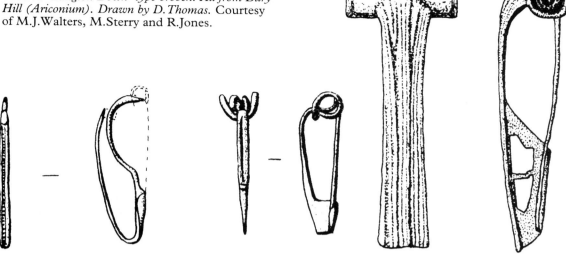

Figure 45. Left: *La Tène II one-piece brooch.* *Centre: Neuheim derivative one-piece brooch. Right: Silvered 'Langton Down' type brooch. All from Bury Hill (Ariconium). Drawn by D.Thomas.* Courtesy of M.J.Walters, M.Sterry and R.Jones.

Similarities between some ancient British (Welsh) and Gaelic words, and even words now part of the English language, especially words connected with agriculture and farming, are to be found in the ancient Sanskrit language. Dr.Steve Jones, reader in genetics at University College, London observed in his 1991 Reith Lecture that half of the world population now speak Indo-European languages. He went on to suggest that: 'Perhaps, then, the first Indo-Europeans were farmers, who brought their language with them as they spread..... The Indo-Europeans may even have been the first farmers.' He added: 'Just like their genes, the language of the Basques seems unrelated to any other. It may be the last remnant of the speech of Europe before agriculture. Safe in their mountains, the Basques resisted being absorbed by the invaders, so that their ancient language, a language of hunter-gatherers, lives on. Archaeology, too, shows that they took up farming much later than the rest of Europe' (122). If the theory is correct then the pre-Roman languages of these islands may have developed during the fourth millenium BC, influenced by immigrant Neolithic farmers, and not during the first millenium BC by invasions of Celts.

Determination of the correct application of the description 'Celtic' and 'Celts' is neatly summed up by Barry Cunliffe and Peter Wiseman in the Introduction to a new translation of Caesar's *'The Battle for Gaul'* (Chatto & Windus, 1980): 'Celts and Gauls were names frequently used by Greek and Roman writers to describe the barbar-

ian peoples who occupied much of northwestern Europe. The words were largely interchangeable and covered a multitude of tribes of different ethnic origin and varying customs. Yet the generalization is a useful one. Archaeological research has shown that by the fifth century BC large parts of Europe from Britain to Romania and from northern Italy to Belgium shared many cultural elements in common. This does not mean

Figure 46. *Stone head from Ruspidge.* Courtesy of Gloucester City Museum .

that we are dealing with a Celtic nation but simply that by the processes of trade and exchange, by folk movement and by convergent evolution, the barbarian communities of Europe had developed a degree of cultural similarity. It was this that impressed the classical observers when they wrote of 'Celts or Gauls'.'

Use of the word Celtic, therefore, should be seen as implying 'Celticization', the acceptance and integration of a set of cultural distinctions by the existing inhabitants of these islands. It would be a nonsense, anyway, to suppose that immigrant Celts totally displaced the native population of any significant part of Britain or Ireland. Their influence, however, was considerable.

The Cult of the Head

There is no doubt that the so-called Celts venerated the human head, but they were certainly not the first peoples to do so. The head was seen as the essence of the being, the 'soul-substance'. It was therefore a symbol of divine powers. The heads of defeated enemies were removed and proudly displayed; the fighting qualities of the dead being transferred to the victor (123).

The Sicilian historian, Diodorus Siculus, wrote of the Gauls in the first century BC: 'When their enemies fall they cut off their heads and fasten them to the necks of their horses. They hand over the blood-stained spoils to their attendants and they carry them off as booty chanting a paean over them and singing a hymn of victory. They nail up the heads on their houses just as certain hunters do when they have killed wild beasts. They embalm in cedar oil the heads of their most distinguished enemies and keep them carefully in a chest: they display them with pride to strangers, declaring that one of their ancestors or their father or the man himself refused to accept a large sum of money offered for this head. They say that some of them boast that they refused the weight of the head in gold' (124).

Should anyone consider this practice as abhorrent and 'barbaric' then it would be well to consider that around 1,000 years before this Celtic practice was recorded the young Israelite, David, having slain Goliath, cut off his head and carried it back to Jerusalem to present it to King Saul (125).

We have no archaeological evidence from this region for severed heads, but there is evidence for the practice of what may be termed head veneration in the form of carved, stone heads, although their real significance can only be conjectured.

Stone Heads

In 1970 five primitively carved stone heads were found in neighbouring gardens in Buckshaft Road, Ruspidge. Three of them are now on display in Gloucester City Museum. Dr.Anne Ross examined the heads and considered them to be of Celtic origin, and the location a possible open-air sanctuary with a sacred spring. Old maps show a nearby well, now covered over. An old trackway connects the site to Soudley Camp and the Dean Road. A crudely carved stone basin was also retrieved from the area in 1990 (126). It must be said that there is still some local scepticism concerning the authenticity of the stone heads, but this must be set against the opinions of some experts in Celtic religions and practices.

There can be no doubting the authenticity of a Celtic-type face carved on sandstone and found in 1991 at Dean Hall, Littledean which is only 2km from Ruspidge and is also connected by a trackway which proceeds through Abbot's Wood and up the ancient Maidenham. The spring-head temple at Dean Hall dates from the pre-Roman period and was developed as a water-shrine

Plate 8. *Primitive face carved on coarse sandstone from Dean Hall, Littledean. Photograph by M.J.Walters.* Courtesy of D.Macer-Wright.

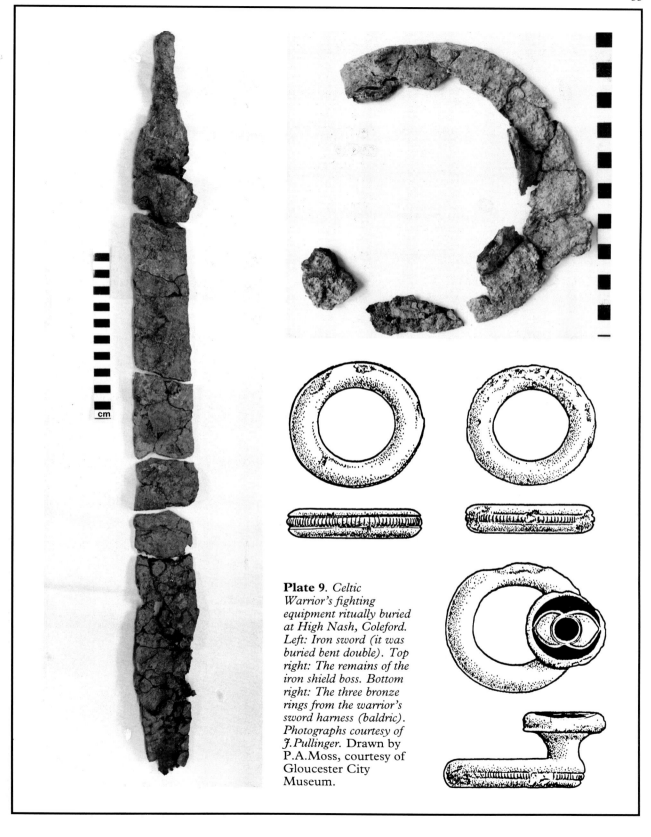

Plate 9. *Celtic Warrior's fighting equipment ritually buried at High Nash, Coleford. Left: Iron sword (it was buried bent double). Top right: The remains of the iron shield boss. Bottom right: The three bronze rings from the warrior's sword harness (baldric). Photographs courtesy of J.Pullinger.* Drawn by P.A.Moss, courtesy of Gloucester City Museum.

through several phases up to the fourth century AD. Excavations by Professor Barrie Jones of Manchester University in 1985 revealed two circular clay-lined pools fed by a spring. Springs are still active on the hill-side (127).

Dating stone heads to the Iron Age is difficult especially when they have not been excavated from definite pre-Roman contexts, but, as Dr.Ross observed: 'Those which come from Roman contexts, which are very numerous, may include some which in fact ante-date the Roman occupation nevertheless' (128). The Romans were remarkably tolerant and even respectful of many aspects of the religions of the people they subjugated, and even though they found the practice of decapitation particularly distasteful, it would appear that they may have tolerated grotesque depictions of the head in stone.

When considering the dating of primitive-looking stone heads and figures it should also be borne in mind that the style persisted throughout the Roman and post-Roman periods up to the 11th century in Wales and along the borders, and such carvings are not uncommon on grave slabs and as church embellishments.

Horned Deity

Part of the head of a horned deity, cast crudely in lead, was found alongside an ancient route on Harrow Hill 2km south of Mitcheldean. Harrow derives from the Old English *'hearg'*, meaning 'land near a pagan sacred grove' and clearly suggests the presence of a Celtic shrine in that area (129). Many ancient springs, renamed after Christian saints, might reasonably be proposed as earlier sacred Celtic water shrines. St.Anthony's Well north of Littledean, St.Bride's Well at St.Briavels and St.Margaret's Well at Stowe are three such.

Celtic Warrior Burial

The most remarkable late Iron Age discovery was that of the buried weaponry of a British warrior found in August 1987 during rescue excavations at High Nash, Coleford in advance of the construction of a housing estate. The equipment included a near metre long iron sword which had been bent double before deposition in the manner of many artefacts found in rivers and lakes, as previously mentioned. Alongside the sword was the warrior's shield of which only a part of the iron boss had survived. On the shield had been placed three decorated bronze rings which had been worn on the warrior's baldric or sword-belt. One of these had a bronze, circular fastening stud which was decorated with a red-enamelled design, unique in Britain. Dr.Graham Webster reported on the burial in *Britannia* (1990): 'In 1987, in the course of building work

along the ancient ridgeway to the Severn Estuary, a late Celtic and Roman settlement covering a considerable area was discovered.....Among the finds was the burial of a warrior which included a typical late La Tène sword...' He described the sword-belt fittings as of 'a type commonly found in Celtic burials, but more often of the horned variety'. He summarised thus: 'There seems a strong presumption that the Coleford burial was that of a Celtic warrior. Although much larger and heavier, this ring and button provides a link between the late La Tène examples in western Europe and those in use in the Roman army' (130).

The excavations also revealed the buried foundations of an early 3rd century AD Romano-Celtic temple and a temenos (consecrated and enclosed ground) ditch which may have incorporated the warrior burial deposit. A spring, now a capped well, lies on the western edge of the site, while a stream flows along the bottom of the slope on the eastern side. It is presumed that the location was a long-established sacred site which continued as such into the early post-Roman period. Fragments of Iron-Age type black native ware pottery were found during excavations as well as prehistoric flint material. It should also be remembered that an early Bronze Age low-flanged axe with a crescent-shaped cutting edge was found in this locality in 1918 and is now in Gloucester City Museum.

The Druids

One cannot conclude this section on Iron Age sacred sites without mention of the Druids even though their presence in Dean and the Wye valley is only a presumption. Neither, therefore, is it appropriate to offer here an extensive account of all that is known, inferred and conjectured from the few historical sources which make reference to them. It is relevant, though, to outline what is believed to be their primary functions in pre-Roman British society because they were undoubtedly the ones who exercised most influence over the population which is why the Romans resolved on their extinction. Readers who wish to avail themselves of a perspicacious and objective analysis of all that is known about the Druids should refer to the brilliant exposition by Stuart Piggott (131).

Graeco-Roman writers agreed that the intellectual elite of the Celticized countries were the Druids, Bards (poets, singers, chanters of eulogies and satires) and Vates, the latter being more concerned with divination and sacrifice. The Druids were male and were ranked above Kings, Bards and Vates. As a result of Caesar's defeat of the Gauls, the British Isles had become the last surviving home of Druidical power in the west, although it would appear that some influence continued in Gaul because it was the Emperor Claudius in AD 54 who 'completely abolished the barbarous and inhuman religion of the Druids in Gaul' according to Suetonius (132).

Figure 47. *Druid's head on an 18th century Anglesey copper token.*

The Druids were held in much honour above the rest of the priesthood and exercised their authority in peace and war, having the power to intervene in war and call off hostilities. Caesar describes them as: having a Druid with chief authority and meeting in an annual assembly in a sacred place, a *nemeton*. Other writers refer to their sacred places as being remote, in forests and associated with groves of oak trees. They were teachers of oral traditions and their students were obliged to commit to memory the epic poems which enshrined the deeds and activities of past generations. In this way they were the keepers and transmitters of all knowledge and learning. They also acted as judges, counsellors, healers, prophets and keepers of the calendar, their unit of reckoning being night followed by day and their months and years being determined by the moon, but being fully aware that intercalary months must be periodically inserted to adjust to the solar year. They communicated and made intercession with the immortal gods, and, with the Vates, offered sacrifices both animal and human. They believed and taught that the souls of humans are indestructible and do not suffer death when the body dies but live on in another form. The belief resulted in a sometimes reckless bravery in war which was noted by some historians when writing about the Celtic nations.

Orally Transmitted Traditions

Organised Druidical teaching and practice must have ended in this region when the Roman military took control in c.AD 50. Ten years later their Anglesey stronghold was captured and the Druids, their followers and many refugees, were slaughtered (133). Because their beliefs and histories were transmitted orally, and not written down, these could not be destroyed either by legislation or the sword. They could, however, become distorted through the embellishments of less-than-meticulous repetition. Centuries later, in Ireland, which was never Romanised, the legendary exploits of the past were recorded in writing. This also happened, much later, in Wales.

Figure 48. *An 18th century depiction of a druid in an oak grove. From the title page of 'Antiquities of England and Wales', F. Grose, 1773-87, Vol. IV.*

These stories, fascinating as they are, can not be considered as historically accurate references to actuality. The strands of truth, which they must contain, have become inextricably woven into a cloak of vibrantly-coloured myth and legend from which many have endeavoured to un-pick the original material, but can never know whether they have succeeded or failed.

For certain many of the beliefs and ritual observances would have continued throughout the Roman period and beyond. Where better to commune with the spirits of rivers, springs, trees, hills and the intimate hearth than the Forest of Dean and the densely wooded slopes of the Wye Valley.

International Trade

Although a certain amount of cross-Channel trade has been logically conjectured for the Neolithic and Bronze Age periods, the first historical mention of trade dates to about 600 BC, the transitional period before the first evidence for British iron-working. The reference is actually in a 4th century AD poem by Rufus Festus Avienus, *'Ora Maritima'*. In the poem fragments of a lost Massiliot sailing-manual known as the *'Massiliote Periplus'* are preserved. This gave an account of a voyage from Massilia (Marseille) down the eastern Spanish coast and included a reference to the islands of Britain and Ireland (under the names 'Albion' and 'Ierne') which were reputed to have trading links with the Oestrymnides, which lay off the coast of Brittany.

A further voyage from Massilia around 325 BC refers to Britain and Ireland collectively as the *'Pretanic Isles'*. This implies that the natives would be known as the *Pritani*. It is easy to see how, by Caesar's time in the 1st century BC, this had come to be recorded as Britannia and the people as Britons. Pritani is the Welsh *Prydain*, and *Prydeinig* is still the Welsh word for British (134).

The Greek geographer, Strabo, who was born c.64 BC and spent a number of years in Rome, wrote of Britain in the early Augustan period and specified its principal exports as: Wheat, cattle, gold, silver, iron, hides, slaves and hunting dogs (135). Whether this included iron smelted from Dean ores can only be conjectured, but much of the silver and gold must have come from Wales. The listing of wheat, cattle and hides is indicative of the surplus produced in southern Britain, and the mention of slaves says much about the presence of a ruling, dominating, rich elite class.

Archaeological research has discerned a number of international trade routes between south coast ports and the coast of Gaul, between Devon and Cornwall to the Iberian peninsula, from Scotland to northern Europe and from the Thames valley to continental ports. Humberside was an important trading area, and in the pre-Roman decades Colchester became a major port. A lead anchor stock weighing 70kg (154lbs) was found at Porth Felen on the Lleyn peninsula, north Wales. It was of Mediterranean origin and dates from the 2nd or 1st century BC. It was presumably lost from a sea-going trading vessel and Welsh metals would have been the obvious trading exports.

By the beginning of the 1st century BC there was a new trade impetus. Excavations on Hengistbury Head in Dorset confirmed the imports, through a nearby harbour, as including Italian wine in huge, heavy ceramic amphorae, pottery from Brittany and Italy, and glass items probably from the Mediterranean (136). Both Strabo and Diodorus record the export of tin from Cornwall to Marseilles (137).

Too little is yet known from the archaeological record of Dean and the Wye Valley to enable any assessment to be made of the extent of local participation in international trade. Wheeler proposed continental origins for some of the Lydney hill-fort brooches. It is impossible to say how many of the Ariconium, late La Tène type brooches, were continental imports. The rare Tregate brooch was unquestionably of continental origin as are many of the Celtic tribal coins that have been found in this region, but none of these are proof of direct cross-channel trade links with this region up the Bristol Channel and into the Severn Estuary. Lydney and Sudbrook/Portskewett are the most likely trading ports on this side of the Severn but the prehistoric and Roman archaeology of Lydney as a potential port has been totally neglected. Monmouth is another possibility, but one has to say that, on present evidence, no international trading port existed in this region although there must have been ports of call for coast-line traders who exchanged goods of continental origin for local products, especially iron.

Mid-First Century BC to Mid-First Century AD Developments

By 51 BC Caesar's conquest of Gaul was complete. Trading patterns changed. The crushing of the seafaring Veneti tribe of Brittany and the destruction of their fleet seriously affected cross-channel trading. Now a province of Rome,

Figure 49. *Portrait of Julius Caesar from a silver denarius.*

Gaulish trade was directed east, rather than west into Britain. Caesar's expeditions to Britain in 55 and 54 BC resulted in treaties being made with the Trinobantes and other tribes who surrendered to him. Caesar described them as 'perhaps the strongest tribe in the southeast of Britain'. He continued: 'Now that the Trinobantes were under our protection and so in no danger of harm at the hands of our troops, other tribes sent embassies to me and surrendered' (138). It may well be that future trading between Britain and Gaul was restricted by the Roman government to trading through the allied Trinobantes and especially through their port of Colchester. As Cunliffe observed: 'Some such explanation would conveniently fit the known facts. It would sup-

pose that the mineral wealth of the south-west was channelled through middle men like the Dobunni, and perhaps along the Thames valley, to the east coast ports, those controlling the trade routes sharing in the wealth that was generated' (139).

The names and approximate territories of many British late Iron Age tribes, along with the often abbreviated names of some of their rulers, are known from a number of sources. Among the principal sources is Caesar's Commentaries and a number of other documentary references and place names. Roman historians writing after the Claudian Conquest of AD 43 added further to our knowledge. Recent information has derived from a study of the distribution of Celtic coins and the concentrated finds of named dynastic rulers. Many small tribal groups existed whose names remain unknown. The existence of some such can be surmised and their boundaries conjectured. Among these can be proposed the ancient people of Dean, but first we must consider what is known about the tribes bordering on this region.

The Dobunni

Dobunnic territory extended from the upper Thames Valley, across Gloucestershire and down into Somerset and northern Wiltshire. Their zone of occupation provided the link between the Severn and the Thames and therefore connected with the lands of the Catuvellauni and the Trinobantes, which tribes were united under the powerful leadership of Cunobelin between c.AD 10-40. Historian Dio Cassius (lx,20) supplies the information that, immediately prior to the

Figure 50. *Known British tribes of the late Iron-Age.*

invasion of Claudius, the Dobunni tribe 'was subject to the Catuvellauni'.

Dobunnic coins of the first century AD have a very distinctive motif on their reverse side: a triple-tailed horse. The names of some Dobunnic rulers appearing in abbreviated form are: *ANTED, EISU, CATTI, COMVX, INAM, CORIO* and *BODVOC*. The find-spot groupings of the coins suggests that the Dobunni were divided under two rulers, one controlling the northern section roughly concentrated in Gloucestershire, while the other controlled the southern section comprised of Somerset and parts of Wiltshire. The western boundary of both divisions of the Dobunni, at the time of the Roman conquest, was almost certainly the Severn Estuary and the Bristol Channel, although, because Dobunnic coins have been found in Dean and Herefordshire, some writers have proposed that their territories extended to the Wye. This is highly unlikely for a number of reasons as will be demonstrated. It is just possible that, after the Conquest for administrative purposes, the Romans may have extended the boundaries westwards.

The Silures

Tacitus (in *Agricola* XI), based on their physical characteristics, suggested that the Silures may have been early Iberian immigrants: '... the swarthy faces of the Silures, the tendency of their hair to curl and the fact that Spain lies opposite, all lead one to believe that Spaniards crossed in ancient times and occupied the land'.

Their eastern boundary was the Wye, and possibly their northern boundary too. The Bristol Channel was their southern boundary offering safe havens for shipping. To their west were the Demetae of Pembroke and Cardigan with their capital at Carmarthen, and whose territory probably extended as far as Loughor according to Ptolemy's *Geography*.

The Unnamed Tribe?

To the northern borders of Dean, in Herefordshire, and south of the Shropshire territory of the Cornovii, there was clearly a tribe whose name does not appear on most tribal maps produced by archaeologists and historians although Dr.S.C.Stanford has proposed the Decangi (140) mentioned by Tacitus in his *Annals* XII.

The Herefordshire hill-forts are well distanced from the most northerly Dean fort on Chase Hill, Ross. The termination of occupation of at least three of these forts excavated under Stanford, at Credenhill, Croft Ambrey and Midsummer Hill on the Malverns, coincided with the arrival of the Romans and, as Stanford adds: 'It would seem that on all three sites the passage of Scapula's troops was marked by the destruction of settlements, the wrecking of communities that had been in place for something like 500 or 600 years' (141). This is in total contrast to what took place in the territory of the northern Dobunni east of the Severn where none of the developed hill-forts show signs of warfare at the time when the Romans entered their lands, neither do the excavated defended enclosures, or any other first century AD site (142). It also contrasts with what little is known from excavations on Dean hill-forts. Neither Symonds Yat nor the Lydney hill-fort produced any evidence of destruction at the hands of the Romans. In fact, as we shall see, several Dean settlements continued to function in the years following the Roman occupation from c.AD 50 and there is strong evidence that they co-operated with the Romans.

Who Were the Ancient People of Dean?

Geographically they were isolated from the Dobunni, the Silures and the Herefordshire tribe

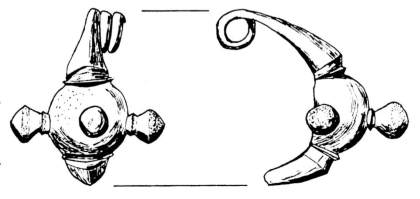

Figure 51. *Iron-Age bronze brooch from Silurian tribal territory (pin missing). Drawn by A.Stait.* Courtesy of MAS.

by the Severn, the Wye, and the Herefordshire plain. Down the Wye Valley, on either side, there are opposing hill-forts. Dean has always been rich in the essential resources of iron ore, timber, stone, coal, fish and animals to hunt. The people, left alone, are self-sufficient and surely always were, and with a surplus to trade. The insularity of the indigenous population is well attested from medieval times. This prevailed well into the 20th century and, indeed, still exists. True Foresters are still a people apart, fiercely proud and protective of their ancient rights and everyone born outside of the central upland area is a foreigner.

The Dobunnic Cotswolds are remote from Dean, as are the Malverns and the Black Mountains; faraway hills, blue with haze even on a clear day. To their inhabitants the Forest of Dean is a foreign land, a place to be visited on a day excursion. It was probably always so. Each area remote from the other. Each with its own concerns, its own strifes. Each with their own allegiances. Perhaps meeting occasionally for commercial transactions and exchange of news and views, but otherwise, independent. Their tribal centres, if the Dean hill-forts can be correctly described as such, surround the upland wooded nucleus and overlook the waters of Severn and Wye and whatever agricultural flat-lands they controlled to the north and east.

The few Dobunnic coins found in Dean do not prove that they were subject to the Dobunni but may well indicate that they were friendly towards, and traded with, that tribe. The same applies to the coin of the Coriosolites, a tribe from the north west of Gaul, which was found at the Bream scowles.

Unless some epigraphic evidence is revealed archaeologically to shed some light on the matter the ancient name for the Forest tribe will remain unknown. People living west of the Wye have no such problem. They live in what was the territory of the Silures.

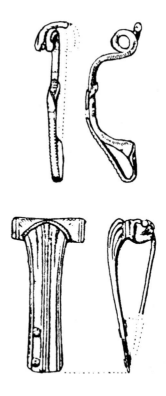

Figure 52. *Two late Iron-Age brooches from Dean. Top: La Tène II one-piece brooch from Lydney hill-fort. Bottom: 'Langton Down' type brooch from Lydney hill-fort.*

The Iron Age and the prehistoric period conventionally ends with the arrival of the Romans in Britain in AD 43. It would be another seven years before the legionaries and auxiliary soldiers entered Dean. In those few intervening years there arose a British warrior whose exploits in resisting the Romans were to become legendary: Caratacus.

Part Two

Roman Dean and the Wye Valley

Was Caratacus In Dean?

Caratacus is the form of the name of the British war leader as recorded by the first century AD Roman historian Tacitus who was the son-in-law of Agricola, the Roman Governor in Britain from AD 78-84. Tacitus' account of the exploits of the man who resisted the armed might of Rome for eight years, from the invasion year of 43 until his capture in 51, is the earliest record to survive.

To the Britons who fought alongside him he was probably known as Caradog. On the tiny silver coins he issued as self-imposed ruler of the Atrebates tribe, who occupied Berkshire and parts of West Sussex and Hampshire, his name is abbreviated to *CARA*.

Caratacus, however, was born north of the Thames (the Tamesa as it was known to the ancient Britons). He was a son of the great British ruler and statesman, Cunobelin, whose kingdom extended from the Chilterns to the North Sea beyond Colchester. For around thirty years Cunobelin had managed to maintain a skilful diplomatic balance between the southern British tribes some of whom were pro-Roman, trading with Roman Gaul and in Treaty with Rome, and the many who were bitterly anti-Roman and fearing a second, conquering, invasion.

When Cunobelin died c.AD 40 his eldest son, Togodumnus, inherited the kingdom, and anti-Roman feelings flared up. He and Caratacus moved to control the south-east coast harbours and landing places. Adminius was replaced as the ruler in Kent and was obliged to flee to the Roman Emperor for assistance to restore his position. Within a year Caratacus is believed to have moved to annexe the Atrebatan territory of Verica which extended to the Channel ports. Verica, too, fled the country and appealed to the newly enthroned Roman Emperor, Claudius, for military assistance. Claudius listened, considered the political benefits, then acted promptly to prepare for the great invasion which took place in AD 43 (142a).

The Roman Invasion

The success of the invasion is history. Close on one thousand ships transported a strike force of around forty thousand elite Roman troops to the shores of Britain under their commander, Aulus Plautius. They were faced by the forces of a confederation of British tribes, including warriors from the northern and southern Dobunni tribes of Gloucestershire and Somerset, all under the

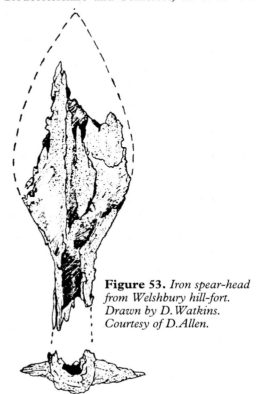

Figure 53. *Iron spear-head from Welshbury hill-fort. Drawn by D.Watkins. Courtesy of D.Allen.*

command of Togodumnus and Caratacus. It would appear that there was no beach-head resistance from the Britons. More probably they adopted the tactics of surprise attack and quick withdrawal but it failed to stop the Roman advance towards the Thames (142b).

The first real blow to the Britons came when the Gloucestershire section of the Dobunni, who probably feared the expansionist policies of Caratacus, surrendered to the Romans. As historian Dio Cassius recorded it, they were: 'won over by agreement' (143), probably a treaty by which their ruler, possibly Bodvoc *(Boduocus)*, would retain his property and receive Roman protection in exchange for the loyalty of himself and his subjects to the Emperor.

Setback For Britons

The second blow came when, having withdrawn to the north bank of a river, probably the Medway, at what they considered was an invulnerable position, the Britons were surprised by Roman tactics and were soundly defeated; Togodumnus dying soon afterwards. According to Dio: 'The Britons then fell back from this position to the River Thames' with Caratacus as their sole leader (144). The Romans advanced as far as the Thames where Aulus Plautius was obliged to call a temporary halt until Claudius arrived from Rome to share the triumph of entry into the tribal capital of Camulodunum (Colchester). There was little more immediate resistance from the Britons. Caratacus, realising that Roman tactics were superior in open conflict, took the opportunity to withdraw his family and loyal troops to a position far west of any immediate Roman threat; to South Wales and the territory of the fiercely anti-Roman Silures tribe. The safe, direct route would have taken him through the Somerset lands of his allies, the southern Dobunni under their ruler, possibly Corio, and across the Severn estuary or Bristol Channel to the Silures. The ruler of the northern Dobunni who controlled the narrow crossing of the Severn near Gloucester, was no longer to be trusted, in fact, he was probably considered an enemy. His lands were soon to become the target for plundering incursions by the warriors of the new anti-Rome alliance.

Growth Of A Legend

The exploits of Caratacus in Wales and the Welsh borders during the years up to his capture in AD 51 made him a folk hero. Poems and songs were written about him. Fortified camps, hills and monumental stones were named after him. History became legend. Legend became myth. The myths grew, were repeated for generation after generation until they were believed and accepted as truth. In Dean some believe the Cradock Stone at Sling to be named after him. It was certainly there in 1282 when the Regard of the Forest of Dene named it as the Cradokestune, on the Bailiwick boundary of Staunton (145). Not far north west of Dean, near Sellack in the Wye valley, there is a Caradoc hill.

A legend that still persists in local literature refers to Caratacus as being forced to retreat by the Romans through the Forest of Dean to the hill-fort at Symonds Yat where his last battle is supposed to have taken place. He escaped to the British Camp across the Wye on the Doward from whence he was lured to the camp of the Brigantian Queen, Cartimandua, only to be betrayed and handed over to the Romans (146).

Another legend, persistently repeated by local authors, is that the Romans used elephants against Caratacus and the Silures, and that, after crossing the Severn at Newnham and having forced the local Britons to retreat into the woods, they erected an altar to the goddess of Victory on the hill behind Newnham (147).

These stories are a blend of folk lore and historical mis-interpretation that has been perpetuated by later writers without reference to source material.

The truth is that the facts are few and the only extant historical account was recorded by Tacitus, however, recent archaeological discoveries, research and logical deduction can, perhaps, flesh-out the bare bones of the historical narrative.

Resistance Strategy

Having joined the Silures, Caratacus had maybe five or six years during which he was able to plan his resistance strategy, arm the Silures and neighbouring Ordovices tribe of mid-Wales, train his troops and familiarise himself with the Welsh terrain of mountains, gorges, bogs and woods; the latter being very much to his advantage.

During this period the Romans gradually advanced their frontier fort and road network to the Fosse way, linking garrisons from Exeter to Lincoln. In AD 47 Publius Ostorius Scapula became the new Governor of Roman Britain and the Commander of the army. The situation he inherited was described by Tacitus as chaotic: 'Convinced that a new commander, with an unfamiliar army and with winter begun, would not fight them, hostile tribes had broken violently into the Roman province. But Ostorius knew that initial results are what produce alarm or confidence. So he marched his light auxiliary battalions rapidly ahead, and stamped out resistance. The enemy were dispersed and hard pressed. To prevent a rally, or a bitter treacherous peace which would give neither general nor army any rest, Ostorius prepared to disarm all suspects and reduce the whole territory as far as the Trent and Severn' (148).

Many historians see the Silures under Caratacus as being among the 'hostile tribes', and the territory of the northern Dobunni in Gloucestershire as being the Roman province that was violently broken into by them. It fits well with the account of Tacitus who continued: 'But neither sternness nor leniency prevented the Silures from fighting. To suppress them, a brigade garrison had to be established. In order to facilitate the movement of troops westward to man it, a strong settlement of ex-soldiers was established on conquered land at Camulodunum. Its mission was to protect the country against revolt and familiarise the provincials with law-abiding government. Next Ostorius invaded Silurian territory' (149).

The fact that Scapula was obliged to extend his front line, beyond the Fosse Way, to the Severn suggests that the Silures were raiding across the Severn into the lands of the new Dobunnic client kingdom. That the garrison established by Scapula was, with some certainty, the Kingsholm, Gloucester fortress, also suggests that Caratacus and his allies were raiding the Dobunni in that location, or at least not far from it. This would have brought Caratacus through, or close, to Dean.

Around AD 48/49 Scapula is believed to have moved his XXth Legion, with auxiliaries, from Colchester to Gloucester in preparation for his invasion against the Silures.

Caratacus And Dean Iron-Workers

There is now enough archaeological evidence to allow the hypothesis that Caratacus, in the intervening years, made use of the skills of Dean ironworkers to arm his allies. The evidence has come from the iron-working settlement of Bury Hill which lies just three miles (5km) north of the ore source at Wigpool and between the villages of Bromsash and Bollitree in the parish of Weston-under-Penyard. It was soon to be known as Ariconium.

In 1785, Mr.Hopkins Merrick, in the course of clearing his land of scrub, uncovered extensive masonry remains of Roman buildings and numerous Roman artefacts from coins to bronze statues. Stone remains were levelled to make way for agriculture. The site was previously unknown to antiquarians but its significance was soon realised and was identified with Ariconium, a place name on a Roman imperial official route guide known as THE ANTONINE ITINERARY (150). The XIIIth Itinerary placed *Ariconio* XV Roman miles from Gloucester and XI Roman miles from Monmouth *(Blestio)*.

All subsequent antiquarian writers commented on the extensive iron-working debris that surrounded the settlement. Thomas Wright in his *'Wanderings of an Antiquary'*, published in 1844, went so far as to describe Ariconium as 'a city of iron workers, and surrounded by forges...'.

Remarkably, after its discovery, it took more than two centuries before enough was known about Ariconium to justify the publication of a monograph confirming its pre-Roman iron working phase, its later Roman military connections, and its subsequent importance as the centre of probably the largest iron producing region in Britain during the second century AD (151,152).

It was during the years after the Roman invasion of Britain, and before the legions and auxiliaries entered Dean, around AD 50, that Caratacus may have used the iron-workers of the Bury Hill settlement to produce weapons and armaments for his guerrilla forces, paying for their services out of the wealth he had accumulated for his war effort. Let us consider the evidence in support of this:

Consultation of the map of the Ariconium area will show the location of the native British settlement prior to the Roman presence. Many hundreds of rim fragments and body sherds of typically late Iron Age, pre-Roman pottery vessels have been recovered from this area. During the long, dry summers of 1989 and 1990 aerial

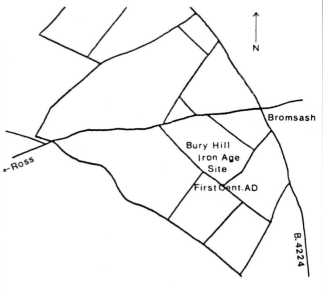

Figure 54. *'Ariconium', Bury Hill. Site of the early 1st century AD British settlement and iron-working area.*

photography revealed a large number of circular native huts and other timber buildings surrounded by ditched enclosures which are typical of early first century British settlements. In very recent years this area has also produced surface finds of many bronze brooches whose manufacture pre-dates the Roman period.

Figure 55. *Gold coin of Massalia (Marseilles) of the 1st century BC. A Massalian coin was found at the Bury Hill settlement.*

Payment For The Manufacture Of Arms?

Of particular significance are the large number of Celtic coins that have been found over the years in the same field and at other nearby locations. Commenting on the 27 Celtic coins actually recorded from the Bury Hill site a decade or so ago, Dr. Graham Webster observed: '... the evidence points towards the existence of a pre-Roman settlement, possibly connected with iron workings' (153). These include Celtic tribal coins from the continent including the Sequani tribe of the French/Swiss borderlands, and the Massalia tribe of the Mediterranean south of France. Two relevant British tribal coins are a copper coin of Cunobelin, the father of Caratacus and a gold ¼-stater of Verica whose Atrebatan territory Caratacus had annexed prior to the Roman invasion. A unique electrum coin, now in Gloucester Museum, was also found on the site. It has been suggested that it could be of Silurian origin, however this is unlikely. For the present it is not possible to identify either the place or region where it was struck.

From the iron-ore source of Bream scowles came the billon coin of the Coriosolites, another Gaulish tribe occupying north west France and the Channel Islands. Two Celtic tribal coins from Dymock, six miles from Ariconium, further confirmed a pre-Roman presence in the area. One was an uninscribed silver stater of the Dobunni tribe, however, it was the context it was found in that is so important: excavated from a level below the earliest Roman road, that is the military-made road from Gloucester to Stretton

Grandison and beyond, and therefore deposited prior to the Roman occupation. Another gold coin from Dymock originated with the Baiocasses of Normandy and was minted around a century before the Romans crossed the Severn.

The foreign coins were probably traded into Britain during the earlier first century AD and it would now seem less likely that the Roman military brought them to Ariconium, as some writers have proposed. All the Celtic coin finds were from the British settlement, not from the Roman fortlets which are 1km away.

Neither can it be argued that the native iron-workers at Bury Hill were trading internationally for, although there is sound evidence for pre-Roman iron-working on the site (154), it is doubtful that it was on such a scale as to have attracted foreign business. A logical possibility is that the coins were payment by Caratacus for services rendered. There is no reason to doubt that Caratacus had the wealth behind him. He would have inherited much of this at his father's death c.AD 40. For many years Cunobelin had been trading with the continent through the port of Colchester, his capital Camulodunum. Later, following his capture, and according to Tacitus, Caratacus addressed a speech to the emperor, Claudius, and his wife, Agrippina which earned for him and his family a pardon: 'I had horses, men, arms and wealth. Are you surprised I am

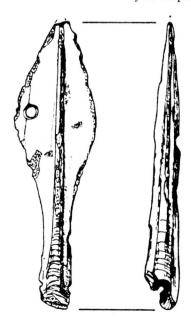

Figure 56. *A rare, pierced bronze arrow or spearhead from the Bury Hill settlement, possibly for ceremonial use. Drawn by A.Stait. Courtesy of T.James.*

sorry to lose them?' (155). Because the speech was recorded many years later it may be viewed as rhetorical. However, it is one of the shortest speeches recorded by Tacitus and may be held to contain the essence of what was said. In any case, it would be hard to dispute that Caratacus must have had at his disposal a generous supply of horses, men, arms and wealth.

One might reasonably surmise, in view of the above evidence, that he used some of his wealth to accumulate arms and that, once he had removed to the Silures, these were provided for him by the smiths at Bury Hill making use of Forest of Dean ores. Nowhere else, west of the Severn, is there evidence for iron-working associated with so many diverse Celtic coins in the mid-first century AD.

Ironically, the Romans were soon to be exploiting the same mining and smithing skills to manufacture weapons which were to be used against Caratacus.

The Romans Seize Dean

Circa AD 50, having established a garrison base at Kingsholm, Gloucester, the Roman XXth Legion along with auxiliaries and under their commander, Ostorius Scapula, crossed the Severn and headed directly for the heart of the Forest of Dean, towards what is now known as Mitcheldean.

There is no evidence that they encountered resistance from the independent tribes occupying the region between the Severn and the Wye. Caratacus would certainly not have chosen the woodlands of Dean for his guerrilla warfare. Had he done so he would soon have been surrounded by the Roman forces because there is evidence that Scapula had commandeered the Iron Age camp at Sudbrook, less than four miles (6km) south west of Chepstow, as a naval and supplies base for a section of his support fleet. This manoeuvre would have allowed for access behind the British lines should there have been resistance within Dean (155a).

No, Caratacus cunningly chose to lure the Roman forces into the hills west of the Wye, stretching their supply lines and obliging them to construct campaign forts in sometimes far from ideal locations such as the fort site at Castlefield, in the Monnow Valley near Kentchurch, which was particularly ambush prone. His tactics were to avoid open confrontation for as long as possible and to harass the Roman foraging parties and fort builders, ambushing small, detached groups of soldiers whenever possible. As Tacitus put it: 'The natural ferocity of the inhabitants was intensified by their belief in the prowess of Caratacus, whose many undefeated battles, and even many victories, had made him pre-eminent among British chieftains. His deficiency in strength was compensated by superior cunning and topographical knowledge' (156).

Before advancing west of the Wye in order to engage Caratacus, Scapula may have spent some months in Dean securing both the iron resources and organising the co-operation of those essential to the success of his campaign, the iron-ore miners, smelters, smiths and charcoal burners who would need to produce the iron, and from it forge the replacement weaponry and fort construction items he would be needing.

Roman Military Roads

It was probably at this juncture that the thirty-feet-wide military road from the Kingsholm base to Mitcheldean was constructed. It took a more or less direct route from the Severn crossing near Gloucester, running below Round Hill south of Huntley, and passing over the gap between Blaisdon Edge and Huntley Hill before descending into Longhope and through the narrowing valley to Mitcheldean (157).

An excavation across a section of this road produced a local copy of a Claudius As in the primary level (157a). These irregular coins, modelled on the official issues of Claudius, are believed to have been struck for, or by the Roman military in order to meet the need for small change. They are commonly found on early military sites and circulated mainly between AD 48 and AD 64 when the official supply of coins was either very limited or non-existent. Nero then established a mint at Lugdunum (Lyons) in Gaul which ensured a plentiful supply of lower value coins and the irregular coins went out of circulation (157b).

Although dating one section of a road need not imply that the whole length was constructed at the same time, in this instance it is difficult to view it otherwise. The road is a relatively short length for a Roman road, just 10 miles (16km). It is also the first and only road running directly west from Gloucester.

At Mitcheldean this primary road was connected to a north-south road that was of strategic importance because it provided a direct link between the Severn Estuary and the iron-working centre at Bury Hill, or, as it will now be referred to: Ariconium. This road was probably an east-of-Forest prehistoric route connecting tribal territories, but was upgraded to a paved and kerbed road eight feet wide which would give clear direction to mounted couriers as well as providing a good surface over which to transport ore from the Wigpool source to the

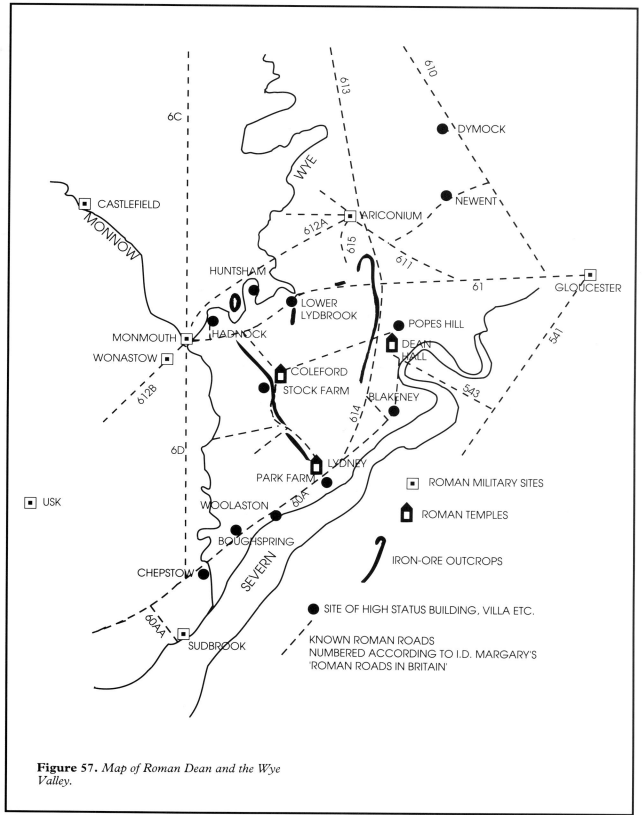

Figure 57. *Map of Roman Dean and the Wye Valley.*

Plate 10. *Roman road at Silver Street, Mitcheldean.* Photograph courtesy of A.P.Garrod.

Ariconium settlement. Should it have been considered necessary to transport forgeable iron bars or manufactured weaponry to the down-river-estuary forts from Ariconium then the road would also have provided the shortest possible route to the Severn. The road was also the first link of an early Roman road system than ran beyond Ariconium up the borders until it joined the west of Wye road from Chepstow which ran northwards through Monmouth. In terms of tactics and strategy these two roads could arguably be viewed as one, and a Scapulan initiative.

'The Dean Road'

To local people the section of road between Lydney and Ariconium is known as 'The Dean Road'. An exposed portion may be viewed at Blackpool Bridge south west of Soudley where it is a scheduled ancient monument. Until the later-1980s there was a sign post alongside the road clearly stating its origins as 'Roman', although it had been wrongly identified as dating from the 2nd century AD. This was subsequently removed and 'Roman' was replaced by the vague and unspecific 'Early'. On the 1988 edition of the Ordnance Survey Wye Valley and Forest of Dean Outdoor Leisure Map the road at Blackpool Bridge had become an 'Exposed Early Road', replacing the 'Roman Road' ascription of earlier maps.

The decision was possibly influenced by the publication of a no doubt sincere but perhaps incautious interpretation of a Carbon-14 dating of a charcoal sample from a Dean Road excavation which proclaimed that the paved road was not Roman, and could not have been constructed before 1660. Regrettably, the press release failed to draw attention to the several alternative possibilities as to how, and when the charcoal was deposited; neither did it allow for the vulnerability to contamination of the sample taken which came from beneath a single layer of paving and from a context that was not sealed (158). It also failed to draw attention to a small pit containing charcoaled wood, immediately outside the kerbing at that point, which was a very recent deposit.

Extensive correspondence with the laboratories and all concerned with the C-14 dating and species analysis eventually proved the sample as unreliable and negated the interpretation, but for a while it did cause some controversy (159).

Aerial photography, environmental survey, numerous recent Roman finds, and excavations alongside the road at Oldcroft and Ariconium have since confirmed the Roman origin of the paved road although many sections of it have since been repaired, stoned, re-laid and causewayed. Long lengths now lie beneath tarmac south of Soilwell Lane and north of Littledean. Where it passes the Roman military iron-working site north of Ariconium, the Dean Road now lies beneath the present B.4224 on its way north up the borders. Other sections have been identified beneath hedgerows (160).

The conclusive evidence finally came late in 1991 following the discovery of a hoard of over 500 fourth-century Roman coins alongside the road near Oldcroft. The site was excavated by Dean Archaeological Group under the direction of Mark Walters in November. Alongside and running parallel to the road was a drystone field

Plate 11. *The Roman military 'Dean Road' at Blackpool Bridge.* Photograph c.1902 by Rev.A.J.Lumbert. Courtesy of the Harris collection.

Instead, as we shall see, by the second century local iron-working centres were arguably producing more iron than any other region of Britain and were making a major contribution to the Roman economy.

boundary wall of Roman-period construction. Mark observed in his published excavation report: 'The most logical deposition location for the hoard would have been within the fabric of the boundary wall... At some point after AD 354 the hoard was displaced from its original place of concealment, possibly because the wall collapsed or because the stone was needed to repair the nearby road surface. The coins were scattered into the adjacent dark, tilled soils... The origins of this boundary wall are probably to be sought potentially as early as the first century foundation of the parallel Roman road alignment which passes the hoard location only 12 metres to the east... The present excavation supports the presence of the Roman road alignment in the fourth century as the boundary wall clearly divided the cultivated land to the west from the road on the east side and had the subsidiary function of preventing hill-wash covering the metalled surface' (160a).

There is no longer any justification for questioning the Roman origin of the 'Dean Road'.

The importance of Dean iron to the Roman military and to the later economy of the country was established at a very early stage. It would be true to state that, without its iron resources, the Roman-period history of Dean and the Wye Valley would have been wholly unremarkable.

ARICONIUM: The Roman Military Take Control

Although Ariconium is now in south Herefordshire in all probability during the Roman period it came under the same administrative authority as Dean and the Wye Valley settlements. Prior to the Roman occupation the surrounding lands may well have been held by the tribal centre on Chase Hill, Ross.

The present archaeological evidence cannot precisely date the beginnings of the pre-Roman iron-working, but an early first century date could reasonably be postulated. It was certainly well established as an iron-working centre by the time the Romans took control c.AD 50.

That there ought to be a Roman military site at or near Ariconium was proposed by a number of archaeologists and historians, foremost among them Dr.Graham Webster who recorded the following observation in 1981: 'The only hint of a military presence are the two Claudian imitation coins and two fragments of samian (pottery) Form 24/25, of Claudian-Neronian date. The deposits of iron ore would certainly have been of

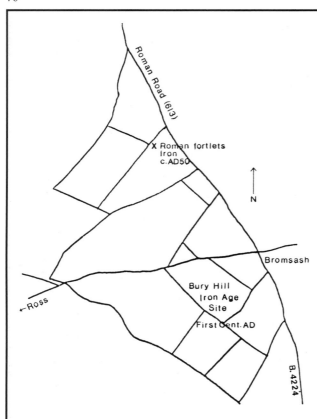

Figure 58. *Relationship of the Roman military iron-working site to the British settlement at Ariconium.*

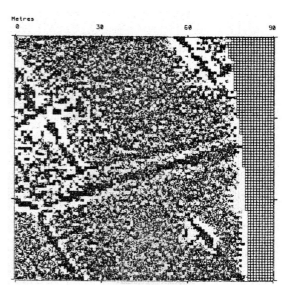

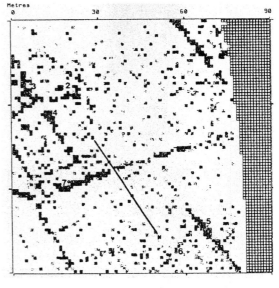

This print-out has eliminated most of the weaker magnetic anomalies caused by the 'floating' slag, thus enhancing the strongest features. Areas surrounded by numbers 2,3 and 4 are of particular interest. Area 1 appears to be outside of the enclosure ditch, however, one must be cautious here because the wide, intrusive ditch, numbered here as feature 7, continues beyond the hedgerow through into the next field. The feature numbered 5 appears to be in one of the fortlet ditches. 6, a straight line (gulley ?) running into the interior of the fortlets at an oblique angle, is doubly anomalous. The position of the 40 metres long excavation traverse has been drawn in.

Magnetometer survey by P.D.Catherall.

interest to the Roman army. A possible site of a fort would be to the north of the settlement, overlooking the Rudhall Brook' (161).

Field surface survey over the following decade produced many more examples of samian wares imported from southern Gaul during the reigns of Claudius and Nero (between AD 43-68), and further examples of poor copies of As coins of Claudius similar to the one found beneath the Kingsholm to Mitcheldean Roman road and others located on the fortress site at Kingsholm. These samian wares, especially when accompanied by the Claudian copy coins, provide even stronger evidence for a Claudio-Neronian military presence.

Aerial Photographic Survey

The very dry summer of 1989 provided Dean Archaeological Group with their first opportunity for productive aerial survey knowing that the drought would reveal where moisture-retaining ditch and pit features lay underground, as well as the close-to-surface stone features which would leave parch marks visible on the ground surface, especially in a shallow-rooted cereal crop. The Ariconium area was given special attention with the key objective being the identification of a Roman fort site. Within a month the objective was achieved, at least partially. The surprise was that no substantial fort was located, but two smaller fortlets were, one overlying the other and therefore not contemporary, also adjacent to what appeared to be a large native enclosure. They were not close by the Bury Hill iron-working settlement, but 1km north, alongside the Roman road from Lydney, and precisely where Dr.Webster had postulated a military site, on high ground above the Rudhall Brook.

Subsequent field survey, followed by geophysical survey with a magnetometer, confirmed the fortlet and enclosure ditches but also showed a very widespread and dense concentration of iron-working slags.

Excavation

The trial excavation that followed in the autumn and early winter of 1989 cut through four different ditches and parts of the interior of the two fortlets. The evidence proved the existence of a major iron-working site in production from the 50s into the Flavian period (later than AD 69). A rejected, faulty spear-tip of Roman type, which was fused to highly magnetic smithing slag and forging debris, may be evidence for the manufacture of weapons. An Aucissa-type brooch, favoured by the military, was also found and much of the stratified pottery could be matched with that found on the fortress sites of

Kingsholm and Usk, the latter thought to date from c.55 (161a). There was also an abundance of local-fabric native-ware pottery confirming the presence of Britons as well as Romans.

The fortlet ditches enclosed around 2,500 square metres, about .6 of an acre and both fortlets were of similar size, large enough to accommodate a century of men. The conclusion reached by the excavators was that they could be viewed as modest-sized administrative centres, staffed with a minimum of manpower and supervising the production, supply and distribution of artefacts and forgeable iron to advance military forts west of the Wye.

One section of the ditch surrounding the much larger, presumed native iron-working enclosure, was excavated and produced only native-ware pottery, however the geophysical survey indicated internal rectangular buildings and solid slag concentrations.

All the evidence gathered from both the military and civilian settlements at Ariconium suggests that there was a compliant work-force co-operating with the Romans and receiving benefits for so doing (162).

Recent fieldwork and excavation in Dean tends to confirm the latter conclusion. There is now evidence that several village communities were permitted, probably encouraged, to smelt ore. With no evidence for forging on these sites it is possible that they supplied their forgeable iron to the smiths at Ariconium for at least two decades following the Roman occupation, thus supplementing the smelting done there and indicating an urgent demand for iron.

Plate 12. *The ditches of two fortlets and an adjoining enclosure showing as crop-marks (centre picture) 1km north of Ariconium. The Roman military road (Margary Route 613), a continuation of the 'Dean Road', can be seen passing the site. Aerial photograph by M.J.Walters.*

Iron-working between the years c.AD 50-75 has been confirmed at Great Howle, which was a small enclosed settlement, Ruardean, Drybrook, on Round Hill, Huntley, at Aston Ingham and within the hill-fort at Symonds Yat. All of these sites produced smelting slags only, with no evidence for secondary smithing (the forging of artefacts). The iron produced can logically only have been supplied to Ariconium for the mineral resources of Dean were now theoretically under the control of the military and belonged to the Roman state (163).

One possibility that cannot yet be ignored regarding the early administration of the Ariconium iron industry is that, under the cover of the military, Roman civilian entrepreneurs were allowed, or encouraged to move in as middle men who profited from both the British producers and the military commanders who may have preferred to deal with them rather than the natives (163a).

The First Two Decades Under The Romans

That weapons were among the artefacts manufactured at Ariconium is supported to some extent by excavated evidence, however, between c.50-60 the greatest demand would have been for millions of iron nails in a variety of sizes for rapid fort construction. The very earliest forts to be constructed during Scapula's action against Caratacus would have been of a temporary nature with turf embankments and with the men housed in tents. These were replaced by more permanent forts with timber palisades and gateways, and with barracks of wood. First, though, Caratacus and the Silures had to be defeated.

Tacitus' account is very informative for the years 50 and 51. The initial Roman advance was westwards from Dean into Silurian territory. Within the year, and possibly because Caratacus saw the danger of having his forces concentrated into too small an area and being surrounded, he made a strategic move northwards with a large force of his men leaving the Romans with a number of temporary forts on the Silures frontier which would still need defending: 'Transferring the war to the country of the Ordovices, he was joined by everyone who found the prospect of a Roman peace alarming'. This took Caratacus into the upper reaches of the Severn, the tribal territory of the Ordovices, and increased support for his cause. It is possible that at this point Scapula moved detachments of his XIVth Legion forward over the north Welsh borders, perhaps in a deliberate attempt to force Caratacus to abandon his hit and run tactics and make a stand, which would be much to the advantage of the Romans.

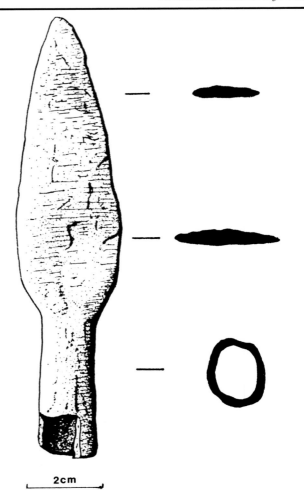

Figure 60. *Roman iron spear from Ariconium. Drawn by D. Thomas.* Courtesy of M.J. Walters.

The Last Battle Of Caratacus

Whatever his reasons were, Caratacus obliged. According to Tacitus: 'Caratacus staked his fate on a battle. He selected a site where numerous factors, notably approaches and escape routes, helped him and impeded us. On one side there were steep hills. Wherever the gradient was gentler, stones were piled into a kind of rampart. And at his front there was a river without easy crossings. The defences were strongly manned' (164).

The precise location of the battle remains unknown although many sites have been postulated. Past historians have favoured one or other of the hill-forts called Caer Caradoc, but none of them fit the description of the location given by Tacitus, who presumably had access to Scapula's despatches sent back to Rome. The site was certainly within the boundaries of the Ordovices tribe which occupied parts of North Wales but the extent of their lands is ill-defined and nowhere does Tacitus make mention of a hill-fort.

Dr.Graham Webster suggested that the river must have been the Severn, and the possible location of the battle as being somewhere between Newtown and Caersws (165). More recently Professor Barrie Jones has proposed a site near Llanymynech on the River Vyrnwy where aerial photographs appear to indicate a series of small campaign forts (166).

Tacitus continued: 'After a reconnaissance to detect vulnerable and invulnerable points, Ostorius (Scapula) led his enthusiastic soldiers forward...... It was a great victory. Caratacus' wife and daughter were captured: his brother surrendered. He himself sought sanctuary with Cartimandua, queen of the Brigantes. But the defeated have no refuge. He was arrested, and handed over to the conquerors. The war in Britain was in its ninth year (i.e. AD 51-52). The reputation of Caratacus had spread beyond the islands and through the neighbouring provinces to Italy itself' (167).

Following a brave speech before the emperor, Claudius, Caratacus was pardoned along with his wife and brothers and, presumably, lived out his life in the rather sunnier climes of Italy. But what of Scapula, and what was the reaction of the Silures to the capture of their leader?

Tacitus further reveals: 'Ostorius received an honorary Triumph. But now his success, hitherto unblemished, began to waver. Possibly the elimination of Caratacus had caused a slackening of energy, in the belief that the war was over. Or perhaps the enemy's sympathy with their great king had whetted their appetite for revenge.'

It is just as likely that Scapula now had the nightmare dilemma of not being authorised by the emperor to complete the conquest of Wales, yet having to hold and defend the newly won lands over a frontier that stretched from the Dee Estuary to the Bristol Channel, a distance of close on a hundred and thirty miles. The Silurians, aware of this predicament when Scapula failed to withdraw his troops, were quick to take advantage of the thinly spread military resources:

Historical Documentary Evidence For Silurian Resistance

In Silurian country, Roman troops left to build forts under a divisional chief of staff *(praefectus castrorum)* were surrounded, and only saved from annihilation because neighbouring fortresses learnt of their siege and speedily sent help. As it was, casualties included the chief of staff, eight company commanders (centurions), and the pick of the men.'

The Legion that suffered this setback in all probability was the XXth which had set out from Gloucester perhaps little more than a year earlier for Dean. One cannot help but wonder if the setback occurred in the narrow Monnow Valley during the construction of the Castlefield fort where it would have been so easy for the Britons to stay hidden among the surrounding hills and bluffs until the Romans were encircled. Further tactical aggression from the Silures came on the heels of their initial success:

'Shortly afterwards a Roman foraging party was put to flight. So were cavalry troops sent to its rescue. Ostorius threw in his light auxiliary battalions, but even so did not check the rout until the regular brigades joined in. Their strength made the struggle equal and eventually gave us the advantage. However, night was coming on, so the enemy escaped almost undamaged'.

The year 51-52 probably saw more military action west of the Wye than any other year in the history of the region:

'Battle followed battle. They were mostly guerrilla fights, in woods and bogs. Some were accidental, the results of chance encounters. Others

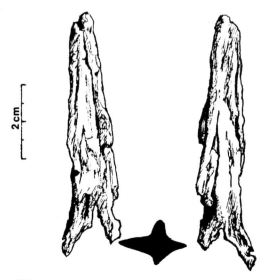

Figure 61. *Quad-lobed missile point from Ariconium.* Drawn by C.Mortimer.

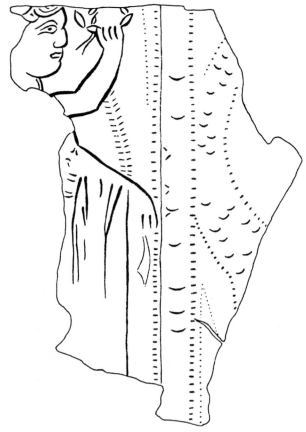

Figure 62. *Victoria holding a laurel wreath and palm branch, punched and inscribed on a fragment of sheet copper-alloy, from Ariconium. Probably a decorative part of some Roman military equipment. Drawn by D.Thomas. Courtesy of M.J.Walters.*

Claudius, upon hearing of the governor's death appointed an experienced and distinguished senator, Aulus Didius Gallus, to succeed him. In the few months it might have taken Didius Gallus to arrive in this region to review his troops there was another defeat for the Romans west of the Wye.

As Tacitus reported: 'Didius made for Britain rapidly. But he found a further deterioration. For in the interval a Roman brigade (legion) commanded by Manlius Valens had suffered a reverse...... Again the damage was due to the Silures: until deterred by Didius' arrival, they plundered far and wide' (169).

The five years of Gallus' governorship are generally seen as years of consolidation during which a forward fortress base was established at Usk (although this may reasonably have been initiated under Scapula), frontier fort construction was completed and supply roads were laid up and down the borders. In his *Agricola* XIV Tacitus summarised his efforts thus: 'Didius Gallus...... kept a firm hold on what his predecessors had won, and even pushed some new forts into outlying districts.'

It must have been an incredibly busy time for the Ariconium iron-workers. During the Scapulan campaigns they would have been fully occupied producing replacement weaponry. Now the greatest demand was for ready-made nails, and forgeable iron bars to be worked in fort fabricas by the military smiths. These would have been transported through Monmouth *(Blestium)* to the new supply base at Usk. Other materials were transported up the west-of-Wye borders road to military sites further north. It is likely that some supplies were transported along the Dean Road to be shipped down the Severn Estuary to Bristol Channel forts.

were planned with calculated bravery ...... The Silures were exceptionally stubborn. They were enraged by a much-repeated saying of the Roman commander that they must be utterly exterminated...... Two auxiliary battalions, which their greedy commanders had taken plundering with insufficient precautions, fell into a trap laid by the Silures. Then they began by gifts of spoils and prisoners, to tempt other tribes to join their rebellion' (168).

So considerable were the spoils, which must have been mainly weapons and armour, that the Silures were able to pursuade other tribes to share in their successes.

At this point, probably late in the year 52, 'exhausted by his anxious responsibilities, Ostorius died.'

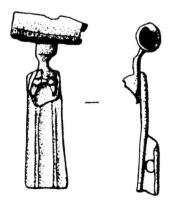

Figure 63. *A repaired hybrid brooch of the Claudian period. The lower part, a 'Thistle' type, has been rivetted to a heavily tooled spring cover. Drawn by D.Thomas. Courtesy of T.James.*

It has been estimated that around 80 furnaces could have been in operation at this time at Ariconium and the other known Dean smelting sites. The furnaces would have required around 400 men to operate them in addition to the smiths who forged the weapons, nails and other artefacts. Others were engaged in mining the ore, producing charcoal and transportation of both. By far the majority of mature males in Dean must have been engaged in some aspect of iron production. (170).

When Gallus died he was succeeded by Quintus Veranius in 57/58 who made more sorties against the Silures. As Tacitus put it: 'Quintus Veranius had only conducted minor raids against the Silures when death terminated his operations' (171). He died within the year and was replaced by Suetonius Paullinus.

The next two years saw renewed aggression under Paullinus who: '... enjoyed two years of success, conquering tribes and establishing strong forts. Emboldened thereby to attack the island of Anglesey, which was feeding the native resistance, he exposed himself to a stab in the back' (172). Tacitus' account implies that Paullinus continued where Veranius left off, in Wales, strengthening the Roman position with further fort construction and the upgrading of temporary forts. Encouraged by his successes he considered that the British tribes in Wales would be totally dispirited and broken if he could destroy the Druid stronghold on Anglesey. This he succeeded in doing during the year 60.

The 'stab in the back' happened while Paullinus was far removed to the west of Britain, and the 'hand' that held the 'knife' was close on 300 miles away to the south east. The hand belonged to Boudica, queen of the Iceni, who, outraged by mistreatment from the Romans following her husband's death, revolted. Tacitus' vividly recorded the events that followed in his *Annals* XIV. He describes the rapid march back from Anglesey with the XIVth Legion, joined by detachments from the XXth, with its central garrison at Usk, along with the nearest available auxiliaries, a total force of nearly 10,000 men. They confronted a British force of six-figure numbers, possibly near Atherstone and the Watling Street, although the precise location may never be known (173).

The Britons suffered a comprehensive defeat and thereby the last hopes withered that the Romans might be forced to relinquish their hold on Britain. The next generation were to look more positively for the benefits which were to be derived from acceptance and co-operation. The Romans, for their part, learnt to deal more fairly and justly with the people of their new province.

'Benefits'

In Dean the natives had already experienced for ten years the benefits that could accrue from co-operating with the Romans. The small communities smelting iron at Ruardean, Drybrook, Great Howle, Huntley, Aston Ingham, Symonds Yat, and probably Coleford could only have been doing so voluntarily, in return for benefits received from the Romans for the iron they supplied to Ariconium. During this ten years of intense military activity it would be unthinkable that even a small military force should be assigned to supervise these scattered communities. There is no such evidence anyway.

Figure 64. *A portrait of the Emperor Augustus (27 BC to AD 14) on a silver denarius from Hangerbury Hill.* Courtesy of N.Webley and Messrs. Symonds.

On the other hand there is evidence for 'benefits' on the British sites. Imported, decorated samian pottery of the Claudius-Nero period has been found in some quantity on the civilian settlement at Ariconium. It can only have originated with the military, or possibly the wealthy Roman civilian middle men. A section of a decorated Form 37 samian bowl was found on the small, isolated settlement at Great Howle. Similar bowls by the same maker were found at Pompeii which was destroyed in AD 69, so the Great Howle bowl probably pre-dates that year. From Hangerbury Hill, where a late Iron Age community may also have been smelting ore on behalf of the Romans at this time, came a very fine, hardly-circulated silver denarius of the first Emperor, Augustus, minted during the first decade of the 1st century. That this also originated with the Roman military must be considered a strong possibility (174). A mint condition gold aureus of Vespasian found near St.Briavels almost certainly did (175).

The mid to late 60s witnessed many troop movements once Nero determined to assemble an army for projected eastern campaigns. The *Legio* XIV was withdrawn from Wroxeter and a new fortress was constructed in Gloucester, c.67, on what was to be the future Colonia site in the city centre. The Usk fortress was temporarily abandoned at the same time, so it was probably to Gloucester that *Legio XX* was now moved. Construction of the new Gloucester fortress would have made fresh demands on the Ariconium iron-workers for nails and other iron fittings.

In 69, following a civil war in Rome, Vespasian, who had commanded the IInd Legion in Britain for Claudius, was installed as the new emperor. He was familiar with Britain and determined to attempt to annexe the whole island. To

of Anglesey was re-captured. By 79 the whole of what is now known as England and Wales was under Roman control.

It took twenty seven years, from the probing resistance of Caratacus to the terminal thrust of Frontinus, before the Silures were totally subdued. During this twenty seven years the people of Dean were becoming well Romanised. The Silures, too, were soon to appreciate the benefits when a new tribal capital was constructed for them by the Romans, at Caerwent *(Venta Silurum)*, a new town only 7 miles (11km) west of Dean and the River Wye.

Developments in Dean and the Wye Valley under Vespasian

It is generally accepted that, once a country became a Roman province, mineral rights came into state ownership. What Vespasian did was to create a powerful bureaucracy to ensure that maximum gains to the Treasury derived from ownership of these rights. To this end he confirmed the policy of Imperial Estates, which included important metal-producing regions, and greatly extended the network (177). Around this time the Dean iron industry was probably nationalised.

The reason for Vespasian's stringent economic moves was revealed by historian Suetonius: '... the emptiness alike of the Treasury and the Privy Purse forced Vespasian into heavy taxation...... he himself had declared at his accession that 400,000,000 gold pieces were needed to put the country on its feet again' (178).

The impact of Vespasian's decrees, especially with regard to mineral rights, are now evident in the local archaeological record both in Dean and west of the Wye. Transformations occurred that were to affect the native population of Dean and

Figure 65. *Vespasian: Commander of Legio II Augusta in Britain at the time of the Roman invasion. Emperor in Rome AD 69-79.*

this end he appointed three highly qualified individuals to govern, Cerialis, Frontinus and Agricola, and then proceeded to increase the British garrison and ordered the contruction of a new fortress at Caerleon c.75. This spelled the end of the protracted opposition from the Silures. Frontinus was the commander who brought it about. Once again Tacitus supplies the information: 'But Julius Frontinus shouldered the heavy burden, and rose as high as a man could then rise. He subdued by force of arms the strong and warlike nation of the Silures, laboriously triumphing not only over a brave enemy but also over a difficult terrain' (176). By 78 the Ordovices were conquered by Agricola and the abandoned island

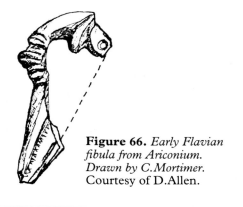

Figure 66. *Early Flavian fibula from Ariconium. Drawn by C.Mortimer.* Courtesy of D.Allen.

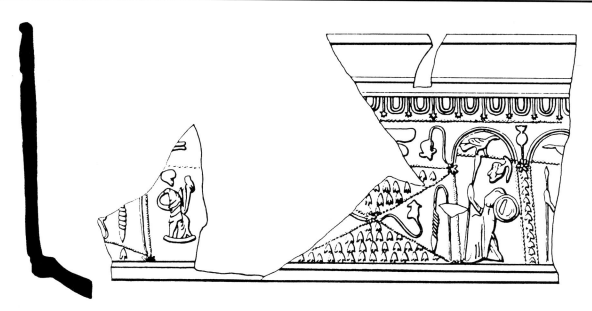

Figure 67. *Part of an early Flavian Form 30 Samian cup from Blakeney. Manufactured in Southern Gaul.* Drawn by D. Thomas.

which also saw significant expansion in the iron industry.

For around a quarter of a century the industry was, with reasonable certainty, either under military control or in the hands of permitted Roman private enterprise. There is not one scrap of evidence to suggest that a state appointed civilian administrator was resident in the area before 75. In any case the iron demands were almost exclusively of a military nature.

An Official's Residence At Blakeney

There is now circumstantial evidence that c.75 a high-ranking state official was appointed to administer the resources of Dean, especially those related to the iron industry. This new evidence emerged as a result of an excavation at Blakeney by Dean Archaeological Group. It revealed traces of a high-status building constructed around AD 75 and in use for around sixty years until it was demolished towards the middle of the 2nd century. It had a heating system, a tiled roof and a stoned courtyard. It was also located alongside the major Roman military road from Newnham, which runs through Lydney to Chepstow, where it bridged the Wye, and continues through Caerwent to Caerleon and beyond. The Bideford Brook flows close by and joins the Severn at Brims Pill. Known ancient trackways also link Blakeney with the river which is less than 2km away (about one mile).

The pottery assemblage confirms the early Roman origins of the site, being rich with early Flavian south Gaulish samian wares and Belgic-type pottery which is common on the Gloucester fortress sites. No other high-status, villa-type building appeared in Dean until the second century. This caused the Director of the excavation, Mark Walters, to observe in his interim report: 'The presence of a substantial building of Flavian date at Blakeney has important implications for the administration of the Forest region in the early years of settled occupation. To find comparable evidence of such building activity at this date elsewhere in Gloucestershire one has to look to military constructions...... The most likely context for the building here is an early administration centre for a high-ranking official, possibly appointed to supervise mining and other economically viable industries in the Forest area. Its termination by the middle of the 2nd century may indicate that economic interests had been handed over to civilian administrative bodies, or the official residence had been re-located' (179).

Another less likely possibility is that the building served as a post house for the *Cursus Publicus*, the Imperial communications' service. The service was founded in the early years of the first century by Augustus and consisted of a system of post houses and inns (*mansiones*) along major roads throughout the Empire at frequent intervals for the change of horses and refreshment. Mounted couriers travelled either alone, in quick-moving two wheeled carts or with passengers on a four-wheeled kind of stage-coach.

Because of its geographic position it is unlikely that the Blakeney building was a post house. It is on a route to and from Gloucester (Margary

Roman Road numbers 541, 543 and 60A) but one which would have required a tidal river crossing at Newnham-on-Severn. The total road distance from Gloucester, via Blakeney to Lydney, is 21¾ miles (35km). The more obvious road route from Gloucester to Lydney, of identical distance, would have been along Margary road numbers 61 and 614 through Mitcheldean. Road 614 runs 2km west of Blakeney, but would have entailed a four miles (6.5km diversion) to go via Blakeney to Lydney. Both routes would have entailed a crossing of the Severn but the Gloucester crossing would be better organised, maintained and most used. A post house at the Lydney, Park Farm villa would be much more logical and practical and is where several roads converge as well as being close to a harbour (see map of Roman road system).

The location of the Blakeney residence *is* well-placed for administrative purposes with road and river links to Gloucester, yet convenient to the east of Forest ore sources.

Its construction probably coincided with the abandonment of the Gloucester fortress, and the installation of the IInd Legion in a new fortress at Caerleon, all of which followed closely on the arrival of Sextus Julius Frontinus as Governor of Britain.

An Official's Residence In Gwent

There is further archaeological evidence for the emplacement of an administrator over mining activities at this time from a little publicised site only 32 miles (52km) west of Blakeney at Lower Machen in Monmouthshire, just 12km from Caerleon. Here a building of comparable specifications to that at Blakeney was built close to the Roman lead mine at Cefn Pwll-Du, near Draethen. The pottery sequence also continued well into the second century but with early Flavian samian dominating the assemblage. Evidence for lead working on site was recorded. The excavator, V.E.Nash-Williams commented: 'The site was certainly in Roman hands by the time of the completion of the Roman military conquest of South Wales (soon after) AD 75, and possibly before...... we may infer a small mining settlement under government control...... the column capitals represented among the Machen finds imply a residential building of more elaborate type, doubtless the residence of the supervising officer' (180). This was probably the residence of a civilian administrator but its proximity to the Caerleon fortress means that a military association must remain a consideration.

These two excavations have produced positive evidence for the application of Vespasianic policies in connection with mineral wealth in, and west of Dean.

Coincident Developments

Recent excavations in Dean and the Wye Valley have confirmed several other major developments which were initiated at this time:

1. A new iron-working centre was opened up at Monmouth.
2. A number of small communities west of the Wye were engaged in smelting ore.
3. Village settlements of central Dean, located within the circle of ore outcrops, were closed down and never inhabited again during the ensuing three hundred years or so of Roman occupation. These included the smelting communities at Great Howle, Ruardean, Drybrook, Huntley and Symonds Yat.
4. Coleford appears to have become the one Dean native settlement with evidence for expansion in the later 1st century and which continued in existence until the late 4th century, and probably beyond.
5. The Ariconium iron-working area expanded into an adjoining field.

MONMOUTH

The Roman name for Monmouth is given as Blestium in the *Antonine Itinerary* XIII. It was part of the long-distance route from Silchester, via Cirencester and Gloucester to Caerleon, and is therefore a settlement where one would expect to find stabling and accommodation facilities in a guest-house *(mansio)* from the second century onwards, if not before.

Massive deposits of iron-working waste underlie the town and the river-bed of the Wye. Excavations by Monmouth Archaeological Society at Granville Street cut through 13 feet (4m) of iron slag layers with sealed Roman contexts at the bottom. Roman furnaces were also revealed there. Much of this slag was unquestionably produced during the medieval period but there is no doubting the Roman origins of much of it.

Flavian Period Smithing Hearth

In 1988 Dean Archaeological Group were invited to assist with rescue excavations on the site of the old Glendower Street School in advance of development. The area excavation to natural layers produced conclusive evidence for iron-working on the site from c.75 to the end of the 2nd century when the area was back-filled and became a green-field, remaining such until the 20th century.

Among the notable finds was an intact primary smithing hearth complete with its last charge of fuel. The hearth had been used to re-heat smelted blooms of iron from a nearby furnace. Once re-heated the iron was hammered on an anvil to release all entrapped and adhering slag,

Plate 13. *Early Flavian period primary smithing hearth at Monmouth, Glendower Street School excavation, 1988.*

then shaped into a small bar of up to 4lbs (2kg) weight, ready for transportation to the secondary smith (now known as a blacksmith) who forged the iron into artefacts. A considerable amount of pottery, small finds and coin evidence confirmed the above dating. The quantity of smelting and primary smithing slags present suggested that the iron-working was extensive. There was also a surprising amount of stratified coal scattered around which could be used for smithing operations, but was not the fuel used for smelting. An analysis of the coal showed that it had been transported from surface outcrops in the Forest of Dean, specifically from the Berry Hill/Bracelands area. No evidence has yet been found for iron-working in Monmouth prior to c.75, so it would appear to have been a new initiative (181).

Pre-Flavian Evidence

A more recent excavation in 1991, on a shop development site in Monnow Street by the Monmouth Archaeological Society, has confirmed a pre-Flavian presence in the town, but not connected with iron-working. The excavator proposed that the evidence for earlier structures, and the small finds of early samian pottery, and bronze brooches were more probably attributable to the Roman army (182). Since then, in September of 1992, a Roman military fort ditch has been revealed on the same site with pre-Flavian imported samian pottery being excavated from the ditch slot, thus confirming what has for long been suspected (182a).

Supplementary Smelting

There is also strong evidence for supplementary smelting on small settlement sites west of the Wye in Monmouthshire for a decade or so after c.75. Smelting slags associated with Flavian period samian pottery and other later first century finds have been found at Gwenherrion Farm, Welsh Newton; at Lower Monkton, Llanwarne; within an enclosed settlement at Lords Wood on the Doward, and at Whitchurch. The iron ore outcrops on the Doward would have been the logical source of supply for the ores which were smelted. The resulting iron bars were probably transported along the Roman road which runs through Whitchurch to Monmouth, or else along the Roman road from Monmouth laid due north from Monmouth towards Hereford.

In the hills to the south of Monmouth, near Trellech, there is also evidence for short-period iron-working from c.75 at Trellech Gaer, Hygga and Great Crumbland. Their forgeable bars may have been sent into Monmouth, but equally they may have gone direct to a new, early Flavian military site that is suspected just south of Monmouth on a hill near Wonastow (183). The latter three sites probably made use of bog ores which are to be found around Trellech.

Of all these Wye Valley sites only Monmouth and Whitchurch continued into the 2nd century as major iron production centres. East of the Wye, in Dean, at some time before the end of the 1st century, all of the supplementary smelting locations were deserted. Their inhabitants must have been re-located, probably to Ariconium or

Figure 68. *From a John Speed map of Monmouth c.1611. X marks the spot of the pre-Flavian Roman finds in Monnow Street. Y marks the site of an early Flavian iron-working site.*

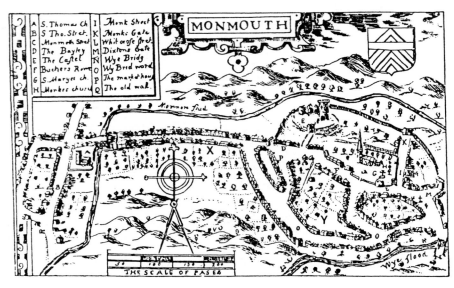

the Coleford settlement, so increasing the work-force there as plans evolved to expand the industry to meet the anticipated civilian needs. That both places clearly expanded around this time is demonstrated by the proliferation and abundance of pottery finds. These co-ordinated changes suggest administrative directives, possibly emanating from an official now resident at Blakeney.

CHEPSTOW

Chepstow has been neglected archaeologically and even in recent years many major developments have taken place without prior evaluation, geophysical survey, excavation or recording. From the rare excavation, salvage work and the isolated find it is clear that Chepstow had an important Roman presence. It is logical that this began between the years 50 and 75. The Roman military road from Newnham to Caerleon crossed the Wye on the river bend north of where Chepstow Castle now stands. It descended through Tutshill on the Dean side, and ascended through Alcove Wood following the present Chepstow/St.Arvans parish boundary on the west side of the Wye. It was almost certainly bridged. Two Roman roads converge at a point about half a mile from the Wye crossing, the one leading through Pwll Meurig to Crick, with a link to Sudbrook, the other runs north to Monmouth via Trellech. There ought to be an early military fort guarding the river crossing.

1st century recorded finds from the town include a Dobunnic gold stater, a coin of Domitian dating to 87, a red and yellow enamelled harness-trapping dated to the second half of the 1st century, a coin of Claudius (AD 41-54),

three late 1st century cremations with contemporary pottery, one of the cremations being surrounded by a timber shrine, and, in 1992, first century material including a mortarium rim of early Flavian date (183a).

Later First Century Iron Requirements

In the last year of the reign of Vespasian, 78/79, Agricola, having brought the northern parts of Wales under Roman control turned his attention northwards to the Brigantian territories. By the year 79 the Roman occupied lands stretched as far north as the Tyne to the Solway, and by 80 from the Forth to the Clyde (184). In the more settled areas to the south Tacitus informs us that: 'Agricola gave private encouragement and official assistance to the building of temples, public squares and private mansions.... Furthermore, he trained the sons of the chiefs in the liberal arts and expressed a preference for British natural ability over the trained skill of the Gauls. The result was that in place of distaste for the Latin language came a passion to command it. In the same way, our national dress came into favour and the toga was everywhere to be seen. And so the Britons were gradually led on to the amenities that make vice agreeable; arcades, baths and sumptuous banquets' (185).

Tacitus was, of course, writing about the effects of Romanisation on the nobles and wealthy Britons, the landowners who had by now accepted that the benefits of co-operation with the Romans far outweighed the certain confisca-

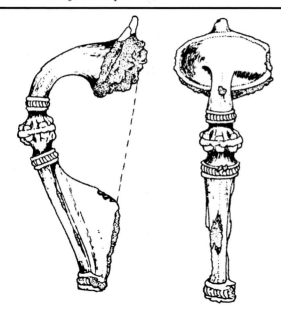

Figure 69. *2nd century AD 'trumpet' type brooch from Chestnuts Hill, Littledean. Brooches were not merely decorative, they were functional, securing loose garments and shawls. Drawn by D. Watkins.* Courtesy of D. Allen.

tion of property that would inevitably follow the slightest demonstration of resistance. It was becoming fashionable to be 'Roman'. Extending benefits to the aristocrats also meant that the dependent lower classes were being controlled, without having to disperse military forces.

It may well have been a trusted, high-ranking British civilian who was placed at Blakeney to supervise state assets. This would have ensured the continued acquiesence of the Dean peoples who were well used to respecting their tribal chiefs. Their work-load would have been heavy, but the necessities at least were ensured and some of the benefits would assuredly have trickled down to them. This much is evident from the quality of the new pottery forms, including imported table wares, which are to be found in some abundance on the later first century iron-working sites both sides of the Wye.

Local Iron Shipped North

Tacitus gives a strong hint as to where some of the Dean iron was directed during Agricola's campaigns in the north: 'Clyde and Forth, carried inland to a great depth on the tides of opposite seas, are separated only by a narrow neck of land. This neck was now secured by garrisons, and the whole sweep of country to the south was safe in our hands...... In the fifth year of campaigning Agricola began with a sea passage, and

in a series of successful actions subdued nations hitherto unknown. The whole side of Britain that faces Ireland was lined with his forces' (186).

It is evident from Tacitus' narrative that Agricola had divided his fleet so as to supply his troops on both western and eastern coasts of Britain. The 'sea passage' mentioned above confirms their presence along the western coast, while Tacitus records the fleet along the eastern coast actively participating in the campaign north of the Forth into Caledonian territory (187). Frontinus would already have deployed a section of the fleet for his final conquest of the Silures and Agricola likewise for his subjugation of north Wales. Forts constructed in the western lands of the Brigantes, in fact all forts along the western coast of Britain from the Bristol Channel to the Clyde, would benefit from supplies shipped by the fleet. Construction nails and replacement weaponry, or at least the forgeable iron which could have been worked by smiths attached to the legions, would be high on the list of necessary supplies. Ariconium and the new centre at Monmouth would be the logical sources for all iron requirements for west coast military action, while the Wealden iron would logically supply the military installations along the eastern coast.

The Civilian Market For Iron

From the mid-80s civilian developments would have made the greatest demands on local iron-workers. Gloucester was to be made a Colonia, a town for veteran soldiers, while new, Romanised tribal capitals were to be constructed; for the Dobunni at Cirencester *(Corinium Dobunnorum)*, and for the Silures at Caerwent *(Venta Silurum)*. Civilian developments at Bath and in the south west as well as northwards up the Severn Valley were probably supplied with all their iron fittings by Dean and Wye Valley smiths.

Some idea of the range of iron objects in everyday use can be gleaned from a glance through the British Museum's *'Catalogue of Romano-British Iron Tools, Fittings and Weapons'* (188). It lists a range of over one hundred and forty items. Reduced to categories they include tools for a diversity of trades from agriculture to metal-working, transport, toilet implements, surgical instruments, styli, locks and keys, domestic equipment, axes, knives, cleavers and a wide variety of structural fittings. The first century requisitions would repetitively have listed: nails, hammers, picks and weapons. Local smiths now had to discover the intricacies of locks, the subtle shapes of strigils and the broader heads of T-clamps for masonry.

By the end of the first century, along with the new stability in Britain, came an optimistic economic climate and visible expansion of the Dean

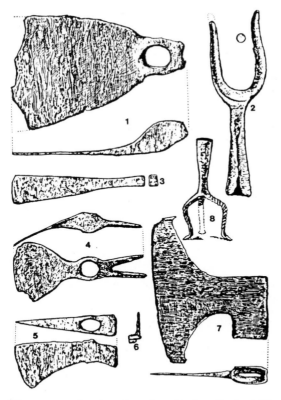

Figure 70. *Iron artefacts from Lydney Park: 1.Hoe 2.Pitchfork 3.Chisel 4.Adze 5.Axe/hammer 6.Ox goad 7.Axe 8.Candle-holder.* After REM Wheeler.

iron industry. The population of the region possibly quadrupled as more new iron-working centres appeared, and a whole new manufacturing settlement was established near Newent. Dean was on the threshold of becoming the foremost iron-producing region in Britain.

Second Century Expansion

ARICONIUM

Two more extensive furnace and smithing areas were opened up during the second century around the civilian settlement, which itself expanded with the construction of high-status buildings, one of which must have served as a guest-house and for stabling in order to justify its inclusion in *Antonine Itinerary* XIII as the first 'stopping-off' place west of Gloucester.

A small part of one of the new iron-working areas was excavated under N.P.Bridgewater in 1963. Although the area excavated measured only 84 feet by 72 feet (25.6m x 22m) the remains of six shaft-type smelting furnaces were revealed alongside primary smithing hearths and a covered charcoal store. As at Monmouth many coal samples were also retrieved. The excavator dated the working period of the site as: 'from before AD 125 until the end of the second century'.

Bridgewater's next comments are worthy of special note here, and will be referred to later: 'A reasonable picture thus emerges of smelting and smithing activities in the second century, leaving hollows partly filled but mostly open. During the following centuries the hollows and the surrounding slag heaps must have become rubbish dumps for the occupants of the houses at Ariconium, but later the land reverted to a scrubby waste' (189).

700m to the south of Bridgewater's excavation there is another large area of iron-working debris at Cinder Hill. Although unexcavated the associated pottery finds are consistently of second century forms, possibly just running into the third century.

MONMOUTH

The excavation in Glendower Street, Monmouth, revealed a similar pattern. The site was rich in second century pottery forms with imported Rhineland wares taking it just into the

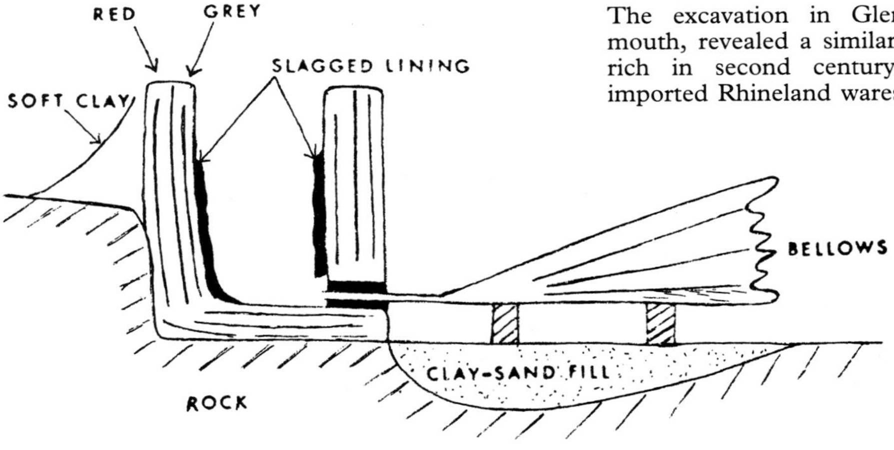

RED   GREY

SLAGGED LINING

SOFT CLAY

BELLOWS

CLAY-SAND FILL

ROCK

Figure 71.
Reconstruction drawing of a Roman iron-smelting furnace at Ariconium. The bellows are conjectural and representative. After N.P.Bridgewater. Courtesy of WNFC.

Figure 72. *Part of a worker's name, probably Cunovendus, inscribed on a cooking pot from a 2nd century AD iron-working site at Monmouth.*

third century, after which the site was deserted. One second century find there supplied us with the only known example in this region of, probably, an ironworker's name. It was inscribed, possibly with a nail, on the outside of a black-burnished cooking pot fragment. Only the letters .VNOVE.... remained but Dr.Roger Tomlin was able to find several parallels in the Celtic personal name C(UNOVE)NDUS (190).

SOUTH HEREFORDSHIRE

About two decades into the second century there was a massive expansion of iron-working activity in south Herefordshire, west of the Wye. The village of Whitchurch overlies a deep bed of Roman iron slags with second century samian pottery identified 8 feet deep in the slag deposits (191). In the 19th century most of the above-ground iron-rich slag heaps were removed for re-smelting in the blast furnaces. The cinder beds were noted as being up to 10 feet (3m) thick and a near-mint-condition coin of Trajan (AD 98-117) was recorded (192). Other massive Roman slag deposits have been recorded in the parishes of Tretire and Hentland associated with second century Roman pottery (193). The 1989 DAG Aerial Survey revealed, as crop marks, a large Roman-period 'structure' with a surrounding boundary ditch at Tre-Addow in Hentland parish. Subsequent fieldwalking confirmed dense slag deposits and Roman-British pottery. In the nearby parish church of Tretire and Michaelchurch an inscribed Roman altar was re-used as a font. The inscription reads: DEO TRIVII BELLICVS DONAVIT ARAM which translates as: 'To the god of the three ways, Bellicus gives the altar'. Three Roman roads are indeed known in the vicinity.

NEWENT provided the most startling evidence for expansion in the second century iron industry when in 1990 a major iron-working area was discovered in a field just south of Newent. Evidence was also also recovered for pottery making and lead and bronze casting in the same field. As the crops were removed in neighbouring fields around 14 acres of concentrated iron slag debris emerged. In other fields roof tile fragments and clay daub identified the location of the workers' settlement and a building of high-status occupied a solitary position in another field. The whole site, which is known to spread over 117 acres (47ha), has Roman roads along each of the three boundaries of its triangular form. The southernmost road, which is raised on an agger, runs in a south west direction towards the ore source of Wigpool. Two roads link it to the major Gloucester to Stretton Grandison road which was laid in the previous century by the Roman military.

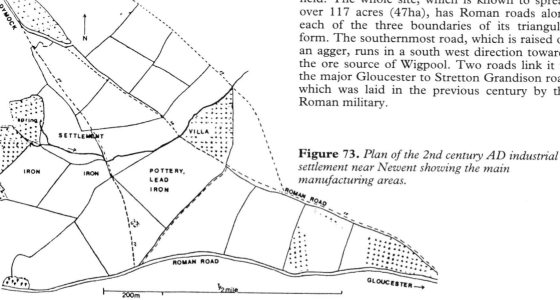

Figure 73. *Plan of the 2nd century AD industrial settlement near Newent showing the main manufacturing areas.*

All of the finds from the site, which were abundant, date unequivocably to the second century, after which the whole settlement was abandoned and became a deserted Roman village.

Apart from iron-working, which was clearly the main activity, there was residual crucible material from which lead had been poured for casting. Among the lead objects found was a damaged lead 'wheel' which had been cast as one of a series in a mould. It was possibly intended as a votive offering to Tanaris, the Celtic god respected by iron-workers and smiths, although the wheel was also a symbol of the Roman deity Fortuna, 'Lady-Luck', and was considered to be a powerful amulet (194).

It has been suggested that this remarkable 'new town' displays all the characteristics of being a 'permitted civilian private enterprise obtaining its main raw materials from a state-controlled industry, the mines. The cost of raw materials would be paid to the state and no doubt a hefty percentage of the profits from manufacture'. These would have been considerable as indicated by the estimated 175,000 tonnes of ore that was smelted during the life of the site.(195).

DYMOCK

Dymock lies only four miles (6km) north of the Newent settlement and its origins are earlier. A first-stage-from-Gloucester fort ought to lie beneath the village. Celtic coins, early Imperial Roman coins including a denarius of Tiberius, coins of Claudius and Nero and several examples of mid-1st century AD south Gaulish samian suggest a Roman military and pre-military presence. Abundant pottery and other small finds of the 2nd to 4th centuries indicate that Dymock continued as a community long after the Newent industrial site was abandoned. Iron slag has been observed on many occasions during small excavations and ground disturbance, but the quantity, spread and dating of the deposits has not been recorded. Dymock has been proposed as the Magalonium or Macatonion mentioned in the *Ravenna Cosmography*, a text compiled by an anonymous Ravenna cleric soon after AD 700 which lists around 300 British geographical locations (195a).

COLEFORD

Rescue excavations in the mid-1980s at High Nash on a late Iron Age/Roman period sanctuary site confirmed an expansion of iron-working activity during the second century with an abundance of typical pottery forms: Black Burnished cooking pots from Dorset, locally-produced flat-rimmed Severn Valley Ware bowls and samian ware from Central Gaul, many of the potsherds deriving from re-distributed iron slags which were used as hard-core.

Coleford town overlies extensive bloomery slag deposits some of which are 3m thick. A certain amount must be assigned to the late medieval period when smelting and smithing is recorded as taking place in the mid-14th, 15th and early 16th centuries, however, the majority of the buried slags can be confidently attributed to the prolonged period of iron production during most of the first four centuries AD (196). Indeed, as will be shown, most of the local outcrop ore deposits around Perrygrove and in Great Lambsquay Wood had been worked out during the second century and had been abandoned.

Villas: High Status Buildings

STOCK FARM VILLA

Apart from the Blakeney villa, all high status buildings of rectangular stone-based construction in Dean and the Wye Valley had their origins in the earlier part of the second century AD. One of them is uniquely placed, only 2km (1¼) miles south of Coleford, at Stock Farm, Clearwell. It was built only 100m west of the ore outcrops, on flat ground in an elevated position with extensive views into Wales as far as the Brecon Beacons.

It is a modest corridor-type villa and was identified as Roman in 1985. Small confirmatory excavations produced pottery of the 2nd to 4th centuries ranging from 2nd century Central Gaulish samian to 4th century Oxfordshire and Nene Valley colour-coated table wares (197). Its positioning, so close to industrial activity, strongly implies the residence of an administrative official connected with mining operations.

PARK FARM VILLA, LYDNEY

Three known villas (a fourth is suspected) were constructed during the second century along the Severn Estuary. Moving westwards from Blakeney, the first was at Park Farm, 1.5km south west of Lydney town centre and close to the now-filled-in Lydney Pill which used to supply local harbour facilities. The villa was part excavated under Dr.C.Scott-Garrett in the late 1950s and early 1960s, but the results were not published. In 1986 M.Fitchett published a site plan from drawings and notes deposited in the Gloucestershire Records Office by Dr.C.E.Hart (198). They reveal that three buildings were located, the main one, of corridor-type measur-

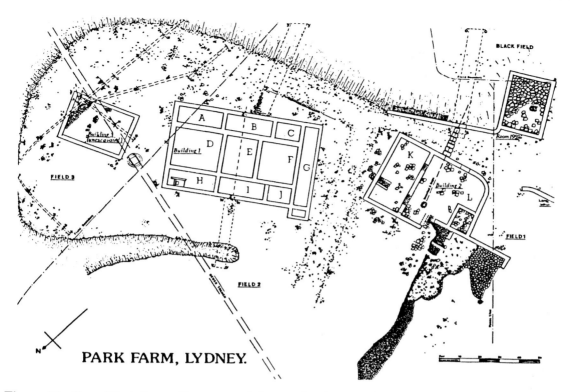

PARK FARM, LYDNEY.

Figure 74. *Plan of Park Farm villa courtesy of the late M.Fitchett who produced it based on drawings by C.Scott-Garrett, donated to the GRO by Dr.C.E.Hart.*

ing 75 feet by 43 feet (23m x 13m). Scott-Garrett, in his notes, continually referred to one of the surrounding walls as being the 'wharf wall' and connected with river traffic. A collection of samian pottery from the site is now in Gloucester City Museum. It is mainly from the Hadrianic/Antonine period although three bowls could have spanned the Trajan/Hadrian period. The foundation of the villa can reasonably be assigned to c.AD 120.

CHESTERS VILLA, WOOLASTON

This villa lies closer to the Severn than the other villas, just 350m from the high water mark and only 15m above OD (sea level). It is located midway between Lydney and Chepstow and is the most imposing of all the villas around Dean. During the 1930s Scott-Garrett, assisted by Frank Harris, excavated two of the buildings and a section of a courtyard wall. One, of developed corridor type, had an associated baths and behind-wall and under-floor ducted heating. Two phases of construction were noted with re-

development in the fourth century. All walls were plastered and painted. Floors were laid with mosaics or sandstone tesserae. Masonry finds caused Scott-Garrett to observe that they bore '...testimony to the former stateliness of the buildings, and proclaim, as the massiveness of the foundations also indicates, that the super-

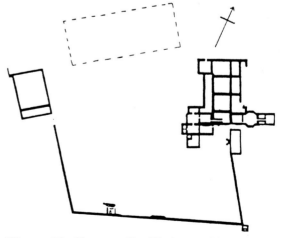

Figure 75. *Chesters villa, Woolaston. Plan of site as excavated by C.Scott-Garrett and F.Harris in the 1930s with outline of unexcavated villa identified by aerial photography in 1989.*

Plate 13A. *Late Iron Age ditched enclosures near the Huntsham villa site.* Photograph by M.J.Walters.

structures were not wooden but built of stone.' The excavator suggested an Hadrianic first phase (199). A nearby tidal Pill (creek) would have provided safe anchorage.

Unknown to Scott-Garrett the largest villa building lay close by at right angles to the one he excavated. This was only revealed by DAG's aerial survey in 1989. Buttresses, visible on its western end as crop and shadow marks, suggest a multi-storey building more than twice the size and length of the developed corridor building. If, as Mark Walters proposed in his report on the Blakeney excavation, the administrator's residence was re-located from there in the earlier second century, then it must have been to Woolaston that he moved, for only at the Chesters villa would status have been maintained.

BOUGHSPRING VILLA

Boughspring is near Tidenham, 3km east of the Chesters. The villa is 1.5km from the Severn, but on higher ground, therefore the succession of owners would have enjoyed the very extensive views across the estuary to the Cotswolds. It also faced south and was set into a bank which provided excellent protection from wind and unfavourable weather.

It was excavated intermittently under T.E.Wilcox between 1976 and 1985 and brief, interim reports were published. In 1990, Joyce Pullinger, with the excavator's co-operation, produced and published the fullest possible excavation report (200).

The first phase building was probably early Antonine and a simple rectangular structure which was extended in the later 2nd century. A corridor was added later and, in the 4th century, wings. The later 4th century saw major developments when the earlier villa was converted to a bath house and a multi-storey building was erected on a platform in front of it. As at Woolaston, the villa had been abandoned and left to decay at the end of the fourth century. In the post-Roman period a woman of about 40 had

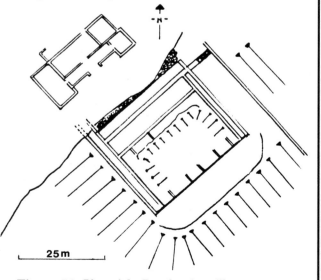

`L___ 25m ___|`

Figure 76. *Plan of the Boughspring villa, Tidenham.* Courtesy of Mrs.J.Pullinger.

been buried in a grave cut through the floor of the north east corridor room.

CHEPSTOW

There would appear to have been at least one high-status building in Chepstow and it would be a reasonable siting for a post-house. There has been a number of 3rd and 4th century coin finds in the town and plentiful Romano-British pottery of similar date. Roman tiles were re-used in the Castle wall along with re-used building stone. Much more attention needs to be given to recording the pre-medieval levels during land disturbance in Chepstow town before any reliable assessment can be made (200a).

HUNTSHAM VILLA

This villa is on the north side of the Forest in the parish of Goodrich, Herefordshire. It is very close to Symonds Yat and occupies slightly elevated ground at the neck of a wide loop of the Wye.

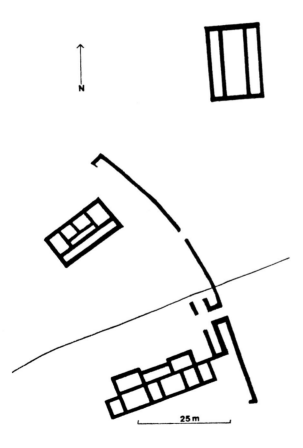

Figure 77. *Plan of the Huntsham villa site. After N.P.Bridgewater. Courtesy of E.Taylor.*

Excavations took place there from 1960 under the direction of N.P.Bridgewater. They revealed a winged corridor villa with one wing extending for around 100 feet (30m). A corn drier was located in a nearby aisled barn and there is evidence for malting taking place. One of a series of nearby ditched enclosures contained timber structures, which are clearly visible on aerial photographs taken in 1989. Pottery from an excavated ditch section was comprised entirely of black native-wares from the Iron Age tradition and probably suggests that the villa developed on the site of a pre-Roman agricultural holding. It would seem that agriculture was the main concern of its owners throughout the Roman period and the land still produces excellent cereal crops on the river alluvium. The actual villa building was constructed in the second century. Interim reports were published by Bridgewater, but no final report. Elizabeth Taylor of the WNFC Archaeology Section is currently preparing a fuller report with a view to publication in the transactions of the WNFC (201).

HADNOCK VILLA

The villa is on gently rising ground on the Dean side of the Wye, but just over the borders in Monmouthshire. It is a little more than 2km (1½ miles) upstream of Monmouth and immediately below the Little Doward hill-fort which stands across the Wye to the west. It is linked by a contemporary road to the cross-Forest Roman route from Mitcheldean to Monmouth, and probably by a trackway to the river crossing at Monmouth which must have been bridged in Roman times.

It was discovered by Monmouth Archaeological Society fieldwalkers in 1981. The pottery from the site is dominated by 2nd to 4th century Romano-British wares and 2nd century samian, although early native-wares are present, including Malvernian 'hammer-rim' storage vessels, which could again indicate late Iron-Age origins. The villa occupants were certainly involved with iron-working, probably during the later third and fourth centuries. Smelting slag deposits abound in the area and especially close to the Wye (202).

LOWER LYDBROOK 'VILLA'

Not a lot is known about this villa-type building which was identified in 1985. It is located on the Stowfield promontory at Lower Lydbrook on the north side of the Forest overlooking a loop in the Wye. It is unexcavated but the rectangular, stone foundations are clearly visible. It was also enclosed by a bank and ditch, traces of which can still be discerned. A small trial excavation within the enclosure proved a long occupation with pottery from the 2nd to 4th centuries including samian and Oxfordshire colour-coated table wares. Iron and copper-alloy slags were recovered from the excavation. The site is on the northern tip of the Hangerbury Hill ridge which has pre-Roman enclosures and iron ore outcrops. The name *'Stow'* indicates the presence of a sacred site in the post-Roman period and it is just possible that the building may have had a religious function in Roman times. More excavation is needed before this can be determined. The same cross-Forest, Mitcheldean to Monmouth route passes the site and ascends the steep slope as a hollow-way, now known as Proberts Barn Lane. A large Roman coin hoard was found nearby in 1848 comprised of mid-3rd century radiates of the emperors Gallienus, Victorinus and Claudius Gothicus (203).

Figure 78. *Fragment of a decorated Samian bowl from Pope's Hill with a dolphin and fish motif. Made in Central Gaul, 2nd century AD.*

POPES HILL

A villa is also assumed close to an iron-working site at Popes Hill near Littledean. This is in an elevated position on the east side of the Forest and has views over the Severn to the Cotswolds. Extensive iron-working was recorded by Dr.Scott-Garrett in 1956, but the quality and quantity of the pottery finds, which included samian and 3rd/4th century colour-coated table wares from the Nene Valley and Oxfordshire, bespeaks the proximity of a high status building whose occupants were engaged in iron smelting (204).

NEWENT

The entrepreneurial iron-working settlement at Newent also had its high status building which was set apart from the workers' village and serviced by its own road. Nothing is yet known about its layout.

DYMOCK

Glimpses of parts of buildings with stone foundations, tessellated floors, hypocausts and ceramic roof tiles have been recorded on a number of occasions, but no plan of any one building exists. Large area exavations, when possible, are clearly needed to begin to unravel the occupation sequences of this very important road-side settlement (204a).

ARICONIUM AND BLESTIUM
(Monmouth)

The inclusion of these two settlements in the *Antonine Itinerary* is a guarantee that both places had buildings of high status.

At Ariconium G.H.Jack part excavated one such residence in the early 1920s by trial trenching. The ample pottery and other small finds indicated 2nd to 4th century use (205). Recent aerial photographic surveys in 1989 and 1990 revealed a complexity of crop and parch marks in the same area including one indicating a rectan-

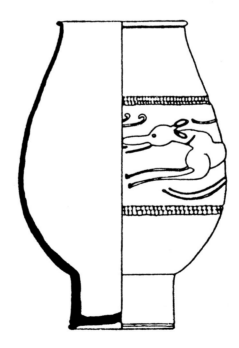

Figure 79. *Reconstruction of a 'Hunt Cup' made in the Nene Valley. From Ariconium, late 2nd century AD.*

gular building with stone coursing and an apsidal west end. This could be a temple.

No certain buildings of high status have yet been confirmed in Monmouth town centre but the most likely place for a *mansio* would be beneath what is now Monmouth School, from the grounds of which considerable amounts of quality 2nd to 4th century pottery have been excavated by A.L.Sockett, assisted by boys from the school.

Who Were the Villa Occupants?

The lack of extensive, or total excavation of any of the high status buildings in Dean and the Wye Valley means that any proposals made here must be seen as conjectural, however, the emerging circumstantial evidence is considerable and makes an hypothesis worthwhile.

Before considering this evidence it would be relevant to outline Roman administrative methods which could shed light on the problem. These are well summarised by Lewis and Reinhold in *'Roman Civilization: Sourcebook II: The Empire'* (206):

'Most mines were government property...... Like the imperial estates, the mining districts were placed under the control of resident procurators, each of whom issued his own local rules to implement general imperial policies. The mining villages were usually not organized along municipal lines; instead, the procurator, like his counterpart on a landed estate, personally exercised the administrative and judicial authority in the village and district...... The emperors (notably Hadrian) encouraged small entrepreneurs by offering those who put unopened or abandoned mines into operation much the same conditions and privileges as were extended to estate tenants who expanded the cultivated area: the mine holding, too, was contingent upon uninterrupted operation; the fisc received a one-half share of the output; the operator was even called *Colonus* (as well as 'proprietor' or 'occupier'); in addition, these operators even had the right to sell their holdings under certain conditions.'

The Newent settlement almost certainly had its origins during the early part of Hadrian's reign with a lessee most likely in charge of operations.

'By far the biggest landowner in the Roman Empire was the emperor. As princeps he possessed estates all over the Empire, some inherited from various local dynasties on their extinction, others bequeathed by or confiscated from private owners. Each estate was operated under the supervision of a resident imperial procurator, who carried out the general policies laid down by the emperors within the framework of local conditions and traditions. We are best informed about the estates in Africa and Egypt, the two major sources of Rome's food supply. The general procedure in these provinces was to lease parcels of the estate to tenant farmers *(coloni)* for varying periods...... In some places the procurators leased large tracts to lessees-in-chief *(conductores)*, who cultivated part themselves and sublet the rest to *coloni*...... The Roman emperors attempted to create a solid and stable class of tenant farmers...... As time passed and the *coloni* handed on their holdings to their heirs, both the holding and the 'owner's' status came to be regarded as hereditary...'

Villa Locations

The distribution of the Dean and Wye Valley villas is striking. All but two, the villas at Stock Farm and Newent, are close to, and overlooking either the Severn or the Wye. None of the high status buildings are located within the ore outcrops surrounding the central woodland area (207).

The villas at Stock Farm and Newent were with reasonable certainty directly involved with the administration of mines and/or iron-working. The villa at Chesters, Woolaston is the most likely residence for a supervising administrator from the early second century onwards following possible re-location from Blakeney. What of the other villas?

The villa at Hadnock, and the conjectured villa at Popes Hill also had iron-working connections, but in a more modest way. A *vilicus* (manager) in charge of the Monmouth iron-working may well have established his out-of-town home at Hadnock. A *vilicus* at Popes Hill

Figure 80. *2nd century AD red-enamelled 'Umbonate' brooch from near Purton Wood. Drawn by C.Mortimer.* Courtesy of N.Butt.

could conveniently have exercised control over the mines from Wigpool to Soudley along the eastern side of the Forest. Another at Park Farm may well have had authority over a supply depot and shipping. As we shall see, Lydney is the most likely harbour on the Severn from which goods were imported and exported during the Roman period.

The villas at Boughspring and Huntsham probably belonged to tenant farmers *(coloni)*. North of Boughspring is a plateau-like area which is bounded roughly by St.Briavels, Bream, Clearwell, Caudwell and Stowe. It is prime agricultural land, mostly on limestones, and even now produces excellent cereal and other crops. Roman pottery sherds are to be found unevenly distributed over many of these fields, yet no concentrations are to be found and no Roman-period building has been located despite extensive ground and aerial survey. This is exactly what one would expect from an intensively farmed area where domestic rubbish is spread over the fields with the manure and midden waste.

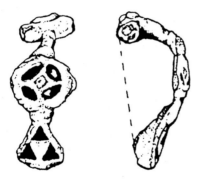

Figure 81. *2nd century AD red-enamelled brooch from Hangerbury Hill.* Courtesy of N.Webley and Messrs. Symonds.

The 'owners' of the Huntsham villa might conveniently have been responsible for iron-working operations immediately across the Wye at Whitchurch and other south Herefordshire sites during the second century, then concentrated on cereal production and malting in the third and fourth centuries. No doubt the tenants also exchanged or traded their various surplus products among themselves.

It should also be borne in mind that, where evidence is available, all but the Chesters villa began as modest residences, then were enlarged and developed as the occupiers became more affluent.

In summary, it seems a reasonable supposition that the villa occupiers were all operating under the supervision of resident state appointed or approved officials for much of the Roman period and between them they administered all the resources of Dean. Dymock is probably the exception. It is on the periphery of the central resource area and is more likely to have had the status of a *vicus* (village or estate) and possibly served as a staging post between Gloucester and Kenchester.

The Second Century Industrial Boom

From c.120, around which time most of the villas were first constructed, Dean and the Wye Valley entered a period of economic prosperity, mainly as a result of the huge demand for iron, although the quarriers and stone-workers also had to meet unexpected demands on a scale never contemplated in the first century. Coal, found on most local Roman sites, was also utilised for industrial and domestic purposes.

Production Estimates

It has been estimated that around one million tonnes of ore were mined during the boom period, an average daily production of around 30 tonnes (208/209). Huge amounts of charcoal were required to smelt the ore and smith the iron (210).

Ore Mining

A recent independent study of surface ore mining at Wigpool estimated that, prior to the end of the Roman period, possibly 600,000 tonnes of ore had been extracted (211). Further research indicates that by the beginning of the 3rd century the Wigpool surface outcrops would have been mined out and exhausted (212). There is evidence that most of the ore outcrops south of Coleford between Perrygrove to Clearwell were also exhausted by the early third century for upwards of 3,000 Roman coins were hidden in three pottery jars in a quarried-out scowle at Perrygrove. They were deposited in the later third century and quite clearly there was no danger of them being found by ore miners because the area was no longer being worked. In fact it was 1849 before they were discovered (213).

It has been deduced, from an estimate of manning requirements for all the known and assumed industries operating in and around Dean during the second century, that there was probably a working population in excess of 2,000 people. Multiply this figure by a factor that allows for women and children and we see that the total population had probably risen to between 8,000 and 10,000, a figure that showed a decline in the succeeding centuries.

The good times were not to last and Dean industries were among the first to suffer from a long and painful recession.

Third Century Recession and its Probable Causes

At the beginning of the third century, within a few years of 210, three of the five main iron-processing areas were closed down, including the oldest and the newest.

Shut-Down

The closures terminated major production on all of the south Herefordshire sites including Ariconium and Whitchurch. As Bridgewater deduced

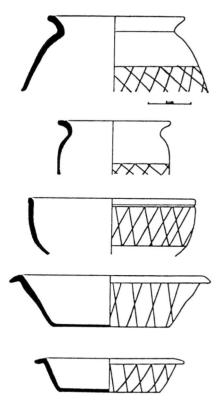

Figure 82. *2nd century AD Black Burnished (BB1) cooking pots and bowls excavated at Monmouth, Glendower Street.*

from his excavation at Ariconium: '... the hollows and surrounding slag heaps must have become rubbish dumps for the occupants of the houses at Ariconium, but later the land reverted to a scrubby waste.'

The other satellite site to the north of the Forest, Newent, even ceased to exist as a settlement. The workers moved away and it became a deserted village.

The Monmouth town centre iron-working ceased and much of the land reverted to a green field. The recession here was to prove not as detrimental as elsewhere. Within a few years the industry revived in the suburb of Overmonnow where it was reasonably prosperous. The move must have been positively beneficial to the town centre dwellers, and visiting officials making use of the guest house.

Possible Reasons For The Recession

The biggest single factor that caused the decline was probably over-production in the latter part of the second century after the consumer market had stabilised following rapid expansion.

When demand exceeds production, especially in monopolised industries where there is no competition (such as the state owned Roman iron industry) the tendency is for prices to rise in the interests of greater profits. Allowing private sector manufacturers to draw an adequate supply of restricted, state controlled raw materials at a time when other producers are fully stretched to satisfy demands sows the seeds for a short-term rich harvest with eventual disaster when supply finally exceeds demand, especially when price-cutting, in an attempt to stimulate consumer demand, fails. The situation is exacerbated when alternative new markets cannot be found, or reached.

Dean and Wye Valley production had been enormous during the second century. The leasing of rights to produce iron at Newent may have seemed a good idea at the time and, indeed, was for many years. Ultimately it proved to be disastrous and resulted in its own closure as well as that of Ariconium which had been established for close on two centuries.

Export markets were beyond the economic reach of Dean due to its geographical location. When the same reduction in demand within Britain hit the Wealden industry there was still the opportunity to export iron to the military garrisons on the Rhine frontier with the shortest of sea crossings to contend with. The long sea journey from Dean, down the Bristol Channel, round the Lizard and up the English Channel even as far as Boulogne is all of 480 miles. A round trip to the Rhine could have taken six weeks, and this given a fair wind and knowledge

Plate 14. *Denarius of Geta (as Augustus AD 209-212) the son of Septimius Severus. Reverse: The goddess of Victory holding a laurel wreath and palm branch. The legend proclaims: VICTORIAE BRIT; celebrating military victories in Caledonia. Coins of Geta have been recorded from Ariconium and Lydney Park.* Photographed by B.Walters.

meant that charcoal was difficult to obtain and would have required carting over longer distances. For certain by the mid-third century, when there was a modest revival of production, new ore mines had to be exploited.

Political Instability

The unstable political situation in Rome's western Empire may have contributed to a lessening of demand for iron during the final decade of the second century. Clodius Albinus, a provincial governor in Britain, certainly had things other than home affairs on his mind. In the year 192-193 three emperors, Commodus, Pertinax and Didius Julianus were assassinated. Septimius Severus became emperor in 193 but discovered that two other provincial governors had Imperial ambitions, one of whom was Albinus who was proclaimed emperor in Britain. Civil war ensued from which Severus emerged triumphant after defeating Albinus in a major battle near Lyons in 197. Severus took control of Britain in the same year and appointed a relative, Sextus Varius Marcellus, as the Procurator of the province.

Reconstruction began on Pennine forts and on neglected installations on Hadrian's Wall. Septimius Severus then came to Britain with his two sons, Geta and Caracalla and determined on a comprehensively destructive campaign against the Caledonian 'barbarians'. A line of forts as far north as the Moray Firth may mark the extent of the rapid campaigns that followed. No great victory was achieved but there was a long peace thereafter. Severus died at York on February 4th, AD 211.

These campaigns were along the east coast of Scotland and supplies of iron would most likely have derived from the sources on the Weald, and carried northwards by the fleet.

Figure 83. Left: *Base silver Antoninianus of Valerian I (AD 253-260). Coins of Valerian have been found at Lydney and High Nash Roman temple sites, and in the Perrygrove scowles hoard.*

Right: *Antoninianus of Gallienus (AD 253-268). Coins of Gallienus have been found at Ariconium, Lydbrook, Lydney Park, Perrygrove, Crabtree Hill, Tufthorn and Parkend.*

of favourable tides (214). It was so totally impracticable that Dean shippers would not even have considered it as a possibility.

More than likely the exhaustion of the major ore sources closest to Ariconium and Newent played a part in their termination as manufacturing sites. The same would apply to the south Herefordshire sites west of the Wye if all the Doward ore had been extracted from the surface outcrops. Woodland depletion would have

Little military building activity occurred to stimulate the Dean economy. Following the Severan campaign there were modest and periodic refurbishments at the Legionary base of Caerleon. The baths were repaired, only to be closed soon after 230. Some new barracks were constructed, others were re-roofed. In the 250s there was a total rebuilding of barracks for the seventh cohort (216). Any iron requirements would have been modest and easily satisfied by the smiths from Overmonnow.

Following the murder of Severus Alexander in 235 there was another period of protracted instability during which seventeen emperors came and went before the accession of Valerian and his son, Gallienus, in 253. In 259 the Empire split and Postumus became the first emperor of the 'Gallic Empire' of Gaul, Britain and Spain. It was around this time that there was a modest revival of fortunes for the iron industry.

A New Temple for the Coleford Community

During the recession a remarkable new building was constructed at High Nash, Coleford; a timber-built temple of considerable proportions. Mature oak trees were cut lengthways and laid snugly in round-bottomed foundation trenches, 60cm wide at the rear of the temple and 50cm wide along its sides. Broad oak beams, either side of the aisles, supported the roof which was tiled with a greenish sand-stone obtainable only 1.5km (one mile) away. At the west end of the temple a semi-circular apse was constructed, 9m wide and 4.5m deep, in which would have stood

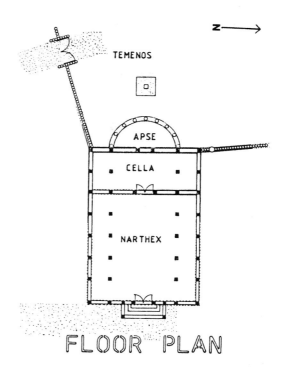

Figure 84. Top: *Plan of the High Nash temple as constructed in the 3rd century AD. The east end entrance, destroyed by roadworks, is conjectured.* Plan prepared by G.Collier.

Figure 85. Bottom: *Artist's impression of what the temple may have looked like in the 3rd century AD looking north.* Drawn by D.Thomas from an architectural reconstruction by G.Collier based on excavated evidence.

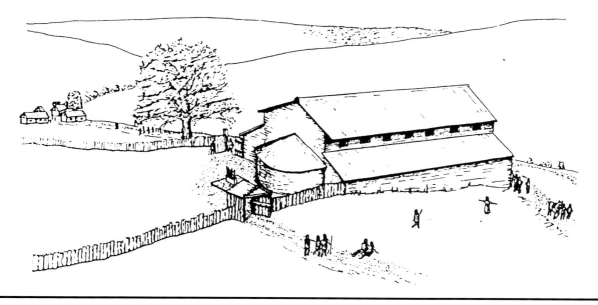

a statue of the deity to whom it was dedicated. The temple itself was 14m wide and may have been 26m long, but its length could not be accurately determined as the temple entrance had been destroyed by the laying of a new road prior to rescue excavations in 1985. 5m behind the apse a buried square stone plinth was discovered on which was probably erected a cult figure. A *temenos* (sacred area) ditch enclosed the land behind the temple.

Opposite the front entrance of the temple was another structure, also rectangular in form, with a shallow central pit in front of a flat, hard-packed surface. Dr.Graham Webster suggested that this too may have been a small shrine. It faced east and was originally constructed in the 3rd century with later 4th century re-construction.

The temple was sited in a location that had been sacred to the local Britons for centuries. The British warrior's weaponry was buried 92.5m behind the apse.

That a new temple should have been constructed during a time of recession, for a community that must have been reduced to a state of extreme pessimism and despondency, may seem strange, however, closer consideration of the circumstances may indicate that, in fact, it was an auspicious time to build one.

Two outstanding possibilities suggest themselves:

First, the impending disaster of impoverishment may have concentrated the minds of the Britons on intercession with their gods who had been so benevolent towards them for generations. Maybe they felt that a new and very imposing structure would placate the deities and restore good fortune. One notable fact is that among the dedicatory deposits found buried in the temple foundations were *two iron horse-shoes*.

The horse played a significant part among the ancient Britons in warfare, hunting, and in their religion. Objects associated with the cult of the

horse have been found in association with depictions of Tanaris, a god favoured by smiths (214). Many Celtic tribal coins of the first century, including those of the Dobunni, featured a horse. An iron horse shoe is still considered a symbol of good fortune and a protection against evil. It may well have been considered such since horses were first shod by the Celts. For certain, horse-shoes had a very special significance for the Coleford community.

The second possible reason for the temple construction at this time could have been an initiative by the controller of the local industries in order to mollify the disenchanted natives. The labour force was restive, available and in need of employment. Even if supplication to their deities failed to invoke a successful response it would, at least, divert blame away from the state for mishandling the economy. The construction of such an imposing edifice would also have introduced an air of optimism when all must have felt an overwhelming pessimism. Perhaps it was all there was left to do.

There was never to be a great revival of the iron industry during the Roman period, however, renewed activity from the middle of the third century has been detected by archaeological investigation.

Iron Mining At Lydney

The early third century recession in the iron industry probably left a stock-pile of forgeable iron bars, which would have meant that mining and smelting virtually ceased for a time until the smiths had used up these stocks.

Mid-Third Century Resurgance

There is archaeological evidence for some resurgance in the middle of the century at Lydney, Coleford, Overmonnow and, for the first time, on some of the villa sites.

At High Nash, Coleford, mid-late third century pottery forms are very numerous, especially Black Burnished cooking pots and flanged bowls. The same can be said for Overmonnow.

During the excavations at Lydney Park the Wheelers' proved iron mining activity and occupation between c.250 and before c.300. What is particularly interesting is that the ore was retrieved by underground mining in the form of tunnels as opposed to digging out scowles from exposed outcrops. As they observed: '... almost the whole of the northern half of the Lydney camp is honeycombed with the hollows which represent blocked mine-shafts... There are, indeed, indications of a mine under the south-western part of the Roman guest-house, but

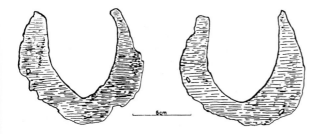

Figure 86. *Securely stratified iron horse-shoes from the High Nash Roman temple excavations.* Drawn by D.Thomas.

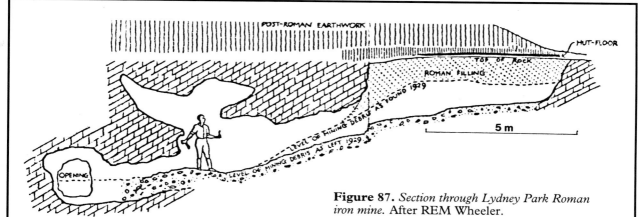

Figure 87. *Section through Lydney Park Roman iron mine.* After REM Wheeler.

these could not be followed up without an extensive destruction of the foundations of that building.'

The Wheelers' summary of the mine that was excavated, which had been sealed by a hut floor, was: 'It may be suggested that the absence of debris in the opening prior to the late third-century filling points to an initial date not long anterior to that filling. Moreover, the coinage indicates a marked general influx of wealth onto the promontory in the same period. On these two grounds, it seems likely that the mine was cut during a period of enhanced activity in the middle or latter half of the third century' (217).

Smelting At Some Villa Sites

The influx of wealth, and the enhanced activity, coincided with smelting activities at the Chesters Villa, Woolaston, and to a lesser extent at the Park Farm Villa, Lydney.

Excavations by M.Fulford at Chesters from 1988 to 1990 revealed an industrial building with sixteen bays, measuring 16.5m by 8.2m. It was of post built construction on two parallel rows of pad-stones. Several shaft-type furnaces were confirmed and an ore-crushing unit. The iron-working phase, on limited pottery evidence, was given a terminus post quem (date after which) of the mid-3rd century (218).

The Park Farm smelting was not intensive, but there is some smelting and primary smithing debris lying around. It is much more likely that Lydney Park ores were being transported away from Dean by river from the Lydney harbour. For a fuller discussion of this see under 'Transportation and Communication' and 'The Distribution of Crude Ore'.

The necessity for mining at Lydney Park strongly suggests that the Bream scowles, less than 2km north west, were also abandoned before the mid-3rd century.

The iron-working at Popes Hill also covered this period although it is not possible from Dr.Scott-Garrett's report to be precise about when it began and when it ended due to the lack of securely stratified evidence recorded (219).

At Hadnock villa the iron-working phase, with some certainty, may be allotted to the mid-3rd century and later, although there is no close dating for the slag deposits.

Estimates indicate that less than 50 furnaces all told were operating on average every day during the latter part of the third century compared with around 300 during peak production in the second century, however, the drop in the quantity of ore mined may not have been quite so dramatic if crude ores were shipped away from Dean during this period, although it is not yet possible to quantify the amount exported.

The Fourth Century AD in Wye/Dean

The last decade or so of the third century sounded echoes of the closing years of the second century with political unrest and a usurping emperor for Britain and parts of Gaul.

Soon after his ascendancy in 284 Diocletian realised that the government and defence of such a vast empire was too great a task for one man. On April 1st 286 he conferred upon Maximianus the rank of Augustus and placed him in charge of the western half of the Empire which included Britain. Soon afterwards, Carausius, now the Commander of a Channel fleet based at Gesoriacum (Boulogne) sailed for Britain, and took possession of the Province, proclaiming himself emperor.

He endeavoured to present an image of one who cared for the rich landowners and those

Figure 88. Top: *Antoninianus of Carausius (AD 287-293). Coins of this usurper have been found at Parkend, Whitecroft and at Lydney Park. Bottom: A coin of Constantine I (AD 307-337). Reverse: Sol Invicto Comiti. The sun-god holding a globe. Mintmark: PLN (London). This is a coin type commonly found in Dean and the Wye Valley.*

with commercial interests by introducing a silver coinage of such fineness that it matched the quality of the Republic and the early Empire. It would not have impressed the working class of Dean and the Wye Valley one little bit for the value of it was way beyond their reach. What it probably did was to ensure the continued use of the third century 'barbarous' radiates of lower value which, through various coin reforms, prob-

ably continued in circulation during the first three decades of the fourth century. The pre-Reform, early issue, copper radiates of Carausius are also frequently found as single-coin finds in Dean.

In 293 Carausius was assassinated at the instigation of his finance minister, Allectus. Three years later Britain was restored to central European government when Constantius Chlorus successfully invaded in 296. So the fourth century began during a period of reasonable political stability.

Temple Alterations

At High Nash, Coleford, within a few years of 300, the apse to the rear of the temple was removed and the foundation timbers at the back of the temple were replaced with slightly wider timbers suggesting a strengthening and renovating of the structure.

During the mid-century years the temple was demolished as was the 'shrine' opposite the temple entrance. The *temenos* timber wall was also removed and the foundation ditches of the temple and the *temenos* filled with silt.

Some years later a new shrine was constructed on the site of the earlier temple, on a slightly different alignment, but still basically east-west. The shrine was simple and small, rectangular in form, set on timber beams laid on the ground surface. The building opposite was renewed around the same time. Beneath a new cobbled surface were some crushed slag fragments which contained a coin of 330-335. The coin had been lost in the slag and re-deposited with it as hardcore and could well have lain around for some years before re-deposition. It is interesting to note that, although the *temenos* timber 'wall' was

Plate 15. *Pottery firing experiment at High Nash in 1988 by Archaeology students from the Royal Forest of Dean College who made the pottery from clay dug from the site.*

never re-constructed, its boundary was perpetuated by a continuous line of large stones which had been placed exactly above the centre of the silt-filled foundation trench.

In the late fourth or early fifth century this small rectangular shrine was in turn replaced by what could only have been an altar or cult figure beneath a covering supported by posts on pad-stones. In the final phase of the site local clays had been used to make pottery which had been fired on the surface in bonfires. Wasters were found which matched nearby clays which were experimentally fired by Archaeology students from the Royal Forest of Dean College. It would appear that Dorset black wares and the popular Oxfordshire colour-coated table wares had ceased to reach Dean by this time for copies of both were found. They had been fired on the site and made with local clays. With reasonable certainty this activity belonged to the earlier years of the fifth century (220).

Dereliction At Ariconium

Ariconium was still in existence as a staging post well into the fourth century but occupation must have been restricted to a few buildings of substance. The settlement centre was well supplied with table wares from Oxfordshire kilns and drinking vessels from the Nene Valley, although the latter are less common as surface finds. Many hundreds of coins have been recovered from the plough soil over the years but none date later than the 360s. The apparent termination of the site within a few years of 370 suggests either the culmination of a gradual decline in official travellers and merchants, or the preference for an alternative route.

No evidence has been recovered for arable farming at any time during, or before the Roman period around Ariconium. In 1988 Dean Archaeological Group undertook a very extensive field survey at the request of English Heritage in advance of a proposed loop road around Weston and in order to determine the extent of Roman-period boundaries. All fields were surveyed, some with trial excavations, between Lea and Weston-under-Penyard. Not one sherd of Romano-British pottery was found away from the known settlement. Normally sherds are scattered about from midden waste and other farming activities on land that is arable farmed. Stock rearing, of course, remains a possibility.

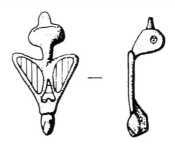

Figure 89. *Fly-shaped, trumpet-headed brooch, enamelled in blue and green. 3rd century AD from Ariconium. Drawn by A. Stait.* Courtesy of M. Sterry.

For the last century and a half of its existence Ariconium must have presented the image of a depressed and depressing area surrounded by slag heaps, rubbish dumps and dereliction, the kind of place that travellers would prefer to pass quickly through.

Overmonnow Flourishes

At Overmonnow, Monmouth there is also ample evidence for iron-working activity through most of the fourth century and, again, Oxfordshire table wares were favoured by the population, however, no coins have yet been found during the several rescue excavations that have taken place that date beyond the 360s.

Hiatus At Woolaston

The villa at Chesters, Woolaston, was deserted for a while in the early fourth century with re-construction on the period 2 baths building beginning after c.320. The excavators' interpreted a platform feature on higher ground just to the north of the villa as being a 'lighthouse' to guide shipping into the Pill around the Guscar Rocks. It was dated as a period 2, fourth century feature. The latest coin in the sequence was of Gratian, minted in the 370s (221).

New Building At Boughspring

At the nearby Boughspring villa there were major developments in the mid-fourth century when

Figure 90. *Section of a geometrically patterned mosaic from the Boughspring villa made from red, black and white tesserae.* Courtesy of Mrs. J. Pullinger.

the earlier winged-corridor villa was converted into a baths and a new multi-storey building was erected on a platform in front of it. Nene Valley and Oxfordshire colour-coated wares were used by the occupants in their elegant dining room which had colourfully decorated, plastered walls with a hypocausted heating system. The latest coin to be found was a well-circulated one of the emperor Valens (364-378).

The villas at Stock Farm and Popes Hill both provided evidence for the ready availability in this region of fourth century Oxfordshire and Nene Valley table wares.

New Fourth Century Iron-Working Sites

The first Roman-period iron smelting site to be excavated in west Gloucestershire proved to be of mid-4th century date. It is also the only excavated iron-working site that can be dated to the fourth century although there is another unexcavated one not far away that was also operating in the same century.

New Furnaces Near English Bicknor

The sites under review are both in the parish of English Bicknor, the excavated one on the slopes of Hangerbury Hill, the other in English Bicknor itself on the other side of the valley.

Several large slag and furnace debris areas are clearly visible on Barnfield which lies on the western slopes of Hangerbury Hill, not far below the summit ridge on which there are scowles, the hollows left by ancient mining of the ore outcrops.

One of the largest slag concentrations was excavated in 1987. It revealed the remains of a shaft-type furnace which had been constructed from clay and erected adjacent to the clay extraction pit. The internal diameter of the clay shaft would have been about 27cm. There was evidence for three different smelts with the slag being tapped away from the furnace into the pit. Romano-British pottery sherds were sealed in the slag and nearby finds of a 4th century colour-coated Oxfordshire mortarium and a Centenionalis coin of Constantius II with a Christogram on the reverse, minted at Trier in 353, would indicate a mid-later 4th century iron-working phase (222). A 2½lb forged iron bar was found close by.

The furnace area at Bicknor, on Cowmeadow Farm, produced a similar mortarium rim of 4th century date and the rim of a pewter dish. Alongside the slag remains was a partly forged iron bar

Figure 91. *Christogram on the reverse of a Centenionalis of Magnentius (AD 350-353), mint-mark TRP (Trier). Two examples of this coin have been found in Dean; on Hangerbury Hill and in the Oldcroft 2 coin hoard.*

(a billet) of similar weight and dimensions to the one found on Hangerbury.

Both of these sites may have been controlled from the only known high status Roman building in the area, at Lower Lydbrook.

An estimate based on the size and depth of the visible slag remains would suggest that around 25,000 tonnes of ore had been smelted (223).

The opening up of this new ore outcrop area on the northern side of the Forest so late on in the fourth century may be a further indication that most of the major outcrops along the east and west sides were seriously depleted.

Fieldwork and some small-area excavation during 1991 and 1992 (unpublished as yet) indicates a modest amount of smelting in the very late third and fourth centuries in the parish of Awre, both close to the village of Awre itself and around Blakeney. No associated structures have yet been located but there could have been a wharf on the banks of the Severn at Whitescourt near Awre.

Historical Events of the Later 4th Century and their Local Impact

By 314 Britain had been split into four provinces, Wye/Dean becoming a part of *Britannia Prima*. Each province had its own governor and a whole new bureaucracy was formed to co-ordinate administration in Britain, each governor now being a civil officer having no command over the military. It could have been at this time that the Chesters villa went through its hiatus of occupation, which could also mean that there was no longer a Dean-based supervising administrator after the early fourth century.

There followed a long period of stability under the Emperor Constantine I (The Great) until his death in 337. His son, Constantine II succeeded as Augustus of the west including Britain, while another son, Constans, controlled Italy and Africa. A third son, Constantine II, held Constantinople and the east. In 340 Constantine II invaded the territories of his brother, Constans, and was killed. Britain thus came under the rule of Constans. He visited Britain in 343 and his sole rule over the western provinces lasted for ten years until the legions revolted against him and joined forces with Magnentius who became ruler over Britain in 350. Inevitably drawn into battle against Constantius II he was finally defeated in Gaul in 353 and the province of Britain came under the control of Constantius.

The next few years may be reflected in some of the archaeologically recorded happenings in Dean.

Temple Closures

Constantius was aggressively Christian with an intense hatred of the old religions. He ordered the immediate closure of all pagan temples and re-affirmed the death penalty for those who made pagan sacrifices or worshipped images of their gods. This not only terminated the state religions but also struck at the heart of the deeply rooted Celtic beliefs of the masses of ordinary people. The civil administrators were obliged to act on the decree out of fear for their lives because Constantius had sent to Britain his Imperial Notary, Paulus, whose reputation for hunting out dissidents and potential opponents to his Emperor was well known by the administrators and land owners of Britain. Tortures, imprisonments and death were common. Innocents became the victims of informers out to protect their own lives. The wealthy suffered most.

The contemporary historian of Roman affairs, Ammianus Marcellinus, vividly recorded the details of this persecution. Of Paulus he wrote: 'He had been sent to Britain to fetch certain officers who had been bold enough to join Magnentius' conspiracy; when he found them unable to resist he went far beyond his instructions, and descending like a sudden torrent upon the persons and estates of many people spread ruin and destruction in various forms. Loading the limbs of free-born men with chains and subjecting some to the degradation of handcuffs, he stitched together a patchwork of charges far removed from the truth...... After these atrocious acts Paul returned to the emperor's quarters steeped in blood and bringing with him a number of prisoners almost crushed with chains, whom he had reduced to squalid misery. On their arrival the rack was put in order and the executioner got ready his hooks and instruments of torture. Of these prisoners many suffered loss of property, others exile, some death' (224).

Julian Eases The Persecution Of Non-Christians

The situation may have eased a little in 355 when Constantius appointed his young cousin Julian to the rank of caesar over Britain and Gaul. Julian was quite a different sort of person to the Emperor having a passionate interest in, and knowledge of Roman history, religion and tradition as well as Classical literature. In 359 he organised for six hundred ships to transport corn from Britain to the lower Rhine armies, which tells us that Britain still had a major reserve of agricultural resources.

In 360 Julian's troops in Britain proclaimed him Emperor and in the succeeding months Constantius II died. Julian immediately restored traditional observances and pagan temples flourished once again.

Probably around 353 the High Nash, Coleford temple was demolished and the *temenos* wall torn down following the decree of Constantius. The lesser, rectangular structure which followed it might reasonably be allotted to c.360 when Julian lifted the ban on non-Christian shrines.

Such changes are also reflected in developments on the Littledean Hall temple site where the final temple phase was given a *Terminus Post Quem* by a coin of Magnentius which was sealed beneath the foundations. This allows for the reconstruction taking place during the reign of Julian. Excavations in 1992 at Dean Hall revealed a remarkable sequence of road surfaces spanning close on 2,000 years with a paved

Figure 92. *Left: Portrait of the Emperor Magnentius (AD 350-353). Right: Portrait of Julian II as Augustus (360-363).*

Roman road clearly serving the site in the fourth
century.

The New Temple
Complex at Lydney Park

The fourth century construction of a magnificent
temple complex consisting of a temple dedicated
to Nodens, a very large multi-storeyed guest
house around a courtyard plan occupying almost
half an acre of land, a generously proportioned
bath house and a long building adjacent to the
baths and close by the temple; all of them richly
furnished, heated and with splendid mosaic
floors, was sited within the old Lydney hill-fort
ramparts, but with its own precinct wall, and
apparently without knowledge that the ground
beneath had been undermined in the quest for
iron ore.

In his excavation report summary Wheeler
observed: 'The building of the settlement was
begun after 364 and more probably after 367.'
Of the later developments and additions he continued: 'These changes are symptomatic of maintained or increasing wealth, The foundation of
this sanctuary within the last generation of
Roman Britain was clearly something more than
a mere flash in the pan.' He described the abundance of trinkets and other minor objects along
with the mass of poor bronze coins as being 'elo-
quent of peasant piety' (225). One could also
add that the fineness of the quality of some of
them, such as the famous cast bronze hunting

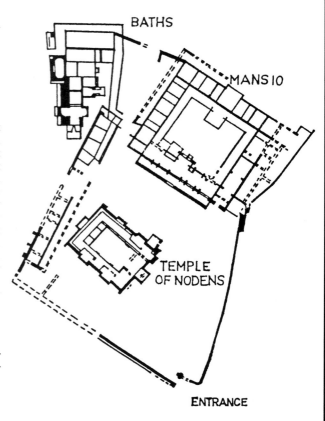

Figure 93. *Plan of Lydney Park temple, guest-
house and baths.* Drawn by R.Eggl after REM
Wheeler.

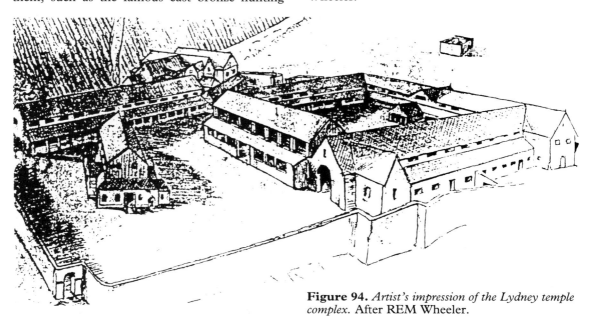

Figure 94. *Artist's impression of the Lydney temple
complex.* After REM Wheeler.

dog, when linked to the expensive elegance of the guest house, bespeaks a wealthy clientele able and willing to pay well in the hope of being healed. It might be reasoned that, although the temple attracted the rich, the poor were not excluded.

Tourist Attraction

The early years of the shrine were probably dominated by pilgrimages of the wealthy from far and wide, indeed the Severn estuary road to and from Gloucester may well have been deliberately selected by travellers because it passed close to the shrine which provided superior accommodation combined with rural peace, fabulous views, medicaments as well as spiritual healing. No wonder travellers avoided the north Forest road to Gloucester via Ariconium. It could have been the construction of the Lydney complex that spelled the end for Ariconium and its doleful guest-house c.370.

Although constructed subsequent to the reign of Julian, it surely owed its existence to the encouragement given by Julian to the revival of pagan temples and worship. The fact that it appears to have functioned well beyond the Roman occupation of Britain indicates that no future emperor was able to effectively revoke Julian's decree.

A Short-Lived Prosperity

For a few years more Britain was very prosperous as Sheppard Frere noted in the introduction to his chapter on The End of Roman Britain in *'Britannia: A History of Roman Britain'*: 'In 370 Britain was once more enjoying firm government and effective defences: forty years later she ceased to be part of the Roman Empire. The civilisation and prosperity of the island during these years had never been higher; but the growing power of external barbarians constituted a danger both to Britain and to the whole western empire which by slow degrees overbore resistance' (226).

It will be recalled that the mid-4th century had seen massive and expensive development of the Boughspring villa. Although not yet confirmed by excavation, the large buttressed building at Chesters, Woolaston which was revealed by an aerial photograph in 1989, also probably belongs to this period. In fact all the villas within Dean appear to have been thriving during the 370s and the wealth to construct the Lydney complex could conceivably have come from an initiative by their occupants to boost tourist trade and industry within Dean. If so, for a while it succeeded. Numerous objects of iron and bronze were recovered from excavations at Lydney Park, many of them no doubt for sale to visitors. The

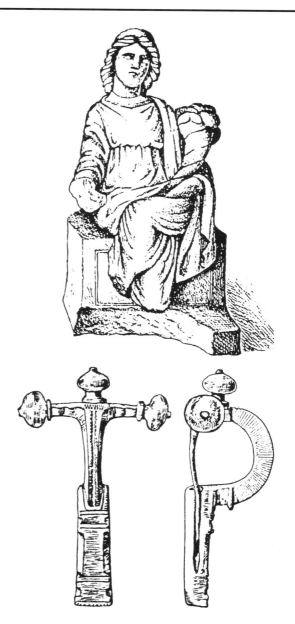

Figure 95. *Top: Stone statue of goddess about 75cm high. Possibly Ceres or Abundantia. Bottom: Fourth century AD brooch, both from the Lydney temple site.*

name of one worker in lead, Doccius, is actually known. His lead votive offerings and curse tablets would have been much in demand (227). We can imagine local people out gathering herbs to concoct potions, salves and medicines for sale. For a while the stone-masons would have been fully employed. Local brewers would for sure have been kept busy. Shell-fish gatherers would have found a ready market for their fresh-water oysters. Transporters between the Lydney harbour and the temple would have been much in demand, not only carrying daily supplies but also assisting the lame and elderly to the hill-top 'hotel'. Severn ferrymen enjoyed a boom period. Official visitors, favoured by the villa occupants, would doubtless have been taken on hunting expeditions in the Forest. The hunting spear of one of the Huntsham villa occupants was actually found during excavations on the villa.

In the closing years of the fourth century there can be little doubt that Lydney was the focal point of Dean, while for those who enjoyed an extended stay there would always be the opportunity to take a trip along the Dean Road from Lydney to Littledean where the other temple could be visited, again with spectacular views over the Severn. Perhaps the first visitors ever to visit the eerie and deserted Bream scowles and Clearwell caves came in the late fourth century. As our own experience shows in the latter years of the twentieth century, the industrial remnants of the previous centuries can prove a powerful attraction to some.

The End of an Era in Wye/Dean

The years of prosperity were to span no more than one generation of people. Early warnings of disruption were sounded as early as 383 when Magnus Maximus, a Spaniard by birth, was commander of the Roman forces in Britain, probably with the title *DUX BRITANNIARUM*. Troops, disenchanted by Gratian, elected Maximus as emperor who promptly denuded many of the British garrisons, including the fortress of Chester from which he took the XXth Legion, to fight on the Continent where he defeated Gratian. He retained power over Britain and in the west until his death in 388. The removal of the force from Chester and the reduction of the Segontium (Caernarfon) garrison allowed Irish tribes to harass the Welsh coast. Some even settled.

By the early fifth century Britain was suffering invasive threats from all quarters. Gaul was overwhelmed by barbarian tribes and communication links with the central government were tenuous. Rome itself was threatened by Alaric the Visigoth until he finally entered it in 410.

The sixth century historian Zosimus records that at this time: 'The people of Britain, taking up arms and exposing themselves to danger on their own behalf, liberated the cities from threatening barbarians; and all Armorica and the other provinces of Gaul, imitating the Britons, liberated themselves in the same way; they threw out the Roman officials and within their power set up their own order' (Zosimus VI,5,3). Frustrated by the lack of response for help, which the emperor Honorius was unable to offer, Britain declared independence. In 410 the Britons were told by Honorius to defend themselves and this they were obliged to do (ibid.VI,10,2).

Collapse Of The Economy

These moves during the first ten years of the fifth century wrecked the British economy. Without an authorised military presence and with no Roman troops to pay, the coin supply to Britain ceased. The latest bronze coins to be sent here from Rome were between 395 and 402. The latest silver and gold coins found in Britain were minted during the first decade of the fifth century. Revenues and taxes ceased to be paid to Rome. Silver and gold coins were hoarded but none have yet been found in Dean or the Wye Valley. There would have been a general reluctance to pay any taxes, so the towns too began to decline. It would seem that some villa occupants of Dean foresaw that the decline would result in eventual disaster and moved away, possibly even before the end of the fourth century. They simply took with them all their valuables, portable goods and their remaining wealth, and deserted their homes.

Villas Abandoned

The Chesters villa was abandoned and soon after was taken over by 'a sort of squatters' occupation' according to the excavator. The roof was still intact and a circular hearth was cut into the floor. No respect was shown for the elegant decor enjoyed by the previous occupants. In 1992 DAG field survey indicated that lead had subsequently been stripped from the main building and re-smelted on site.

The Boughspring villa too was deserted; the decorated wall-plaster left to crumble as the roof deteriorated and leaked rain.

The same applied to all the villas for no post-Roman material has been found to suggest continued occupation. Only at the Coleford settlement and at the Lydney and Littledean temple sites is there any evidence for continued activity. Coins of Arcadius have been found at both of the latter, and coins of Honorius at Lydney.

Figure 96. Right: *Excavation plan of Littledean Hall Roman temple provided by the late Maurice Fitchett who recorded it in 1984. The post-Roman timber structure (see post-holes on plan) occupied the narthex area of the earlier temple.*

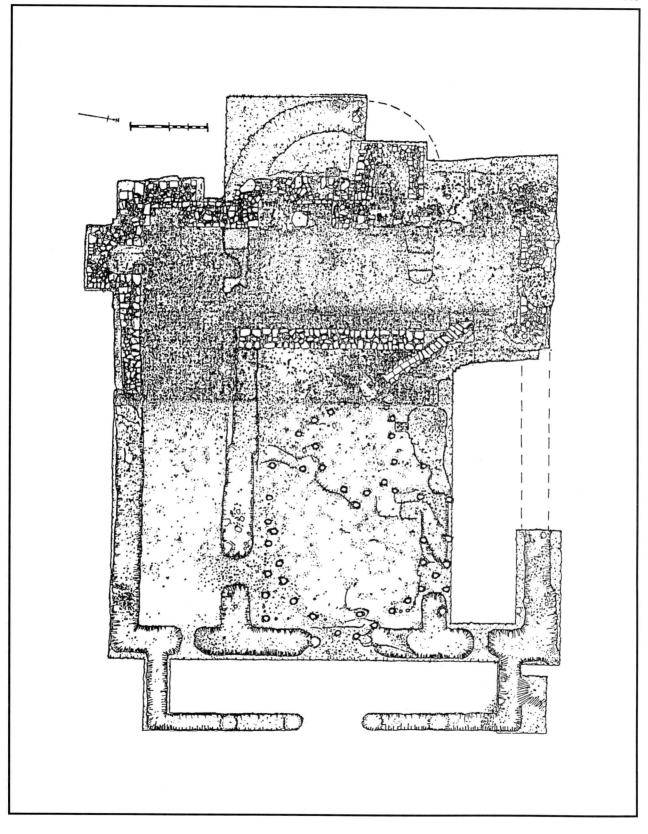

Table Wares Acquire Rarity Value

Any usable pottery and equipment left behind by the villa occupants would have been plundered by the local people. Sometimes, as we shall see, isolated finds of the valued Oxfordshire colour-coated table wares may indicate the siting of fifth and sixth century dwellings constructed of timber. Just as we value Georgian and Victorian heirlooms and antiques, so the local Britons living in the post-Roman era would probably have treasured those colourful and elegant table wares that were no longer being produced. In Dean and the Wye Valley the discovery on a field surface of sherds of this distinctive pottery may be the first, and possibly the only visible indicator of a post-Roman settlement nearby. When found during an excavation, they could indicate a site that extended into the 5th century. In May 1992 Mr.B.Johns, while excavating a Roman site on his own land near Blakeney, found a rare and complete exotic bead of slightly biconical form. It was black with applied yellow and white spirals and chevrons. Little is known about this type of bead but it became more common after c.AD 400 and is thought to be of European origin, possibly Teutonic. It was found in association with Oxfordshire colour-coated table-ware sherds.

Before considering the centuries following the departure of the Romans it would be well to review the legacy they left to the local Britons.

Figure 97. *Late fourth or early fifth century glass bead from Blakeney. It is opaque black with yellow and white spirals and chevrons.* Courtesy of B.Johns.

Transportation and Communication

The rivers bordering Dean, especially the Severn, played a strategically vital role in Roman military operations against the Silures. Later, both the Severn and the Wye were heavily utilised for the distribution of the area's resources, thus contributing substantially during the periods of economic prosperity.

Prior to 1842 when part of the Severn was canalised between Gloucester and Stourport much trade was carried on by Severn trows and barges over this stretch and far beyond; up to Pool Quay, some four miles below Welshpool in Montgomeryshire' (228).

The Severn was tidal as far as Upton but beyond that laden or part-laden boats would be dependent on 'freshes' (a river rise due to heavy rain at the Severn source in mid-Wales).

Gloucester became a key port and distribution centre in Roman times. Recent excavations on and near the Roman waterfront in Quay Street confirmed aspects of earlier excavations and further increased knowledge of the Severnside docks and wharves (229).

The Wye, which flows into the Severn estuary near Chepstow, is tidal as far as Tintern, which is halfway in river distance to Monmouth. Monmouth was an important port until relatively recent times (230).

Lydney Port

There can be little doubt that Lydney was the key port of Dean although there is a dearth of excavated archaeological evidence to support this. Dr.Scott-Garrett certainly believed that his excavations had revealed a wharf wall adjacent to the Park Farm villa.

The 'Regard of the Forest of Dene in 1282' records: 'At Lydney is a port called Nerene (Newerne) at which boats call'. It also listed eight people who moored boats there (more than at any other Dean port) and also recorded that they were all dealers in wood.

The Rev. W.M.Hiley Bathurst, writing of the *Roman Remains in Lydney Park* in the mid-19th century observed: 'It is probable that the river (Severn) flowed nearer to Lydney in former times by at least half a mile, for a large tract of alluvial ground is known to have been formed by deposition from the river within the last 150 years, and tradition reports that the water once came up within a short distance of the churchyard at Lydney (231).

The assumption was quite correct. In 1664 Daniel Furzer, a hired master shipwright, informed Samuel Pepys that Lydney '...is not so fit a place now for building a ship as formerly, on account of the growing of the sands, not known in man's memory before' (232). Lydney harbour from prehistoric times was entered by a pill or inlet from the Severn into which flowed two major streams. In more recent times it was still an important harbour and the Admiralty used it for ship-building in the 1650s. That pill, although long silted up, abandoned and overgrown, is still clearly visible on aerial photographs winding from the Severn south of Lydney towards the present Lydney railway station. Canalisation and development may have

destroyed much of the Roman evidence but many undeveloped open spaces still remain.

The truth is that, like Roman Coleford, Lydney has been largely ignored by planners as a site of special archaeological interest. All future development in these towns that involves earth removal should be observed with archaeologically experienced eyes.

Newnham-on-Severn, as a crossing point, and approached by Roman roads to both banks, probably also had wharfage facilities. The Chesters villa certainly did. During the later first century and early second Brims Pill may have had a wharf which served the Blakeney officials' residence. Flag-stones, masses of slag and mostly later Roman pottery found in the river bank at Whitescourt, Awre, could indicate the presence of an eroded wharf there (233).

Roads

Ivan D.Margary produced a definitive work on *'Roman Roads in Britain'*, first published in two volumes (1955 & 1957) and in one volume in 1967 by John Baker. To produce the books he travelled arout 20,000 miles, visiting every known or conjectured road. Those which met with his approval were given a number. These numbers are still standard references (even though more roads have been identified since his death) and are used in this book.

As Margary was well aware, there is no such thing as a 'typical' Roman road although most have paving (in some form), plus kerbstones, and revetting stones to keep the kerbstones in place. Margary listed twelve different recorded methods of construction ranging from the wide, long-distance roads of early military construction (usually with a well-prepared base, camber and side-ditches) to narrow roads with their paving laid directly onto sub-soil, and roads metalled with iron slag in industrial areas.

Several of these different types are to be found in Dean and the Wye Valley. Not all followed routes newly determined by the Romans. On both sides of the Wye long sections of some existing pre-Roman trackways were upgraded and paved by the Romans. In this region only the first century roads would have been constructed by and for the military. Later roads were ordered by the civil authorities for the convenience of industrial and agricultural transportation. Some Forest trackways were probably for easy access to hunting lodges. Some roads, such as the one to the Hadnock villa, were linked to major cross-Forest roads. All of the roads on the accompanying map have confirmed sections of paving or metalling, and more important, all link known Roman settlements or industrial sites.

One glance at the map will indicate which are the main Roman centres for several roads converge on Monmouth, Ariconium, Coleford and Lydney. During the second century Newent had its own road links connected to either its ore source, or to Gloucester towards which most of its manufactured products would have been directed for distribution.

The Distribution of Crude Ore

Until recently there has been little convincing evidence that crude ores were shipped away from Dean to be smelted elsewhere. In the Weald ores were smelted close to the ore sources and the same practice was assumed for Dean. The practice in Dean is now proved to be totally opposite to this, and smelting sites adjacent to, or even very near the ore sources are extremely rare. Ore (and charcoal) was moved several miles to the key centres of Ariconium, Monmouth and Newent. Dean ores have been recognised at Worcester (probably to supplement leaner local ores) and on many villa sites east of the Severn. Following their researches along the Severn estuary Allen and Fulford observed: 'Our estuarine sites, along with Worcester, can be seen as part of a more widespread practice of exporting the ores away from the ore-bearing formations to be smelted elsewhere...... Clearly the Severn and the Wye played a major role in the distribution of ore away from the producing area' (234).

Ores were still being shipped away in 1282. 'At Aylburton is a port called *la Were*, and boats call there for iron ore' (235).

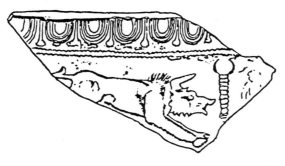

Figure 99. *Wild boar from a hunt scene on a 2nd century Samian bowl from Monmouth.*

The Central Woodlands of Dean

In a triangle formed by the Severn and the Wye, and on the north side by a line drawn from Ross-on-Wye, through Newent to Gloucester there is around 100,000 acres (40,000ha) of land. Dr.Cyril Hart, in his book 'Royal Forest' (1966), estimated that, at the time of the coming of the Romans, about 80,000 acres of this may have been woodland, 'in some places dense, in others thinly stocked, the whole being interspersed with scrub, thicket and patches of ground vegetation other than trees' (236). As a result of more recent research Dr.Hart now feels that the woodlands may have been substantially less than he originally estimated (pers. comm.).

Much of this woodland and scrub would have been lost to the charcoal burners, especially during the second century, when the regrowth of coppiced trees would not have kept pace with the massive demand for charcoal to fuel the furnaces and smithing hearths. The woodlands west of the Wye would almost certainly have been cleared to fuel the south Herefordshire and Monmouth iron-working sites. So would woodlands north and north west of Newent which would have been utilised to fuel the Newent and Dymock furnaces. These were outside of Dr.Hart's assessment area.

Figure 100. *A hunting spear from the Huntsham villa excavation.* From a photograph kindly supplied by E.Taylor.

The lesser demands during the third and fourth centuries probably allowed for some regeneration.

Hunting Lodges

There is sound evidence, though, that much of the central woodlands area was reserved for hunting by the administrator of Dean's resources and his appointees. As we have seen, no settlement was permitted within the central woodlands after c.75. Access must have been allowed for quarrying of Pennant sandstone, especially east of Coleford. The grey-green, easily-split, stone was much sought after for roof-tiles and for flooring on villa sites and in towns many miles from Dean. The access and quarrying, one must presume, was stringently monitored. There were no such problems of access for those who quarried the conglomerates and finer sandstones to make quern-stones. These rocks all occur around the Forest's edge.

Four coin hoards have been found within these central woodlands for which no one has yet offered an explanation. Of the thirteen Roman coin hoards recorded from Dean nine are located near to known or suspected buildings and all were either on, or outside of the ore outcrops. Of the other four, insufficient information was recorded about the recovery of two of them: more than 1,000 coins from Parkend deposited around the time of Allectus (late 3rd century), and at Kidnalls, 80+ silver denarii deposited in the later 2nd century. The latter hoard, along with the one from Bream scowles, contained coins of high silver content and were deposited at a time when the coinage was in decline and the percentage of silver was being reduced. The circumstances of the other two hoard discoveries record the presence of building stone.

At Crabtree Hill, in Cinderford parish, around 500 mid-3rd century bronze coins were found in a pottery jar among 'several heaps' of stones, most of which stones were removed for building purposes. This suggests that the stones were already partly dressed and had formed part of a Roman building in which the coins had been hidden (237).

Figure 101. *Coin hoard research and graph presentation by M.J. Walters.*

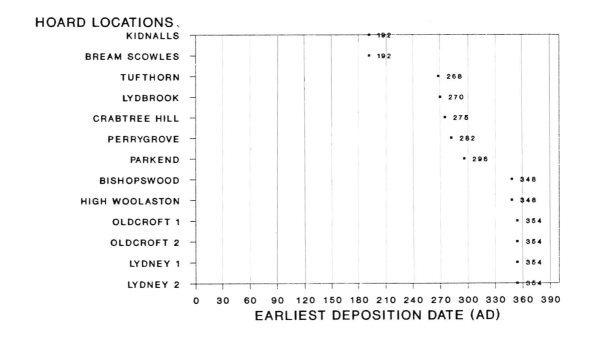

COIN HOARDS IN THE FOREST OF DEAN
Dates after which deposition of hoards
occurred based on date of latest coin

HOARD LOCATIONS

Location	Date
KIDNALLS	192
BREAM SCOWLES	192
TUFTHORN	268
LYDBROOK	270
CRABTREE HILL	275
PERRYGROVE	282
PARKEND	296
BISHOPSWOOD	348
HIGH WOOLASTON	348
OLDCROFT 1	354
OLDCROFT 2	354
LYDNEY 1	354
LYDNEY 2	354

0 30 60 90 120 150 180 210 240 270 300 330 360 390

EARLIEST DEPOSITION DATE (AD)

At Bishopswood, in woodlands near the Wye between Lower Lydbrook and Ross, over 17,000 mainly fourth century coins were discovered. The date of the latest coins in the hoard coincided with that of five other Dean hoards; two from Oldcroft, two from Lydney Park and one from High Woolaston, all of them within two or three years of the Constantius II/Magnentius period of disruption.

It is interesting to note the details of the Bishopswood hoard recovery as recorded by M.E.Bagnall-Oakley in the Transactions of the Bristol and Gloucestershire Archaeological Society for 1894/95, page 399: 'The coins were found by some workmen who were getting surface stones to mend a road, when an accidental blow from a pick struck a large earthenware jar in which they had been placed, and scattered the coins in all directions. All had been enclosed by rough walling built against the hillside.' Note: walling *'built against the hillside'*. In other words, the coins had been deposited within the walls of a building set into the hillside of which little remained. The removal of the stones by the workmen also removed the evidence of where these two buildings once stood. The buildings were clearly of modest proportions offering shelter rather than permanent living accommodation, both in areas where villas were not permitted to be built anyway. Only 2km away from Bish-

opswood was the first century enclosed building at Great Howle. The residents had been obliged to move once an official administrator took control soon after c75.

The inference is that these buildings were allowed by the controllers because they were for their own use. The logical use would have been as hunting lodges. The hoards could only have been deposited by local men of some wealth and standing. They would have been hidden within buildings that they felt were secure from thieving by the natives, simply because no unauthorised natives were permitted to enter these preserved woodlands.

At least two more hunting lodges may exist within the woodlands at Moseley and Saintlow. The *'Regard of the Forest of Dene in 1282'* mentions *'castra'* in the Bailiwick of Blakeney at 'Seyntelescastel' and at 'Moseleye' (238). Dr.Hart also draws attention to a document in the Public Record Office which mentions 'at Moseleyes castell' (E32/258-AD 1333) and adds the footnote: 'Castell was used often of the remains of a Roman dwelling'. Neither of these sites has yet been identified, and, as a useful source of building stone may have long since been robbed, leaving no trace.

These same woodlands were to become the Royal Forest of the Norman kings, but what of the intervening years?

Part Three

Post-Roman Dean and the Wye Valley

The Fifth Century to the Norman Conquest

Ecclesiastical References

Whereas the evidence for prehistoric occupation and activity in this region, and indeed elsewhere in Britain, is almost totally dependent on archaeological discoveries, for the Roman period it is possible to combine and compare archaeological evidence with some written historical records. Information on the succeeding six centuries relies heavily on preserved documents and to a much lesser extent on archaeological evidence. This particularly applies to the Wye Valley for which there are many ecclesiastical references under Gwent and Ergyng (Archenfield).

Few of the surviving documents can be considered contemporary accounts of events, and most have had their historical content questioned.

The intention here is not to to discuss the merits, or otherwise, of the post-Roman source material, but simply to attempt to bring together, for the first time, all recorded mentions of Dean and the Wye Valley that are known.

The many learned expositions of these sources express a wide diversity of opinions and frequent disagreement, especially with regard to dates. There is a labyrinth of information from which one must extricate material relevant to this region. The situation also resembles a minefield in which any frame-work laid down is liable to be exploded by those with opposing preferences. The intention is to discuss all the local archaeological evidence and seek to place it within an historical frame-work which has been retrieved through a minefield in a labyrinth.

The Fifth Century

Internal Disputes

The repulsion of Saxon raiders c.410 brought a few years of respite to the Britons. It gave time for necessary administrative re-organisation now that Imperial officials had been expelled, or recalled. This process was not without disputes according to a British Bishop named Fastidius who recorded the violent deaths of magistrates c.411. Britain, as represented by most of the nobles and aristocrats, was still essentially Roman in outlook. The natural inclination was to have an emperor, but it was not easy to agree on anyone who could command the respect of both aristocratic civilians and the military. Gildas, writing c.540, confirms a succession of locally appointed rulers who failed to unify: 'Kings were anointed not in God's name, but as being crueller than the rest; before long, they would be killed, with no enquiry into the truth, by those who had anointed them, and others still crueller chosen to replace them. Any king who seemed gentler and rather more inclined to the truth was regarded as the downfall of Britain: everyone directed their hatred and their weapons at him, with no respect' (240). Procopius records concerning the years following 410: '... from that time onward (Britain) continued to be ruled by tyrants' (241). One such local tyrant, Aurelius Caninus (a pun on the Welsh Conan), who probably ruled in the Severn Valley, was the subject of one of Gildas' invectives. He accused him of murder, fornication, adultery and of having an unjust thirst for civil war and constant plunder (242).

The disputes may be better understood if we accept that the aristocrats and landowners were divided between those who still hoped for a restoration of the Empire, or at least a continuation of a Roman-type constitution, and a

Figure 102. *Distribution map of church and monastery sites of pre-Norman foundation.*

powerful anti-Roman faction, also with an aristocratic background, but perhaps supported by those of lower social status.

Pelagius

The latter group appear to have been heavily influenced by the teachings of the British-born monk, Pelagius, who settled in Rome in the closing years of the 4th century. He acquired a reputation as a spiritual guide and was befriended by aristocratic families. He left Rome before the arrival of Alaric in 410 and settled in Palestine. His views were that individuals were responsible for their own actions and not irrevocably committed to sin because of the action of their first parents in Eden, which act was followed by God's pronounced curse upon mankind. He was horrified by the teachings of Bishop Augustine that good life and good works were of no avail without God's grace, and that children were damned at birth unless they received grace through baptism. Pelagius' beliefs were outlawed and banned in 418 by an imperial edict, but this had no immediate effect on the church in Britain where the Pelagian supporters were dominant in the anti-Roman faction.

Tracts published by a British emigrant to Sicily, a follower of Pelagian doctrine, condemned the social inequality that prevailed throughout the Romanised world and was therefore popular among those of lower status, but also appealed to many of the families of diminishing wealth and increasing Christian conscience. His indictment and appeal highlights the social distinctions of the early 5th century in the Roman world: 'One man owns many large mansions adorned with costly marbles, another has not so much as a small hut to keep out the cold and heat. One man has vast territories and unlimited possessions, another has but a little stretch of turf to sit upon and call his own ...... Mankind is divided into three classes, the rich, the poor, and those who have enough' (243).

Fastidius, already quoted, was a British Pelagian. At least one of the aforementioned tracts circulated in Britain for it was later cited by Gildas (244), who incidentally, had been born north of the Roman frontier, in the region of the Clyde, but was brought south to the shores of the Severn Sea to receive his education in the Roman tradition before becoming a monk (245).

The rulers, or emperors, of early fifth century Britain were probably appointed by, what came to be referred to as: 'The Council', a representative body of influential people drawn from the centres *(civitates)* of the former Roman province.

Vortigern

Out of the conflicts for acceptance and supremacy came Vortigern c.425, the son of Vitalis (Vitalinus) who had Gloucester associations (246). Vortigern was not his given name but was a title meaning 'High King'. Its widespread use implies that he was popular with the people who spoke British rather than Latin. His real name may well have been Vitalinus but he clearly identified himself with the British tradition and gave two of his sons British names, Vortimer and Cateyrn (247).

Britain was again under threat from the old enemy, the Picts from north of the Clyde-Forth line and the Irish, both using the coastal seaways and plundering inland from the shores. 'Our citizens abandoned the towns and the high wall...... the disasters from abroad were increased by internal disorders' was the way Gildas summarised the situation (248).

Nennius adds further detail: 'Vortigern ruled in Britain, and during his rule in Britain he was under pressure, from fear of the Picts and the Irish, and of a Roman invasion, and, not least, from dread of Ambrosius' (249). This Ambrosius, probably the father of Ambrosius Aurelianus (see below), was a Rome-orientated 'king' who opposed Vortigern. Gildas records that Aurelianus' parents 'wore the purple', implying the status of emperor, and that they were slain (250).

Figure 103. *Dinas Emrys, near Beddgelert in Snowdonia, is the legendary domain of Vortigern and is also associated with Merlin.* From an engraving by E.Evans 1879.

Saxon Settlers

Nennius then outlines Vortigern's solution to the Irish and Pictish problem: 'Then came three keels, driven into exile from Germany. In them were the brothers Horsa and Hengest...... Vortigern welcomed them and handed over to them the island that in their language is called Thanet, in British Ruoihm'. The year of the Saxon landings was c.428 (251: See comments on date).

Vortigern no doubt viewed these Saxons as allies against those he considered his real enemies, the Picts and the Irish. The Council of the Britons, or most of them, must have supported his decision to allow them marginal land and immediate essential supplies. Such a small contingent seemed to offer effective defence at a low cost; however, things got out of hand.

'And it came to pass, after the English were encamped in the aforesaid island of Thanet, that the aforesaid king promised to supply them with food and clothing without fail; and they agreed, and promised to fight bravely against his enemies. But the barbarians multiplied their numbers, and the British could not feed them. When they demanded the promised food and clothing, the British said 'We cannot give you food and clothing, for your numbers are grown. Go away, for we do not need your help.' So they took council with their elders, to break the peace.

The passage suggests a disagreement of policy between the king and The Council of the Britons, perhaps between the followers of Vortigern and the supporters of Ambrosius. Despite the threat to 'break the peace', Hengest held his hand for a few years more.

Sizing up the king's impotence, and the military weakness of his people, he held a council, and said to the British king: 'We are few; if you wish, we can send home and invite warriors from the fighting men of our country, that the number who fight for you and your people may be larger. The king ordered it to be done, and envoys were sent across the sea, and came back with sixteen keels, with picked warriors in them' (252). There is no evidence that this decision by Vortigern was supported by The Council.

The new arrivals included Hengest's daughter, whom Vortigern promptly seduced. He then married her in exchange for the region of Kent, which he handed over to the Saxons without even consulting the encumbent British local king (253), a clear indication of the authority invested in him as High King.

Hengest then said to Vortigern: 'I am your father, and will be your adviser.... I will invite my son and his cousin to fight against the Irish, for they are fine warriors. Give them lands in the north about the Wall...... He invited Octha and Ebissa, with forty keels. They sailed round the Picts and wasted the Orkney Islands... So Hengest gradually brought over more and more keels, until they left the islands whence they came uninhabited (254).

At this point Vortigern could well have claimed success, for the Saxon buffer zone on the Pictish borders effectively terminated the Highlanders' attacks on the northern British.

In 429 the bishops of Gaul sent Germanus of Auxerre to combat the effects of the teachings of Pelagius in Britain; this closely coincided with the arrival of Hengest and Horsa. He visited again in the mid-late 440s but found a totally different situation prevailing in Britain.

In 437 the struggle between Vortigern and Ambrosius had reached a head: 'And from the beginning of the reign of Vortigern to the quarrel between Vitalinus and Ambrosius are 12 years, that is Wallop *(Guoloppum)*, the battle of Wallop' (254). The outcome of the battle is not given.

Figure 104. *Artist's impression of an early Saxon hall.*

The Saxons Revolt

Soon after, the Saxons revolted against the British. They '... complained that their monthly allowance was insufficient, purposely giving a false colour to individual incidents, and swore that they would break their agreement and plunder the whole island unless more lavish payment were heaped on them, There was no delay: they put their threats into immediate effect...... a fire heaped up and nurtured by the hand of the impious easterners spread from sea to sea. It devastated town and country round about, and, once it was alight, it did not die down until it had burned almost the whole surface of the island and was licking the western ocean with its fierce red tongue...... All the major towns were laid low by the repeated battering of enemy rams; laid low, too, all the inhabitants; church leaders, priests and people alike, as the swords glinted all around and the flames crackled...... So a number of the wretched survivors were caught in the mountains and butchered wholesale. Others...... went to surrender to the enemy...... Others made for lands beyond the sea...... Others held out, though not without fear, in their own land, trusting their lives with constant foreboding to the high hills...... to the densest forests, and to the cliffs of the sea coast' (255). These were Gildas' shuddering words written about a century later.

Ambrosius and his wife were slain during this revolt, but his son, Ambrosius Aurelianus, emerged in the succeeding years as a potent leader of the resistance against the spread of Saxon settlement and plundering (256).

The Saxon revolt began around 442. The Britons subsequently appealed to Aetius, the commander in Gaul, for military assistance c.446. The appeal went unanswered.

The 'Others who made for lands beyond the sea' recalls a well attested migration of Britons to Gaul in the late 450s (257).

Nennius records the attempts of Vortimer, the son of Vortigern, to resist the revolt. Four battles are named, in the second both Horsa and Vortigern's son Cateyrn were killed. 'But Vortimer soon after died' (258).

Saxon Treachery

'So it came to pass that after the death of Vortimer, son of king Vortigern, and after the return of Hengest and his hosts, they (the English) instigated a treacherous plan, to trick Vortigern and his army. They sent envoys to ask for peace and make a permanent treaty. Vortigern called a council of his elders to examine what they should do. Ultimately one opinion prevailed with all, that they should make peace. The envoys went back, and conference was convened, where the two sides, British and English, should meet, unarmed, to confirm the treaty.

But Hengest told all his followers to hide their daggers under their feet in their shoes...... All the three hundred Seniors of king Vortigern were murdered, and the king alone was taken and held prisoner. To save his life he ceded several districts, namely Essex and Sussex, together with Middlesex and other districts that they chose and designated' (259).

This massacre, which took place around 458, must have been a devastating blow for the British, and terminal as far as Vortigern's credibility as a leader was concerned. All the key representatives of Britain's surviving local councils had been eliminated. Britain's decision-making body needed fundamental re-construction. It was to happen under Ambrosius Aurelianus, not Vortigern. Discredited and desperate, by all accounts his death, within a year or so, was a violent one.

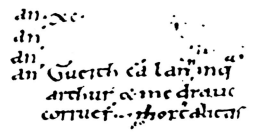

Figure 105. *An extract from the 'Annales Cambriae' which records the names of Arthur and Medraut (Mordred) who fell at the battle of Camlann.* Courtesy of the British Museum.

Vortigern's Death

Nennius offers three different versions. The first has Vortigern pursued by the castigating St.Germanus and the British clergy as a result of his illicit union with his own daughter. He 'fled in desperation to the country that is called Gwerthrynion after him, and hid there with his wives.' He was followed by Germanus. Unable to endure the forty days and nights of preaching inflicted on him, he fled again, this time to 'the fortress of Vortigern, which is in the country of the Demetians, on the river Teifi.' Relentlessly Germanus pursued him...... 'and on the fourth night, about midnight, the whole fortress was suddenly destroyed by fire sent from heaven...... Vortigern was destroyed with all who were with him, and with all his wives' (260).

The second account has Vortigern as a hated man wandering 'from place to place until at last his heart broke, and he died without honour'.

'Others say that the earth opened and swallowed him up on the night when his fortress was burnt about him, for no trace was ever found of those who were burned with him in the fortress' (261).

One other account, which moves the action into the region of Dean and the Wye Valley, is perhaps the most contentious and therefore deserves a lengthier discussion. It is found in Geoffrey of Monmouth's *'History of the Kings of Britain'* which appeared early in the 12th century, around three hundred years after Nennius' *'British History'* and *'Welsh Annals'*. Geoffrey, probably born in Monmouth, lived for many years in Oxford where his friend, Walter, was Archdeacon. Geoffrey claimed that his source material was 'a certain very ancient book written in the British language' presented to him by Walter who had brought it into Britain *('ex Britannia')*. The problem is that this book is not known for research and analysis. But, as Lewis Thorpe observed: 'the fact that we do not possess this book does not rule out its possible one-time existence. It would have been a manuscript, of course, and maybe a unique copy; and far more medieval manuscripts have been destroyed than have come down to us' (262). Brynley F.Roberts, in a recent, well-considered analysis

of Geoffrey's work commented: '... there is nothing inherently impossible in the suggestion that Walter should have brought from Brittany a manuscript which contained native historical material relating to Brittany and south-west Britain. Genealogies and traditional history were the common stock of Breton and south-west British culture...' (263).

Whatever, Geoffrey produced a splendidly readable work of historical fiction. It could be that archaeology will yet reveal as fact much of what has long been considered fiction by the analysts of literary sources.

Ambrosius Aurelianus

To return to Geoffrey's account of Vortigern's death, we find Ambrosius Aurelianus, with his brother, Uther Pendragon, returning from exile in Brittany. They were welcomed by the Britons and Ambrosius was anointed as King by the clergy. Before turning his attention to the Saxons he determined to hunt down Vortigern to avenge his father's death.

'In order to carry out his design, he marched his army into Kambria (Wales) and made for the castle of Genoreu (Ganarew), for it was there

Plate 16. *'Castle Genoreu', the Little Doward hillfort; legendary site of Vortigern's defeat and death.* Photograph by M.J.Walters.

that Vortigern had fled in his search for a safe refuge. This castle, which belonged to the Erging country, was beside the River Wye, on a hill called Cloartius (the Little Doward)'. Ambrosius was accompanied by Eldol, Duke of Gloucester, whose brother is named as Eldadus, Bishop of Gloucester.

'They lost no time, but moved into position with their siege-machines and did their utmost to break down the walls. When everything else had failed, they tried fire; and this, once it took hold, went on blazing until it burned up the tower and Vortigern with it' (264).

The 'castle' is the hill-fort on the Little Doward close to which lay the Hadnock villa on the other side of the Wye. The remains of four robbed barrows lie inside the fort. They have been assumed to be prehistoric, but round barrows are also known to belong to the Roman and post-Roman periods. There is no dating evidence for them.

'When news of this reached Hengest and his Saxons, he was greatly frightened, for he dreaded the courage of Aurelius.'

Gildas takes up the account: 'After a time, when the cruel plunderers had gone home, God gave strength to the survivors. Wretched people fled to them from all directions...... Their leader was Ambrosius Aurelianus, a gentleman who, perhaps alone of the Romans, had survived the shock of this notable storm: certainly his parents, who had worn the purple, were slain in it...... Under him our people regained their strength, and challenged the victors to battle. The Lord assented, and the battle went their way.

From then on victory went now to our countrymen, now to their enemies...... This lasted right up till the year of the siege of Badon Hill, pretty well the last defeat of the villains, and certainly not the least. This was the year of my birth; as I know, one month of the forty-fourth year since then has already passed' (265).

So Gildas, who wrote c.540, provides a key date, the battle of Badon c.495. Badon was the twelfth of Arthur's great battles as recorded by Nennius (266). To the years between c.460 and c.495 belong the heroic campaigns of Ambrosius and Arthur. Did they affect Dean and the Wye Valley? A consideration of documentary evidence combined with recent archaeological discoveries will show that some light is now being shed on this dark period.

Resistance Of The 'Fellow-Countrymen'

The last vestiges of independent Roman Britain, such as they were, died with Vortigern. With Ambrosius grew a resistance among the landowners, nobles and local kings of the south west, west and north west (probably by now call-ing themselves the *Combrogi*, 'fellow-country-men') which sought to contain any further Saxon advances into their territory, which had so far remained virtually unscathed. Dean and the Wye Valley lay well ahead of the Saxon advance lines of the fifth century, safely in British hands.

The *Combrogi*, the modern form of which is Cymry in Wales, and Cumbri in the north west, was the identity adopted by people throughout the former Roman territories of Britain to distinguish themselves from the English, and to indicate severance from their Roman past.

Their tactics in war centred on mobile cavalry groups supported by scouts who were able to identify weaknesses in the enemy formations. The Saxons utilised infantry only. Their villages were vulnerable when their men-folk gathered for war and advanced to meet the British, whose cavalry officers could choose to ignore the Saxon warriors and strike at the villages instead. Smaller plundering parties on foot were deterred by the possibility of being surprised by a mounted unit. The British mobility also enabled them to travel great distances the length and breadth of the land in order to rapidly counter new threats.

Arthur: The New Resistance Leader

No record or indication exists as to how long Ambrosius campaigned before Arthur took over as the commander of the British forces. Nennius summarised events thus: 'On Hengest's death, his son Octha came down from the north of Britain to the kingdom of the Kentishmen, and from him are sprung the kings of the Kentish-men. Then Arthur fought against them in those days, together with the kings of the British; but he was their leader in battle' (267). His list of battles seem to begin in Saxon territory to the east of England, then move further north, culminating in Badon, believed to be near Bath.

From Nennius it appears that Hengest was dead when Arthur took control. Geoffrey places the death of Hengest as being during the reign of Ambrosius (268), and then has his brother, Uther, as king prior to Arthur (269). Arthur's leadership would seem to have begun in the later 470s. Gildas, c.540, looked back on the period with nostalgia and described it as a time 'of such unlooked for recovery' that led to 'the calm of the present' (270). Arthur had probably died when Gildas was a youth. He was remembered as being 'victorious in all his campaigns' (271).

Arthur In The Forest Of Dean?

Of the many later tales and legends concerning Arthur, there is one that is set in the Forest of Dean. It is found in the 'Mabinogion', a recent name given to a collection of stories preserved in

Figure 106. *After an illustration from a MS of 'The Hunting Book' now in the Biblioteque Nationale, Paris.*

The White Book of Rhydderch and *The Red Book of Hergest*, the extant manuscripts of which date from around 1300. The story itself, 'Geraint son of Erbin' is much older. It begins thus:

'Arthur was accustomed to hold his Court at Caerlleon upon Usk...... And on Whit-Tuesday, as the King sat at the banquet, lo! there entered a tall, fair-headed youth, clad in a coat and a sur-coat of diapered (embroidered) satin, and a golden-hilted sword about his neck, and low shoes of leather upon his feet.' He announced himself as '... one of thy foresters, Lord, in the Forest of Dean, and my name is Madawc, the son of Twrgadarn.' Asked what his errand was by Arthur, he responded: 'In the Forest I saw a stag, the like of which beheld I never yet....... He is of pure white, Lord, and he does not herd with any other animal through stateliness and pride, so royal is his bearing. And I come to seek thy counsel, Lord, and to know thy will concerning him.'

Arthur determined to hunt it the following day when 'they took the road to the Forest'. Gwenhwyfar (Arthur's queen), following later, met Geraint son of Erbin on the way and they proceeded together to the edge of the Forest. Meanwhile the story tells of how Arthur took the stag: 'The men and the dogs were divided into hunting parties, and the dogs were let loose upon the stag. And the last dog that was let loose was the favourite dog of Arthur. Cavall was his name. And he left all the other dogs behind him, and turned the stag. And at the second turn, the stag came towards the hunting party of Arthur. And Arthur set upon him. And before he could be slain by any other, Arthur cut off his head.

Then they sounded the death horn for slaying, and they all gathered around' (272).

The road taken to the Forest would have been the old Roman military road from Caerleon, through Caerwent with a crossing of the Wye at the Chepstow bridge. Although the story was not recorded until perhaps two centuries after the Forest of Dean had become a Royal Forest for the Norman kings, it may well preserve a tradition of the Forest being reserved for royal hunting from pre-Norman times.

'Wonders' In The Wye Valley

The section of Nennius' *Historia Brittonum* on **The Wonders of Britain** (Mirabilia) was originally written by someone who was very familiar with this region. The fifth 'wonder' mentioned is: *Dau Ri Hafren*, that is, 'The Two Kings of the Severn'. When the sea floods into the Severn estuary in the Bore, two heaped-up wave crests are built up separately, and fight each other like rams. One goes against the other, and they clash in turn, and then one withdraws from the other, and they go forth again at each tide. This they

Plate 17. *The site of the spring at Gamber Head.* Photograph by B.Walters.

have done from the beginning of the world to the present day' (273). This marvellous metaphorical description could hardly be bettered and probably derives from a very ancient legend.

Another 'wonder' must have been located in the Chepstow area: 'By the river called Wye, apples are found on an ash-tree, on the hill-side by the river estuary' (274).

Yet another is located at Pwll-Meurig just one kilometre south west of Chepstow: 'There is another wonder in the aforesaid country, called Gwent. There is a spring by the wall of Pydew Meurig (Meurig's Well), and there is a plank in the middle of the spring, and men may wash their hands and their faces, and have the plank under their feet when they wash. I have tested it and seen it myself. When the sea floods at high tide, the Severn spreads over the whole shore, and touches it, and reaches to the spring, and the spring is filled from the Severn Bore, it draws the plank with it to the open sea, and it is cast about in the sea for three days, but on the fourth day it is found in the same spring. Now it came to pass that a countryman buried it in the ground to test it, and on the fourth day it was found in the

spring, and the countryman who took it and buried it died before the end of the month' (275).

The final wonder relates to the region called Ergyng, or, as it was later called, Archenfield. The site of the wonder is a spring located at Gamber Head, the source of the Gamber Brook, near the northern boundary of Llanwarne parish, and it again relates to Arthur: 'There is another wonder in the country called Ergyng. There is a tomb there by a spring, called *Llygad Amr*; the name of the man who is buried in the tomb was Amr. He was a son of the warrior Arthur, and he killed him there and buried him. Men come to measure the tomb, and it is sometimes six feet long, sometimes nine, sometimes twelve, sometimes fifteen. At whatever measure you measure it on one occasion, you never find it again of the same measure, and I have tried it myself' (276).

Interestingly, in the story of 'Geraint son of Erbin', Amhar is named as the son of Arthur, and, at the time, he was one of Arthur's four pages.

'King Arthur's Cave', or 'Hall', as it used to be called, close to the hill-fort on the Little Doward, preserves legendary, probably medieval, associations of Arthur with this region. There is, however, more solidly based archaeological evidence for activity in Dean during the Arthurian period.

Arthurian-Period Lydney

The Wheelers' excavations at Lydney Park confirmed a post-Roman reinforcement of the hill-fort defences. The ramparts of the re-modelled earthwork contained 4th century pottery, a coin minted in 361, and, more significantly, building debris from the adjacent temple complex indicating that the ramparts were re-constructed after the baths, guest-house, and probably the temple, had fallen into disuse. Their report also observed that the earthwork was entirely un-Roman. Closer dating of the post-Roman occupation was assisted by the find of a bronze brooch of a Gothic type found in the early Saxon-occupied counties of Britain, and more commonly, in the Rhine valley. It was dated to the latter part of the 5th century, the Arthurian period in Britain (277).

For what purpose might the hill-fort have been utilised at that time?

John Morris, in his *'The Age of Arthur'*, logically reasons the problems a cavalry force might have had in protecting their horses over-night when an enemy might be expected to attempt to either disperse or hamstring them, thus rendering the force ineffective. He proposed that sound tactics would have required the men to seek out suitable fortified enclosures and ready-made defences when the shelter of a walled-town was not available. Iron Age hill-forts offered such security once their defences had been reinforced.

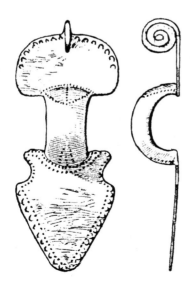

Figure 107. *Later 5th century AD brooch from Lydney Park hill-fort.*

Lydney hill-fort would have been an obvious choice lying as it did close to a main east-west Roman road and mid-way between two walled towns. Excavations at Lydney did not produce evidence for fifth century buildings and long-term occupation within the fort, as excavations on several other south-western re-occupied forts did. Rather the evidence suggests that the ramparts were strengthened so that it could have been used for temporary stays, perhaps over-night, or for a few days, the sort of time a cavalry force might have needed to occupy it for security reasons (278).

There is no way of being certain how the brooch came to be at Lydney, but it might reasonably have been lost there by a British cavalryman, acquired as spoil after a defeat of the Saxons, or a British-made copy of a Saxon brooch that had been similarly obtained. One thing is certain; it belonged to the age of Arthur and it was found in Dean.

Defaced Roman Altar

Another enigmatic stone find which may be connected with this period is a Roman-type altar 67cm high. On four sides had been cut an abbreviated inscription that has so far defied interpretation. The letters: NO are repeated, but there is also a simple cross of early form. It has been suggested that it is an illiterate copy of a 5th century Christian memorial stone. What is particularly curious is that it was dredged up from a sacred spring area between Bream and St.Briavels, on Closeturf Farm. The disposal of it there, intact, suggests a respectful belief in Celtic traditions, possibly combined with a nominal acceptance of Christian beliefs. The inscription, therefore, may be valedictory. Until someone can provide an acceptable interpretation we are left with an intriguing mystery. The altar may now be viewed in the Dean Heritage Museum, Soudley.

Very late in the Arthurian period, perhaps culminating in the early years of the sixth century, there is a tradition that the strong colony of Irish settlers in Demetia, Pembrokeshire and parts of Carmarthenshire, were removed by military action that could have involved troop movements through Dean and the Wye Valley. The British and the Irish independently preserved their lists of the succession of Demetian kings. In both versions the kings have Irish names to c.500 and are then replaced by names of Romano-British origin. In the fanciful Brychan (Brecon) documents a general named Theodoric (a Gothic name; the Welsh form is Tewdrig) advances along the Roman road from Gloucester, through Newent and Stretton Grandison (Margary route 610 and 63a) to Kenchester, and from there, via Clyro to Brecon (Margary route 63b). Memories of the

Theodoric campaigns are also to be found in Cornish, Breton and Irish traditions. All place him around the time of Arthur (279).

Local Saints and Kings of the Fifth and Sixth Centuries

This section of the labyrinth contains the densest concentration of mines. The primary source is the *Liber Landavensis*, 'The Book of Llandaff', an early 12th century Register Book of the Cathedral of Llandaff which embodies memoirs of famous prelates and grants of land to the church. It contains the 'Lives' of the early saints and alludes to many historical events which affected Wales and the border country. Concerning this region there are many references to the Wye Valley, to Upper and Lower Gwent and to Ergyng.

Ergyng (Archenfield)

Almost all references to Ergyng or Archenfield state that Ergyng derives from Ariconium, the Roman-period settlement east of the Wye and within the medieval bounds of the Forest of Dean, but no one gives the etymological development.

Nennius, in his early 9th century collection of 'British History' in the section 'The Wonders of Britain' (Nennius 73) refers, in Latin, to 'Ercing', which is usually translated as Erging. Ercing is the earliest known form for the tract of land later referred to as Archenfield. It is still Erging in the 12th century 'Liber Landavensis'.

Archenfield, in the Anglo-Saxon Chronicle of 915 is *Ircingafeldes* and variously *Yrcingafeld* and *Iercingafeld*. In Domesday Book it is *Arcenefelde*, and in 1316 *Irchinfield*. Leland, in the 16th century, rendered it *Herchinfield*. *Feld* is early English for 'open country/land'.

It must be considered that these renderings are further examples of how the English have corrupted Welsh place-names without knowledge or consideration of their original meaning. One cannot help but feel that the etymological origins of 'urchin' (hedgehog) may better indicate the source of the name Archenfield. In Middle English a hedgehog was *urchon/yrichon* and later *hirchon/irchoun*. The Roman form was *hericionem* from the Latin *hericius*. The Latin for 'hedgehog' bears a distinct resemblance to Ariconium which may be why the English rendered the region Archenfield. However, Ercing was not Welsh/British for hedgehog and may have derived from the definite article *yr*, 'the', followed by a noun, the meaning of which is now lost to us.

In fact the only explanation as to how how the Bury Hill settlement may have got to be renamed Ariconio (this is how it appears in the *Antonine Itinerary XIII*) is proposed by S.Applebaum and repeated by Anthony Birley. L.Aruconius Verecundus was a mining contractor and is known to have leased the rights to mine lead in the Peak District. It is quite possible that he was also involved with mining on the Mendips in the first century AD. Applebaum's suggestion was that Aruconius Verecundus may also have been connected with the iron-working industry of Dean, and that Ariconium may be named after him. The name is certainly unusual and is only recorded elsewhere in Rome (280). Rivet and Smith in 'The Place-Names of Roman Britain' suggest that Ariconium may be derived from the British *are-/ari-* meaning 'in front of', and *conio* of unknown meaning. So, did Ariconium imply 'Hedgehog Country'? Was it named after a Roman citizen, or was it a descriptive British name? Also, what was the original British meaning of Erciing/Erging?

There is a further problem to be faced when attempting to equate Ariconium with Archenfield. In the medieval territories of Ergyng, as given in the *Liber Landavensis* X.7, all the churches listed are within boundaries embraced by the Monnow, the Black Mountains and the Wye. Ariconium was east of the Wye, and if Ergyng/Archenfield was derived from Ariconium, then it would hardly have given its name to the area unless it was situated within it. Fenn argued that the early boundaries of Ergyng were much more extensive and that the Wye only became a later, eastern boundary as a result of subsequent territorial contraction (281). It is also possible that early ecclesiatical foundations east of the Wye were not mentioned in the *Liber Landavensis* because there was little chance of having them restored to the See of Llandaff in the 12th century.

These arguments are not without support as we shall see, however, there still remains the problem that there is not a single scrap of archaeological evidence to indicate a post, or even very late Roman presence from the Ariconium settlement, although the nearby place-name, Eccleswall from Latin: *ecclesia*, Welsh: *eglwys* (church), suggests that there could have been. As we have seen, the coin sequence ends in the 360s, there was dereliction everywhere around the site and the *mansio* had probably closed because the route that passed through Ariconium was out of favour.

If the name Archenfield was derived from Ariconium then it would only seem to be perpetuating a memory, not an existing, thriving centre.

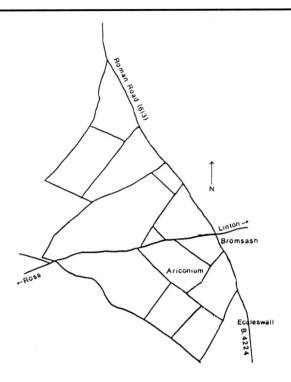

Figure 108. *Eccleswall and its relationship to the fourth century Ariconium site.*

Eccleswall

Before passing on from this subject it would be well to observe that Eccleswall is now in the parish of Linton, probably from OE *lin-* flax farm or enclosure. Other possibilities are: OE *hlyn-* a maple tree, and OE *lynd-* a lime tree. The OE *hlinc-* a hill-side terrace from which 'lynchet' is derived, is less likely as it is usually found as the second element in a place-name, not the first. There are two Aston place-names to the east of Eccleswall; Weston to the west of it; Sutton (in the Hope Mansel valley) to the south of it, and Upton to the north of it. This suggests that Eccleswall was the centre of several small Saxon communities. Which raises the question: Could a post-Roman Christian settlement have been established just to the east of Ariconium, away from, and out of sight of the former iron-working settlement, and immediately alongside the Roman road from the Severn? If so, did it perpetuate the name of Ariconium at the time? More ground and aerial survey, possibly combined with some excavation, might resolve the problem.

The Early 'Celtic' Church

The concept that there was ever a 'Celtic' Church in the sense of a unity of beliefs, prac-tices and structure that was common to Britain, Ireland and Europe, is best avoided. So is the notion that it was fundamentally dissimilar to the Church of Rome although it did take many centuries before all regions of these islands fully accepted the authority of Rome.

By the seventh century there were clear differences and diversity of thinking and practice. By the eighth century there was a distinctive divide between the British and Irish approaches to Christianity and Rome. During the fifth and sixth centuries there were already differences in doctrinal acceptance, as we have seen, however these were probably less obvious than in later centuries due to the common objectives of the early missionaries.

The earliest saints, churches and monastic foundations associated with this region will now be considered although it will soon be apparent that most sites and dates are conjectured.

Nowhere can it be said with absolute certainty: There is where the earliest building was constructed (281a).

Saint Dubricius (Dyfrig)

Dubricius' main sphere of activity was unquestionably Erging and the part of Gwent that lies in, or close to, the Wye Valley. Most of his ecclesiastical foundations are to be found in this area. What is still very much in dispute is the approximate date of their foundations, and this is due to the uncertainty surrounding the date of Saint Dubricius' death which is given very precisely as 'Sunday, the 14th day of November, in the year of our Lord, 612' in the section of the *Liber Landavensis* on: (Readings from) 'The Life of St.Dubricius' (II.VIII). This has been viewed as almost a century too late by most chronologists and commentators, but has been defended by others (282). The 'Life' also adds the information that Dubricius: '... being weary through infirmities and old age, resigned the laborious office of a Bishop, and for many years lived solitarily, leading the life of a hermit... (on) the isle of Bardsey.' The length of his years on Bardsey are unknown, but the inference is that the main years of his ministry were in the 6th century and that he was of advanced years when he retired. On this reckoning his ministry could hardly have begun before c.540.

One of the chronological problems is that the earliest and most reliable 'Life' is that of St.Samson which was recorded by a relative c.600, some thirty to forty years after Samson's death in old age. This has Samson, as a young man, being consecrated by Dubricius and also places him as a younger contemporary of St.Illtud. Samson is independently attested as being present at a church council in Paris, c.557. Gregory of Tours dates the events that brought him back to Brittany to the last weeks of 560, shortly after which he died (283). If these dates are to be accepted then Dubricius must have been alive, as Bishop, to consecrate Samson in the early years of the 500s, and Dubricius' ministry would have begun well before, in the mid-later 5th century.

It is perhaps perverse at this point to add that Geoffrey of Monmouth firmly places Dubricius as a contemporary of Arthur and has him crowning the fifteen-year-old Arthur as king (284).

There is also a disputed, if not discredited, tradition closely linking both Dubricius and Illtud with Saint Germanus who unquestionably is associated with the first half of the fifth century when there was still a strong Romano-British society.

The story surrounding Dubricius' birth, as it appears in his 'Life', is typical of the fantastical embellishments that grow within folk-lore before it is finally written down, yet it may be held to contain some elements of historical accuracy.

He is portrayed as the illegitimate son of Ebrdil, the daughter of Peibio who was the son of Erb, king of Erging. His place of birth is given as Madley, seven miles from Hereford:

'And when he became a man in growth, age and wisdom, and skilful in both the modern and ancient law, his fame extended throughout all Britain, so that from all parts, not only scholars who were uninstructed came, but also learned men and doctors flocked to him for the sake of study, particularly St.Teilo and St.Samson, his disciple...... And with those he retained two

Figure 109. *A 19th century drawing of Hentland church by W. Raffles Davison.*

thousand clergy for seven successive years at Henllan, on the banks of the Wye' (285).

Henllan is Hentland, 4½ miles (7km) north west of Ross-on-Wye, and the seminary is believed to have been located at Llanfrother, close to the Red Rail ford (Rhyd-yr-Heol) of the Wye, which is served by Roman roads to both banks.

It became the custom, in Wales, for some of the kings, nobles and wealthy landowners to grant to the Church a portion of their land on which to establish a monastery or ecclesia, in expectancy of heavenly favours. Sometimes a grant of land was made to an already-existing ecclesiastical community. The main purpose of the grant of land would be for supporting the community by means of arable and livestock farming. Some religious orders provided their own labour, others were helped by nearby residents who received essential supplies in return for their labour.

Monastery (epicopalis locus) Founded At Welsh Bicknor

One of the earliest recorded grants of land to Dubricius, in this area, was at Welsh Bicknor. In the Charters it is recorded as Llangystennyn Garthbenni in Erging. Cystennyn is Constantine, so it signifies the Church of Constantine. Garth is an enclosure. The wording of the grant is important: 'Be it known to you that King Peibio son of Erb, granted the Manor of Garthbenni, as far as the black Marsh beyond the wood, and field, and water, and the property of King Cystennyn, his father-in-law, beyond the Wye, to God, and Dubricius, Archbishop of the See of Llandaff, and to Iunapeius his cousin, for his soul, and the writing of his name in the Book of Life...... And Peibio held the written deed upon the hand of St.Dubricius, that the house of prayer and penance, and the episcopal residence might belong to the Bishops of Llandaff forever. And in testimony thereof, he consecrated the church, and left there three of his disciples' (286). The names of fourteen men, including Dubricius and Cystennyn, are listed as witnesses.

Constantine is here given as the father-in-law of Peibio and therefore a contemporary of Erb, Peibio's father, who was King of Gwent and Ergyng. Constantine's property is given as being 'beyond the Wye'. As most of the land granted to Dubricius is the elevated peninsula within the loop of the Wye that faces Lower Lydbrook, it follows that Constantine was an owner of land within the Forest of Dean on the other side of the Wye, although it need not imply that he actually lived within Dean. His lands may have included the Huntsham peninsula with its earlier Romano-British associations.

Plate 18. *Welsh Bicknor church and the River Wye.* Photograph by M.J.Walters.

The name, Constantine, was Roman and very popular in the fourth and early fifth centuries. All things considered the date for the giving of this grant fits more comfortably into the latter part of the fifth century, although Prof.W.Davies suggests good reasons that would place it a century later c.575 (287).

Where Was The Church Sited?

It has been assumed by some that the site of the church foundation must be where the present Welsh Bicknor church stands, which is very close to the river Wye and only marginally above flood level. DAG's 1990 aerial survey revealed a much more likely possibility, although it should be borne in mind that both a church and an episcopal residence were referred to in the grant, and they may not have been located immediately next to each other.

Courtfield House, now part of a monastery complex, stands at the head of the promontory facing Lower Lydbrook. An earlier Courtfield House, on the same site, is the traditional place to which the young Henry V was taken as a child from his birthplace in Monmouth. Leading up to Courtfield House is a trackway from the former ferry crossing of the Wye at Lower Lydbrook. It

was in use well into the 20th century. To the east of Courtfield House is a semi-circular field, still bounded by a hedgerow which follows the contours around the hill, well above the river. In the bottom corner of this field, where it abuts the recent track, is a double-ditched enclosure, partly curved, about one acre in area which shows as a distinct parch-mark from the air. Running from the enclosure is a filled-in hollow-way, which is also clearly visible from the air, but not noticeable at all from the ground. The hollow-way filling is ancient and the route has been disused for a very long time. It meets the river bank at a point almost opposite Vention Lane which itself connects to the cross-Forest route from Mitcheldean to Monmouth, a prehistoric route paved in sections during the Roman period. It suggests a very ancient ferry crossing at this point where the river flows deeper and slower.

The enclosure is at the centre of the loop, and well elevated above the Wye. It is the perfect positioning for a *llan* within a *garth*. While ploughed in 1987 the field was walked and produced a hemispherical bowl rim of Oxfordshire colour-coated ware, usually a fourth-century import into this area. There is no known Roman site on the peninsula and the pottery fragment may well represent an example of choice fourth century Romano-British table ware being pre-

been identified with names given in the Charters. There are abbots recorded at *Lanndougarth*, the Doward, in the 5th/6th centuries, but whether the site of the monastery was Whitchurch, Ganarew or some other location is uncertain.

Figure 110. *Saint Teilo (after a MS in the Hengwrt Library).*

St.Teilo succeeded Dubricius to the See of Llandaff '... in which he could not long remain, on account of the pestilence which nearly destroyed the whole nation. It was called the 'Yellow Pestilence...' (289). The plague hit Britain c.547. Teilo fled to Brittany until it was over.

Saint Tecla

A little-known early saint, whose name does not appear in the Llandaff charters, is perpetuated in 'The Isle of St.Tecla'. This tiny tidal islet is just off the Beachley peninsula, where the Wye joins the Severn estuary and south of the Severn bridge. The ruins of St.Twrog's chapel can still be seen on it.

Tecla or Tecychius was a disciple of St.Tatheus who was recorded in the sixth century as being 'entertained by a rich man near Chepstow, who still heated his bath on Saturdays in the manner of his Roman forbears' (289a). A St.Tegla is also known as being the martyred daughter of an early king of Gwynedd with churches named after her at Llandegley in

Plate 19. *Courtfield House on the hill overlooking a loop of the Wye and Lower Lydbrook.* Photograph by M.J.Walters.

served and used well into the fifth century, or later.

A further grant of a dwelling and land was given by Peibio to Dubricius a few years later at Llandinabo (Lann Inabwy), 6½ miles (10km) north west of Ross-on-Wye. Inabwy, the priest, was a witness. Woodland is again mentioned ('the great wood') in the grant of land which began at a ford of the Wye, near Hoarwithy, and looped back to the Wye (288).

The earliest recorded grant of land was made by Erb to Dubricius at a place called Cil Hal in the Charters. Recent research by David Hancocks of DAG would seem to place this in the lower Monnow Valley near St.Maughams, although W.Davies suggests Pencoed, now a parish in south Herefordshire between Llanwarne and Hentland, but adds a question mark (288a). The wording of the grant describes the land as Erb's inheritance, which may suggest that it was his family seat.

The church at Whitchurch, by the side of the Ross to Monmouth road, is dedicated to Dubricius but there would appear to be no mention of it in the Charters. There are, however, a number of churches and land grants that have not yet

Powys, and Llandegla in Clwyd. St.Twrog, c.600, was a disciple of St.Beuno.

Another saint whose name is perpetuated in Dean is St.Brioc. Briavel derives from Brioc. E.G.Bowen in his 'Saints, Seaways and Settlements in the Celtic Lands'(289b) describes Brioc as one of the *peregrini*, holy men, possibly monks, who travelled alone or with a small group of followers. In suitable places they would set up 'cells' and preach, teach and heal. When they moved on the place where they had dwelt was sometimes sanctified and became a church. The *peregrini* spread the Celtic form of Christianity widely, even across the seas. Dedications to Brioc are to be found in west Wales, at St.Briavels, in Cornwall, and mostly in Brittany, but he is believed to have originated from Wales.

Because they were humble, travelling men, the *peregrini* did not attain the fame of such as St.Dyfrig to whom grants of land were made for the benefit of the church and its resident encumbents. Bowen also observes that their cult was unlikely to be revived in the Middle Ages to such an extent that later dedications were made in their name as was the case with major saints such as David, Brigid, Illtud and Patrick whose names were associated in a dedicatory way with many Norman and later churches. Brioc may be viewed, according to Bowen, as a holy man who travelled from Wales, through Dean, Somerset, Devon and Cornwall to Brittany, establishing cells en route, some of which became churches which perpetuated their founder's name.

In a recent joint paper by Dr.Nancy Edwards and Dr.Alan Lane they commented that Bowen's: '... rather uncritical use of dedications and suspect historical sources to write an account of the peregrinations of the early saints and their supposed foundation of early church sites, have proved particularly misleading' (289c). Clearly the origins of St.Briavels and its association with St.Brioc must remain in doubt.

Another saint with dedications in Brittany is St.Méen who traditionally is stated to be an immigrant from the kingdom of Erging (Archenfield). He was a close relative of St.Samson and at least one famous Breton monastery founded by him still exists.

The West Saxons Enter Gloucestershire

In 577 'Cuthwine and Ceawlin fought the Britons, and killed three kings, Conmail, Condidan and Farinmael, in the place called Dyrham. They took three cities: Gloucester, Cirencester and Bath' (290). The West Saxons entered the Vale of the Severn for the first time but there is as yet no evidence that they penetrated west of the Severn into Dean or the Wye Valley at this date. Local British kings still had control.

The Battle Of Tintern

Ceolwulf became king of the West Saxons in 597 and it might have been he who decided to probe the strength of the British kings west of the Wye in Gwent. In the 'Grant of King Meurig son of Tewdrig', when Teilo's successor Oudoceus was Bishop of Llandaff, a battle against the Saxons is described; the location: Tintern. King Tewdrig had given up his kingdom to his son, Meurig and had '... commenced leading a hermetical life among the rocks of Tintern. When he was there resident, the Saxons began to invade his land against his son Meurig, so that unless he individually would afford his assistance, his son would be altogether dispossessed by foreigners...... and

Figure 111.
Saxon spear from Tutshill.

5cm

being armed, he stood in the battle on the banks of the Wye, near the ford of Tintern; and on his face being seen, the enemy turned their backs, and betook themselves to flight; but one of them threw a lance, and wounded him therewith.'

The next day Tewdrig died at what is now called Pwll Meurig, near Chepstow. 'His son Meurig being informed of the death of his father, built there an oratory and cemetary, which were consecrated to Oudoceus and the Church of Llandaff' (291).

A Saxon spear-head, dated to this period, was found at Tutshill, close to the old Roman bridge near Chepstow in 1951 (292).

King Meurig is also recorded as granting the land of Porthcasseg with 'two wears for fisheries' (on the Wye) to Oudoceus. Porthcasseg is just north of St.Arvans, about three miles north of Chepstow (293).

Churches And Monasteries Founded

About this time further monasteries were founded at Lanndougarth (Doward), Lann Loudeu (Llancloudy), and Lannenniaun (Llandogo). Churches (ecclesiae) were founded at Merthir Teudiric (Matharn) and Cynmarchi (Chepstow), all of these being in the Wye Valley.

Figure 112. *Ganarew Church. Possibly the site of the 6th/7th century monastery of Llandougarth (Doward). A 19th century drawing by W.Raffles Davison.*

On the Dean side of the Wye an abbot of Lannceuid (Llan Cewydd), Lancaut, is referred to c.625 and there was a monastic settlement there c.703. A recent survey of the ruins of the church that still stand at Lancaut failed to discern any feature that pre-dated the late 12th or early 13th century, although a lead font from the church, now in Gloucester Cathedral, has been dated to c.1130-1140 (293a).

In c.703 King Morgan of Glywysing (Glamorgan) granted the ecclesia (church) of Tidenham (Istrat Hafren) to Bishop Berthgwyn (294). This infers that at least part of the Severn side of Dean was still in Welsh/British hands throughout the 7th, and into the 8th centuries. Again there is no certainty that the present church is on the site of the earliest foundation, but it may be assumed to be so.

The Mercians Take Control

In 628 Gloucestershire, east of the Severn, changed hands again when 'Cyngils and Cwichelm fought with Penda at Cirencester' and surrendered their West Saxon domains in Gloucestershire to Penda of Mercia, and that part of Gloucestershire became part of the Mercian sub-kingdom of the Hwicce; but they did not control Dean (295).

It is unclear how the Dean region was divided up at this time and who the rulers were. It has been proposed that part, at least, belonged to the Western Hecani of Herefordshire whose first recorded ruler was Merewalh (c.625-c.685). According to Goscelin, he was the third son of Penda. In the *'Tribal Hidage'* (8th century) the Hecani are referred to merely as *Westerna*. In a charter of 811 they had become *Magonsetum* (295a).

In a recent study of Anglo-Saxon Gloucestershire Carolyn Heighway held that: 'The rest of Dean was in the kingdom of the Magonsaetan. The Magonsaetan were, like the Hwicce, a sub-kingdom of Mercia, and just as the boundaries of the Hwicce were preserved in the medieval diocese of Worcester, so the boundaries of the Magonsaete were preserved in the diocese of Hereford (created c.675). The territory comprised west Gloucestershire, Herefordshire, and south Shropshire...... there can be no doubt that the Forest of Dean had different origins from the rest of Gloucestershire...... The ancient Anglo-Saxon dialect of the Forest of Dean area was a Mercian one, but it was different from the more East Midlands version spoken in north Gloucestershire. The more Midland speech of the Dean probably derives from its take-over in the 600s by the Mercian Magonsaetan' (296).

Fenn takes a different view about the language of the Magonsaete as a whole: 'With a Welsh element in their folkname, the Magonsaete must have become predominantly Welsh in blood and speech...... In fact most of the land of the Magonsaete lies within an area whose dialect bears marked peculiarities which can only be explained by the descent of its speakers from speakers of Welsh (297).

Plate 19A. *Soil marks of probably pre-Norman broad ridge and furrow field-strips near Alvington Court.* Photograph by M.J.Walters.

It is appropriate here to add that, just as the dialect of the upland Foresters differs from that of Gloucestershire east of the Severn, so also does it differ from the dialects of Herefordshire and the borders further north. No one knows how, and when the dialect developed in the Forest. Could it have been as a result of an influx of people into the sparsely populated Dean uplands to meet a specific industrial or political need? If so, when?

Considering that Dean is Welsh border country, remarkably few of the indigenous population have names of Welsh/British origin. Of the many names listed on newly acquired documents of miner's Mine Law Court records of the Forest of Dean for 1469-1470, only one name, Morgan, is Welsh (298). Interestingly, Morganwy and Madog, who held English Bicknor and Rudford before 1066, are the only Welsh names attested in the Domesday Book for pre-Norman

Figure 113. *Lancaut Church and the cliffs of Wintour's Leap above the Wye. The Piercefield hill-fort is on the cliffs to the right of the Wye.* Drawn by Eric J.Rice.

landowners in Dean and west Gloucestershire. The same can be said about field and place names. Whether drawn from the Parish Tithe Map apportionments, a 1608 map of west Dean, ancient land transactions, or the 10th century Saxon charter for Tidenham, field names derived from the Welsh are comparatively rare. This is in direct contrast to place and field names west of the Wye, even in Herefordshire.

If there was an influx of people it would be reasonable to deduce a Mercian origin, but perhaps not a Magonsaetan one. Could they have been the people referred to as the Dunsaete, a name only known from an Ordinance believed to date to c.926? The name is possibly derived from OE *dun*, 'a hill, a tract of high ground', and *saete* 'settlers/dwellers' (299). They were certainly associated with this area as we shall see.

Eighth Century Developments

While Berthgwyn was still Bishop, and Ithael, king, there were further Saxon probings across the Wye, which, according to the *Liber Landavensis* 6.24, affected Llandinabo, Llancloudy, and Llangarron in the Wye Valley, as far inland as

Figure 114. *A representation of Saint Cadog.*

Llanardil, near Usk, and up the Herefordshire borders to the Dore Valley and Llanddewi Mochros. The Saxons were eventually repelled and the lands restored to their owners 'although destroyed and depopulated by foreign people'. These troublesome years, in the early 8th century, caused an alliance of the Britons to be formed in these parts in order to resist future Saxon incursions.

Despite the border disruptions further monasteries were founded near Monmouth c.733, and at Dixton c.735. Churches were constructed at Wonastow c.750, Trellech c.755, Llanwarne c.758 and Llangovan c.775. By the 8th century too, a church dedicated to St.Cadoc is believed to have been sited to the north west of Monnow Street in Monmouth. The Breton lord, Withenhoc, in the late 11th century, described the site as being: 'on ground near my castle in my manor, where the monks were first accommodated before the church of Monmouth was finished' (299a).

During the course of the eighth century the lands of Tidenham became a part of Mercian territory. As though to emphasise this, the greatest of all Mercian kings, Offa, caused one of the most impressive sections of his dyke to be constructed within that territory.

Offa's Dyke

Offa ruled from 757-796 and by the middle of his reign the impressive earthwork, attributed to him, between Wales and Mercia was under construction. Sir Cyril Fox's survey of the Dyke, published in 1955, viewed the positioning of the Dyke as representing a boundary or frontier negotiated with the Welsh. This has since been questioned by Frank Noble who saw sections of it as having clear advantages as a military barrier (300). This particularly applies to the section between Dennel Hill and Madgetts (Modesgate) where it is built along the crest of steep slopes and cliffs, facing Tintern. Equally it could be said that it is massive where it least needed to be. Also puzzling is the fact that the Lancaut settlement was separated from some of its open fields by the Dyke which seems to have used the eastern rampart of the Spital Meend fort to isolate the peninsula and leave it in Welsh hands. The 'missing' sections of the Dyke beyond Lower Lydbrook, and the many unimpressive lengths in between there and Sedbury, on the Severn, still leave one feeling that only more archaeological investigations on the Dean side of the Dyke might eventually unravel its many enigmas.

A silver penny of Beorhtric, king of Wessex from 786-802, is the only published find of a Saxon coin from Dean. It was found at Stowe (301).

Figure 115. Top: *Coin of Beorhtric (AD 786-802). Bottom: Coin of Burgred (AD 852-874).*

The Anglo-Saxon Chronicles record for 853 that: 'Burgred, king of Mercia, subjected the Welsh with king Aethelwulf's help.' Aethelwulf was the king of Wessex and Burgred sealed an alliance by marrying his daughter. At this time Burgred also gave Lidenige (Lydney) to his brother-in-law, Aethelred of Wessex (302).

By this time the Vikings were sorely troubling the Mercians, especially with regard to their eastern territories. They joined forces with the West Saxons under Aethelred and his brother, Alfred, in an effort to stem the raids. Between 866 and 874 there were constant battles until finally Burgred fled to Rome, and the Danes appointed Ceolwulf as king of Mercia so that, effectively, Mercia was now under their control. By 877 the Danes 'went into Mercia, shared some of it out and gave some to Ceolwulf.' He was left with the western part up to the Welsh borders.

The Vikings in Archenfield

In 910 they 'ravaged greatly by the Severn' and returned again in 914 when they 'ravaged in Wales everywhere along the coast where it suited them. And they captured Cyfeiliog, Bishop of Archenfield...... and King Edward ransomed him for 40 pounds. Then after that all the army went inland, still wishing to go on a raid towards Archenfield. Then the men from Hereford and Gloucester and from the nearest Boroughs met them and fought against them and put them to flight and killed the earl Hroald and the brother of Ohter, the other earl, and a great part of the army, and drove them into an enclosure and besieged them there until they gave them hostages' (303).

At this point it might be worthwhile to consider the alternative routes that may have been used by the Danes during this incursion. This is, of course, speculative, but the possibilities are very limited.

The Saxon Chronicles record specifically that it was Archenfield (Erging) that was the target for the Viking attack. There is no mention of Gwent, or travelling through it. They would have disembarked well down river from Gloucester which was, by now, a defended garrison town; so was Hereford. The exceptional mobility of the Vikings, once on shore, meant that they would have made good use of Roman roads and pre-Roman trackways, especially those which avoided the Saxon urban areas (304).

This leaves two outstanding places for disembarkation on the Severn side of Dean. The first is the former Roman harbour at Lydney which offered them two routes for penetration into Archenfield. One of these would have taken them to Coleford with a choice of either descending into Monmouth, or passing Symonds Yat and crossing the Wye on the Huntsham peninsula. The other would have taken them along the Dean Road through Soudley, Littledean and Mitcheldean to Ariconium, and from there to Ross.

The second suitable landing place would have been Brims Pill with road links to Blakeney and from there to the Dean Road near Blackpool Bridge. The Dean Road would then have been followed to the site of Ariconium and Ross. It is also possible that, by this time, there were good post-Roman trackways linking Weston to Ross. A post-Roman slag trackway is known that is heading in that direction from Lea. Mooring at Newnham would have been another possibility, then marching the short route up-hill to Littledean. The disadvantage of this would have of where the Bishop was at the time. It appears that his capture and subsequent ransom was planned. His ransom for 40 pounds of silver was paid then: 'Shortly afterwards, the whole army landed and marched towards the aforesaid plain'.

The time taken to collect and deliver the ransom had given the Saxons the opportunity to co-ordinate an offensive. They either knew, or guessed that the Vikings would return to plunder the monasteries, churches and manors of Archenfield. So they 'went out suddenly to meet them'. This suggests an element of surprise. Also the account says that the raiders 'marched towards the plain' and were met.

Figure 116. *Viking longship (Oslo Museum.*

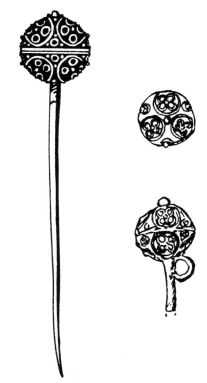

Figure 117. Left: *Silver pin from near Welshbury. Drawn by D.Thomas. Courtesy of D.Allen. Right: Silver-gilt pin from near St.Anthony's Well. Drawn by C.Mortimer. Courtesy of M.Hill.*

been the narrowness of the river at Newnham and the fairly direct road link to Gloucester from Arlingham on the left bank. The fact that 'all the army' went inland to Archenfield on the second sortie would have left their ships particularly vulnerable to sabotage once the men at Gloucester were alerted.

Whether the ships were moored at Lydney or near Blakeney the Vikings would have had to have passed through Littledean, close to Cinderford and beneath Edge Hills to Mitcheldean before entering the territory of Archenfield.

It is interesting to compare the account of the raid as recorded by Florence of Worcester who died in 1117. He possibly had a copy of the Saxon Chronicles, which he used as a basis for his history of the period, and which contained details that have not survived in later copies. He records that Cyfeiliog was captured '... at a plain called Yrcenefeld' and was carried to their ships, then ransomed. He continues: 'Shortly afterwards, the whole army landed, and marched towards the aforesaid plain for the purpose of pillage; but the men of Hereford and Gloucester, and very many men from the neighbouring cities, went out suddenly to meet them, and fought a battle with them' (305).

The outcome of the battle was as noted in the Saxon Chronicles already quoted. The added details clarify that two sorties took place and that Cyfeiliog was in Archenfield when he was captured, probably by an inconspicuously small group of Vikings who may have had intelligence

Battle, Flight And Siege

There is a tradition that the battle took place at 'Kill Dane Field' between the old Ariconium settlement and Kingstone. It would be a reasonable place for the armies of Gloucester and Hereford to meet, and is where the Roman roads from the Hereford direction and Gloucester conjoin. It is, however, rather too open for a surprise attack. One may also suspect the anglicisation of a

Welsh name: *Cil*, for example is Welsh for a corner or retreat, and *an, danas*, deer, implying a field frequented by deer.

The Viking leaders and many men were killed. The rest 'were put to flight'. They would have fled towards their ships, along the old Roman Dean Road. Before they could reach them they were overtaken and driven into 'an enclosure and besieged'. The enclosure they resorted to was possibly the disused, multiple-banked hill-fort at Welshbury, near Littledean. The only alternative was the diminutive, univallate Soudley Camp immediately alongside the Dean Road. Either could have withstood a limited period siege; Soudley the more vulnerable to missiles hurled over the single rampart. Neither would have offered any protection apart from the eroding, surrounding banks. The account does not say specifically how long the Viking raiders held out, but it could not have been for long. They were besieged until 'they gave them hostages, (promising) that they would leave the king's dominion'.

It is particularly interesting that the only Viking-period, or Viking-style artefacts to be found in Dean have all come from within 1km (¾ mile) of the Dean Road, three of them from within the parish of Littledean.

The first of these is a silver dress pin with superb filigree tracery on the head. It was found on the slopes of a hill to the south of Welshbury and within sight of the fort (306).

A smaller pin, of silver-gilt, with a retaining loop and similar filigree work, was found at the foot of Edge Hills alongside a Roman road just 600m from Welshbury. The pin had been damaged in antiquity but the pin-head and loop was in perfect condition (307). Both of these pins could have been used to hold together shoulder clasps which were often made from precious metals and inlaid with enamel or bejewelled.

The third item is a very rare find indeed in this part of England. It is part of an ornamental bronze fitting with an animal head combined with foliage, either a decorative surround for a chest lock, or the end piece from a horse's bridle bit, re-used, and attached by an iron rivet to a wooden chest or something similar. The British Museum identified it as of Scandinavian *Ringerike* style and usually dating in Britain to the earlier part of the 11th century (308).

From the late 9th to the mid-11th century Scandinavian designs in jewellery became very fashionable, especially after Cnut became King of all England. Viking art was in vogue with the moneyed Saxons. Communities of craftworkers were to be found at manorial sites and in monasteries. The bronze piece, found on the ridge to the west of Littledean, could then have been

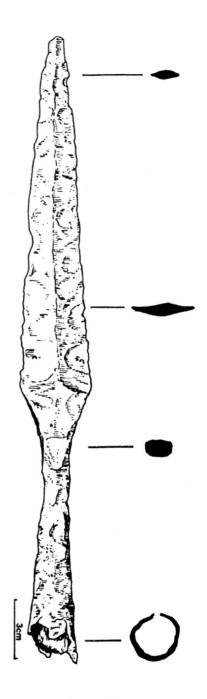

Figure 118. *Saxon spear from woodlands alongside the 'Dean Road' between Soudley and Blackpool Bridge. Drawn by W.J.Laughlin.* Courtesy of Gloucester City Council Museum Archaeology Unit, and B.Johns.

either of Viking manufacture, or made by an English craftsman to a Viking design. The motif, though, is distinctly Scandinavian and specifically of a type frequently found in Norway (309).

One further local artefact find probably relates to a Viking-period context. It is a socketed iron spear, the incomplete remains of which are 30cm (12 inches) long. The spear was found in the early years of this century within a few metres of the Dean Road between Soudley and Blackpool Bridge. It is on display in the Anglo-Saxon showcase of the Gloucester City Museum and 'is considered to be Saxon' (309a).

West of the Wye, in south Wales, there was growing consternation among the minor rulers in the 9th century due to the expansionist policies of Rhodri Mawr of Gwynedd (844-878) and his sons. Some of these kings turned to King Alfred of Wessex (871-899) for protection against the Vikings whose frequent raids along the south Wales coast were proving difficult to contain. Alfred, too, wished to encourage and foster a pro-English party in the south.

Under Hywel Dda (died c.950) relations with Wessex were further cultivated and finally effected with Aethelstan (924-939).

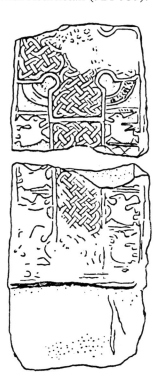

Figure 119. *10th century cross-slab from St.Arvans Church (after V.E.Nash-Williams 1938).*

A grant of c.878 shows that Istrat Hafren (Tidenham) had been returned to Welsh hands. A monastery had been established at Sellack (Lann Suluc) c.866 and at Foy (Lann Timoi). Another monastery was founded at St.Maughan's (Lann Bocha) c.860. It is claimed that the font in the present church is of 9th/10th century date. It is circular with convex sides. Churches are recorded at Llangynfyl (Methirch-infall) on the Monnow just north west of Monmouth c.860, (Tipallai) near St.Maughan's, Dingestow (Dincat) c.872, St.Mary's near Monmouth? c.910, Penterry (Lannuedeui) and St.Arvans (sanctorum Iarmen et Febric) c.955 (310). Part of what was possibly a carved headstone of the tenth century is now to be seen inside the church of St.Arvans built into the sill of the east window of the south aisle. It has, on both sides, a Latin wheel-cross of Celtic type. Double-beaded plaitwork is a feature along with bird-headed angels.

Curvilinear Churchyards

Prof. Charles Thomas has proposed that curvilinear (circular, partly-rounded or oval) churchyard and monastery enclosure boundaries indicate pre-Norman foundations. In Dean, Hewelsfield church has a circular walled enclosure. A recent study by Diane Brook shows that around two thirds of the Gwent churches with partly curved or largely curved surrounds can be proved to be of pre-Norman origin including, in the Wye Valley, the churches of Llandogo, St.Maughans, Llandinabo, Llanishen, Penterry, Dingestow, Llangovan and St.Arvans. To these could be added the church at Wonastow. Aerial survey suggests that the churchyard was originally curvilinear in plan, a feature that has been obscured by the adjacent farm outbuildings. East of the Wye, in addition to Hewelsfield, the churches at Bulley, Linton and Kempley have partly curved churchyards. The research, however, also revealed that some pre-Norman church sites have quadrangular enclosures and that a small number of almost certain Norman foundations have curvilinear boundaries, with excavation reports making it clear that such forms were being constructed as late as the twelfth century (310a).

Without documentary or archaeological proof it cannot be assumed that the Hewelsfield church had pre-Norman origins, although it must remain a possibility. It should also be noted that there is no curvilinear bank on its northern half, only a dry-stone wall, and the curvilinear slopes on its southern side are as a result of diverging small hollow-ways and not earthwork banks.

As previously observed, the ditched enclosure in fields close to Courtfield House, Welsh Bicknor, based on aerial survey results, is also partly curved, so is the possible larger enclosure boundary, but these have not yet been proved by excavation to be associated with the early Dubricius foundation. The south Herefordshire churches of Pencoyd (Pencoed) and Marstow also have partly curved enclosures. There are probably more, but no study comparable to that of Diane Brook has yet been published on the churches of Ergyng and west Gloucestershire.

The Ordinance Concerning the Dunsaete c.926

From around 775, when Ffernfael ap Ithel of Gwent died, no grants of land are recorded for Ergyng. Ergyng was to become the Archenfield of the diocese of Hereford and would cease to come under the ecclesiastical organisation of Llandaff.

Offas Dyke (c. the 780s) was set well back from the Wye in Mercian territory in our region. The Wye would appear to have been left in Welsh hands. So, apparently, was Ergyng which bordered Gwent at the Monnow and included south Herefordshire west of the Wye. By the early 10th century, when the Ordinance was probably prepared, it would seem, on initial reading, that either Offa's Dyke was no longer being maintained as the boundary between the Welsh and the English, or the Ordinance was introduced to apply where the Dyke was nonexistent and the river Wye formed the boundary. There is a third possibility: that the 'river' referred to in the document was not the Wye.

Figure 120. *Coin of Offa (AD 757-796).*

'The Ordinance Concerning the Dunsaete' (311) is believed to have originated following a meeting between Aethelstan and the Welsh princes near Hereford c.926 in order to define laws concerning border relations between the Welsh and the English. Aethelstan succeeded as king following the death of Edward the Elder in 924. The Chronicles record that: '... all the kings on this island were brought under his rule: first Hywel, king of the West Welsh...... Uwen, king of the people of Gwent...'

The Ordinance begins: 'This is the agreement which the English Witan and the counsellors of the Welsh people have established among the Dunsaete:' (312).

The regulations first deal with cattle stealing by driving the beasts across the river 'from one river bank to the other', then outlines surveillance procedure when Welsh or English wish to cross over into the territory of the other.

The Ordinance concludes: 'Formerly the Wentsaete belonged to the Dunsaete, but more correctly they belong to the West Saxons: and they have to send tribute and hostages there. But the Dunsaete also need, if the King will grant it to them, that at least they should be allowed hostages for peace' (313). The 'Wentsaete' were the people of Gwent.

The surviving manuscript is frustratingly ambiguous because it had no need to define for future generations what everyone concerned knew at the time. The river is not named. Who the Dunsaete were, and what their territorial boundaries were is unclear. Were they comprised of English and Welsh subjects, or were they solely English? Is the mention of the Wentsaete an afterthought, unrelated to the Ordinance, or is it central to the understanding of it?

If the river referred to is the Wye then it is unlikely that the regulations were drawn up to apply to the river below Redbrook because there is no easy way to drive cattle across it and up, or down, the steep slopes and sheer cliffs on the Dean side of the Wye between there and Chepstow. The only valley access is from Bigsweir to Mork. Between Redbrook, Monmouth and upstream of Lower Lydbrook there are many such opportunities. Also, as far as any substantial earthen barrier is concerned, Noble observed: 'None has yet been found which is a convincing portion of Offa's Dyke in its own right, and it is probable that if any full-scale Dyke existed between Redbrook, Symonds Yat and Lydbrook it would have been recorded by earlier surveyors and antiquarians' (314).

One of Noble's theories was that the medieval Deanery of Archenfield, which included Monmouth, could well have been the territory of the

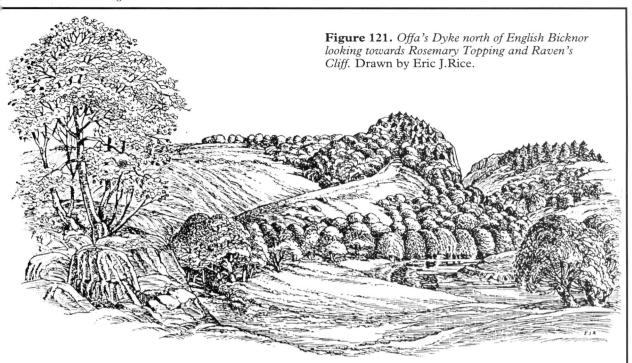

Figure 121. *Offa's Dyke north of English Bicknor looking towards Rosemary Topping and Raven's Cliff.* Drawn by Eric J.Rice.

Wentsaete, while the Deanery of Ross, which extended from Redbrook, through Newland, English Bicknor, Ruardean, Hope Mansel, Aston Ingham, and as far as Mordiford, might provide a better indication of the extent of the English Dunsaete (315).

He was also inclined to the belief that the people of Upper Gwent may have been under the direct control of the Mercians from at least the time of Offa, and in this way had formerly 'belonged to the Dunsaete' (316). The problem here is that Upper Gwent traditionally lay south of the Monnow and Monmouth, and bordered the Wye where it would be extremely difficult to drive cattle across. If Noble's theory were followed through then the river referred to in the Ordinance would more likely be the Monnow than the Wye. It would be extremely easy to drive cattle across this ancient territorial boundary at almost any point.

Elizabeth Taylor, an historian and excellent archaeological field-worker associated with the Woolhope Club's Archaeological Section, views the Dunsaete as occupying both sides of the Wye in south Herefordshire; as far south as the Monnow west of the Wye, and probably as far south as Redbrook in Dean. She sees the Wye as dividing the English part of the Dunsaete from the Welsh element of the Dunsaete, a kind of racial segregation upheld by the Ordinance. The only problem here is that we would also apparently have the Welsh part of the Dunsaete requesting the English King that 'they should be allowed

hostages for peace' from the Welsh Wentsaete of Gwent.

Historian Arthur Clarke's observation concerning Aethelstan may reflect the truth of the matter: 'He fixed the River Wye as the boundary between the Welsh and the English, thus recognising the districts of Erging, between the Monnow and the Wye rivers, and Ewias, at the foot of the Black Mountains as part of Gwent. These were added to Herefordshire before the Norman Conquest' (316a).

Much more research is needed before all of these problems can be resolved. What can be proposed, with reasonable certainty, is that part of Dean, and south Herefordshire, was either occupied or settled by the Dunsaete during the middle to late Saxon period, or else the indigenous population of these areas were referred to as the Dunsaete.

Under the Welsh King Hywel Dda there was a major shift of political power from north to south Wales. Friendship was cultivated with Wessex. He gave active co-operation to Aethelstan, introduced English institutions into Wales, and personally signed many of Aethelstan's charters. Tradition also credits Hywel as introducing the earliest written code of Welsh laws.

After his death c.950 there followed a century of feuding and warring between the Welsh kings which continued virtually up to the time of the Norman Conquest. Thirty five Welsh rulers met violent deaths, four more were blinded and four were thrown into prison. The Vikings gave them constant trouble as well. St.Davids was sacked four times in seventeen years and many hundreds were captured and carried off into slavery.

Tenth Century Tidenham

In 955 Eadwig (Edwy) was crowned King of the English. The following year he granted Tidenham to abbot Wulfgar and the monks of St.Peters, Bath. The parish was made up of four tithings or divisions, Stroat, Bishton, Sedbury and Beachley. The boundaries were appended to the charter:

1. 'From the Mouth of the Wye to the Headland (of a ploughland) where the Yewtree grows'.
2. 'From the Headland where the Yewtree grows to the Row of Stones'.
3. 'From the Row to White Hollow'.
4. 'From the White Hollow to Yew Valley'.
5. 'From the Yew Valley to Broad Moor (swampy ground)'.
6. 'From Broad Moor to Double Ford'.
7. 'From Double Ford to the Pill of the East Island? (or edge?) to the Severn' (317).

A section of the 'Row of Stones' may still be seen alongside a stream above Stroat Farm. The Pill referred to is Horse Pill, near to the 'Broadstone'.

Saxon Fields

The 'Headland (of a ploughland)' is a sure indication that many of the fields that contain broad ridge and furrow along the Severn could have originated in the Saxon period, especially when the headland (a bank of soil formed where the plough turned at the end of a furrow) is still traceable. Many such headlands were noted during DAGs aerial surveys in 1989 and 1990. They showed up, not as crop marks during the dry summers, but as soil and shadow marks in the early autumn when the fields were ploughed. Some of them now show only as soil marks from the air and are not detectable from the ground; the raised ridges and the headlands having been totally levelled by more recent ploughing.

The charter also shows that Tidenham was back in English hands. It remained thus just over a century later when 'Abbot Aelfwig and all the community of Bath...... let 30 hides of land at Tidenham (Dyddanhamme) to Archbishop Stigand for his lifetime...' This lease was drawn up within five years of the Norman Conquest. In 1070 the estate was forfeited by Archbishop Stigand to a Norman earl (318).

Danish Domination

The Welsh were not the only ones to be threatened by Danish raids. The English now found themselves confronted by Danish armies, often under the leadership of members of the Danish royal family. In 997 'The Danes went around Devonshire into the mouth of the Severn, and there ravaged in Cornwall, Wales and Devon.' King Aethelred II (978-1016) was to suffer greatly at their hands. The rapid movements of the Danes left the English bewildered. 'When the (Danish) force was in the east, the (English) troops were kept west, and when they were in the south, then our troops were in the north' (Chronicles for 1010).

Figure 122. *Coin of Aethelred II (978-1016).*

Saxon Coin Hoard

Very recently there was a remarkable and very rare find of twelve silver pennies, all of them thought to be of Aethelred II, close to a Roman route just 2km north of Monmouth. Several mints are believed to be represented including Hereford (319). The find spot was also around 2km east of the site of the early church of Llangynfyl, which had been given, with its territory, to bishop Grecielis by Britcon in c.860.

Cnut

By 1013 the western thanes had submitted to the Danish King Swein at Bath. In 1016, the year that Aethelred died, the Danes were still ravaging under Cnut, Swein's son. It was in this same year that ealdorman Eadric, with levies from the 'Magesaet tribe from Herefordshire and south Shropshire, betrayed his natural lord and all the nation. Cnut had the victory and with that won all England.' Eadric had fled the field of battle against the Danes, not for the first time. Cnut met the English King Edmund near Deerhurst in

Gloucestershire. Edmund received Wessex and Cnut Mercia, however, on Edmund's death the following year Cnut became the first Danish King of all England. He made Eadric, earl of Mercia, but a few months later had him murdered.

Worcester And Hereford Plundered

Cnut died in 1035 and was followed by Harold and Harthacnut. The Magonsaete received a further less-than-honourable mention in 1041 when Harthacnut became enraged because two of his tax-collectors had been slain in Worcestershire while collecting the tribute he had imposed. To avenge the deaths of these men he sent all of his earls to Worcestershire 'with orders to slay all the inhabitants if they could, to plunder and burn the city, and lay waste the country round about.' Among the earls was 'Roni, earl of the Magesetas (men of Herefordshire)....' (320).

By the late 1040s Gruffydd ap Llywelyn, the overlord of Wales, was making frequent raids across the borderlands into England. In 1049 he joined forces with Danish settlers from Ireland to attack this region. Florence of Worcester recorded the incident thus: 'In the month of August...... some Irish pirates with thirty-six ships entered the mouth of the Severn, and landed at a place called Wylesceaxan, and in unison with Griffin (Gruffydd), king of the South Britons, plundered the neighbourhood and did considerable damage. Then the king and they joined their forces, and crossing the river called Weage, burned Dymedham, and put to death every one whom they found therein. They were quickly opposed by Aldred, bishop of Worcester, and a few of the natives of Gloucestershire and Herefordshire. But the Welsh who were with them, and who had promised to be faithful to them, sent a messenger privately to Griffin, requesting him to attack the English as quickly as possible. Griffin flew to their assistance with his own men and the Irish pirates, and rushing at day-break on the English, slew many of them and put the rest to flight'. Dymedham is believed to be Tidenham and the attacks are thought to have spread from the mouth of the Usk across the Wye into Dean (320a).

In 1055 Gruffydd attacked Hereford and 'Great slaughter was made there, about four or five hundred men'. Hereford was refortified by earl Harold and the battles continued for a number of years until 1063, when 'Gruffydd was killed on August 5th by his own men' and his head brought to the English king. Much of south Wales subsequently passed into English hands for a short while, before being annexed by the Normans. Archenfield must have been badly affected by these raids for the Domesday recorder (Herefordshire 49) observed: 'King Gruffydd and Bleddyn laid this land waste before 1066; therefore what it was like at that time is not known.'

The last act of aggression, before the Norman Conquest, recorded in the Saxon Chronicles for this region was in 1065: 'Earl Harold commanded building done in Wales at Portskewet, now that he had conquered it, and there brought many goods, and thought to have king Edward there for the matters of hunting. But when it was all ready, Caradoc son of Gruffydd went to it with all the force he could gather, killed almost all those who worked on the building, and seized the goods which had been prepared'.

Early in the following year Edward died. Earl Harold was proclaimed King 'and he had little peace during the time he ruled the kingdom.' The last aggression went unpunished.

Mid-11th Century Landowners in West Gloucestershire

There was a manor at Alvington in the late Saxon period. Brictric held it in 1066 according to the Domesday Book which also informs us that it was included in the Bromsash, Herefordshire Hundred. It had 'In Lordship 2 ploughs; 12 villagers with 9 ploughs; they pay 20 blooms of iron and 8 sesters of honey'.

An aerial photograph of the land near Alvington Court shows remarkably the evidence of this ancient ploughing and the headlands between the pre-Norman landholdings. Nothing is discernible at ground level and, but for the colour changes in the soil noticeable only from the air, one would be totally unaware of these historical features. In a few years these soil marks will probably disappear because the fields are now being ploughed in a totally different direction to what they were in the Saxon and early medieval periods.

Other people named as holding land in Dean immediately before the Norman takeover were, as noted in the Domesday Book:

Aelfric, Alfward and Brictsi who held manors at Lower Redbrook. Hadwig held Ruardean. Brictric held a manor at Staunton, which, along with Redbrook, was also in the Bromsash Hundred of Herefordshire. The Canons of Hereford also held land at Whippington, through which flows the Whippington Brook from Staunton to the Wye. Another entry which also appears in the

Plate 20. *Ridge and furrow field-strips showing beneath Lydney golf course.* Photograph by M.J.Walters.

Plate 21. *Ridge and furrow field-strips alongside Plummer's Brook, Lydney, a site scheduled for development.* Photograph by M.J.Walters.

Figure 123. *Royal seal of Edward the Confessor (1042-1066) holding the dove of peace and the sword of war.*

Hereford Domesday survey is for 'Newarne'. This is thought to be in the Speech House area, close to the Cannop Valley in the central woodlands.

King Edward (the Confessor) held the manor of Westbury-on-Severn, which had a thriving community with much ploughland.

King Edward also held the manor of Awre in the Bledisloe Hundred. The church is recorded, and so is a salt-house. The earthwork remains of the saline-collection area are still visible in fields close to the Severn, immediately to the west of the lane that runs southwards to the river from the church, near Whitescourt.

King Edward also held the manor of Dymock in the Botloe Hundred, another thriving community. There are claims that the chancel of the present church of Dymock was probably the original Saxon chapel.

Earl Harold held Nass, near Lydney but in the Bledisloe Hundred. It was to be joined to the manors of Poulton and Purton by Earl William. Siward and Winstan held undesignated land in the Bledisloe Hundred, possibly Allaston. Palli also held undesignated land along with a mill, but this can reasonably be assigned to Ruddle.

The Bishop of Hereford held land in Lydney (in Lydney Hundred) from which Earl William 'made a manor'. Aerial photography has revealed that some of these fields are now preserved beneath Lydney golf course, where ridge and furrow, and trackways are still visible from the air. Unfortunately, several other historical fields, which border Plummers Brook where it flows into the harbour, are now scheduled for industrial development. It is these same lands that were given by King Burgred of Mercia to his brother-in-law, Aethelred of Wessex around 853. They were, shortly afterwards, transferred to the monks of Glastonbury, and later to the Bishop of

Hereford. It is rather sad that they now seem to rate as of little historical importance to development planners.

The manor of Highnam was in the Longbridge Hundred; Upleadon, with its mill, in the Botloe Hundred, and Churcham in the Westbury Hundred. A note on the latter adds 'The Church had its hunting here in 3 hedged enclosures before and after 1066.'

Alfwold also held a manor in the Westbury Hundred. Tovi held Bulley from King Edward and also held Ruddle.

Also in the Botloe Hundred was Newent, held by King Edward until it was handed over to the St.Mary's Church of Cormeilles by Earl Roger. There was a manor there before 1066. In the porch of Newent church there is a portion of a carved cross-shaft which is thought to be of 9th century date. It depicts Adam and Eve with a serpent entwined around the Tree of Knowledge. There is also an 11th century funerary tablet known as a 'pillow stone'. This was found at a depth of five feet during excavations for a new vestry in 1912. Two skeletons were recovered, the skull of one of them resting on the stone. Along with carved representations is the name: EDRED (320b).

Bondi is recorded as holding Alverston (Aluredstone) in the Lydney Hundred before 1066. Aluredstone (Alfred's Farm) is Plusterwine where there was a moated mansion. It lies just to the north of the site of the Chesters, Woolaston, Roman villa (321).

Alstan held Wyegate at the north west corner of Lydney Hundred before 1066.

Brictric, son of Algar, held Woolaston in the Twyford Hundred, and Madgett.

Wulfhelm held Tibberton in the Botloe Hundred 'from King Edward and could go where he would.' Alwin held Huntley in the same Hundred 'from Archbishop Aldred and could go where he would.' He also held Taynton. (Little) Taynton was held by Wulfgar from King Edward. Kempley, Oxenhall and Carswall, were also in the Botloe Hundred. Edric and Leofric held Kempley as two manors from King Edward; Thorkell (a Scandinavian name) held Oxenhall from Earl Harold and Wulfhelm held Carswall (just east of Newent) before 1066. Land at Pauntley, Kilcot, Ketford and Hayes was held by Wulfhelm, Alfward and Wiga as four manors. Madog, one of only two Welsh names, held Rudford before 1066.

Longhope, Stears and Newnham were in the Westbury Hundred. Forne and Wulfheah, thanes of King Edward, held Longhope; Wulfheah held Stears and his predecessor is named as Wihenoc

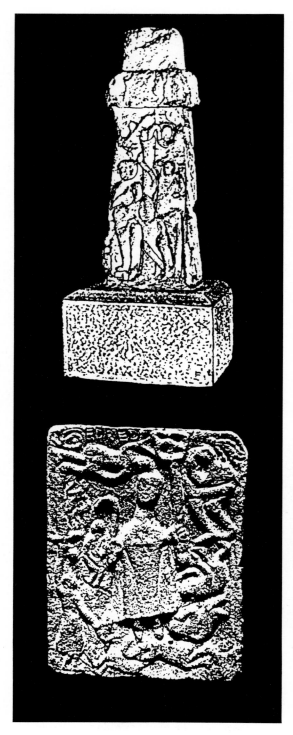

who also held land at the Hill House estate in Newnham. Alfwold held a manor in the Westbury hundred believed to be at Minsterworth.

Little Lydney, later St.Briavels, was in the Lydney Hundred and was held by Alfhere before 1066. Wulfheah also held Hewelsfield in the same Hundred.

English Bicknor was in the Westbury Hundred and was held by Morganwy before 1066, as mentioned earlier when considering Welsh names east of the Wye.

Three thanes, Godric, Alric and Ernwy held Mitcheldean in the Westbury Hundred. It should be noted that in Domesday Book it is named simply as 'Dene', and that Mitcheldean is an interpretation. There is reason to think that Dene may have extended from Littledean (Dene Parva) to Mitcheldean (Dene Magna) and possibly as far as the boundary with the Lea. This could well account for the need of three thanes to control it, one possibly with a residence at Littledean, and another at Mitcheldean. A third may have resided in the Abenhall area. It should also be noted that the earliest post-Norman castle in Dene was at Littledean, not Mitcheldean, and there is some evidence for pre-Norman occupation at Littledean Hall. It is interesting that these lands were assigned by King Edward to these named thanes as being 'exempt from tax in return for guarding the Forest.' King Edward is believed to have hunted frequently in the Forest of Dean (322).

Figure 125. *King Edward the Confessor (from the Bayeux tapestry).*

Figure 124. Top: *Late Saxon cross-shaft. Bottom: 11th century 'pillow-stone' of Edred. Both in Newent Church.*

Archenfield in the Years Before 1066

The Herefordshire Domesday survey is informative about a number of villages north of Dean in south Herefordshire:

There was a Saxon manor in Linton before 1066. This would seem to have been located on the aforementioned Eccleswall site, near Bromsash, and the former Ariconium.

The important manor of Clive was close to Ross-on-Wye and held by Earl Harold. Lea was held by Ansgot; Leofric and Edwulf held Hope Mansell as two manors; Gunnar (another Scandinavian name) held Pontshill, Weston and Coldborough in Upton. Estune (Aston Ingham) was held by King Edward.

The survey also clearly points up the divisions between Welsh and English in Archenfield. There is little doubt too that, at the time of the survey, much of the Forest of Dean, and Gloucestershire between the Leadon and the Wye, were part of Herefordshire.

One further snippet of information concerning the people of Archenfield is contained in section 179b.9 of the survey: 'When the army advances on the enemy, these men by custom form the vanguard and on their return the rearguard. These were the customs of the Welshmen in Archenfield before 1066' (323).

Hundreds

A Hundred was a sub-division of the landscape, later, a district within a shire. It was was the first fundamental form of English government, but was earlier a widespread European institution.

The original purpose of a Hundred is not clearly discernible; perhaps it was to provide a

Figure 126. *King and Witan (from the Cotton MS, British Museum).*

hundred fighting men, with one man from each family, which, in principle, meant that a Hundred represented a hundred families with a similar number of supporting land areas.

The later Hundreds were also administrative units which held an assembly of notables and village representatives usually once a month. Each Hundred had a 'vill', a royal centre at which dues were paid, usually produce, livestock, or other non-perishable assets like iron and timber. These required much storage space. A Hundred assembly day was an essential event to attend. Laws and orders were explained. Legal matters were dealt with and, more informally, gossip and news was exchanged. Wales had a similar system but it owed nothing to the Saxons, and confirms that the idea of Hundred equivalents had pre-Saxon origins.

Place-Names

Some time around 600, perhaps a little later, the Saxons began to establish their settlements in Dean and south Herefordshire. Most would have been very small, a homestead in a clearing on the edge of the Forest with the benefit of a few surviving Roman field systems perhaps. These settlements rapidly grew in number and are reflected in the place-names ending with -*ham* (a dwelling or homestead), -*leah*, -*ley* (a clearing in woodland, sometimes a wood), -*tun*, -*ton* (a farm or enclosed land). -*Bury* endings came from burh, (a fortified place, often one long disused but with visible remains). -*Hlaw* indicated either a burial mound or a hill and is found in place-names ending in -loe and -low. -*Stow* indicated a holy place. -*Wic* (wick, wich) names refer to a dwelling, farm or village, but, surprisingly, very many -wick names are also Roman-period dwelling sites, possibly from the Latin *vicus*, which was a small settlement.

The -*bury* place names have been discussed earlier in this book because so many of them have produced evidence for pre-Roman occupation. *Stow* names, like Stowe itself, can suggest holy places that had wells and springs which were respected as sacred long before the Saxons ever took control of England. Marstow and Merstow indicate a sacred place on a boundary. St.Anthony's Well was Merstowe before it was given its present name in the later medieval period. Stowfield, at Lower Lydbrook, faces the Dubricius foundation at Welsh Bicknor and may have taken its name from there, however, it might equally have had some connection with the Roman-period site at The Mount, Lower Lydbrook. Bridstow and Peterstow, near Ross-

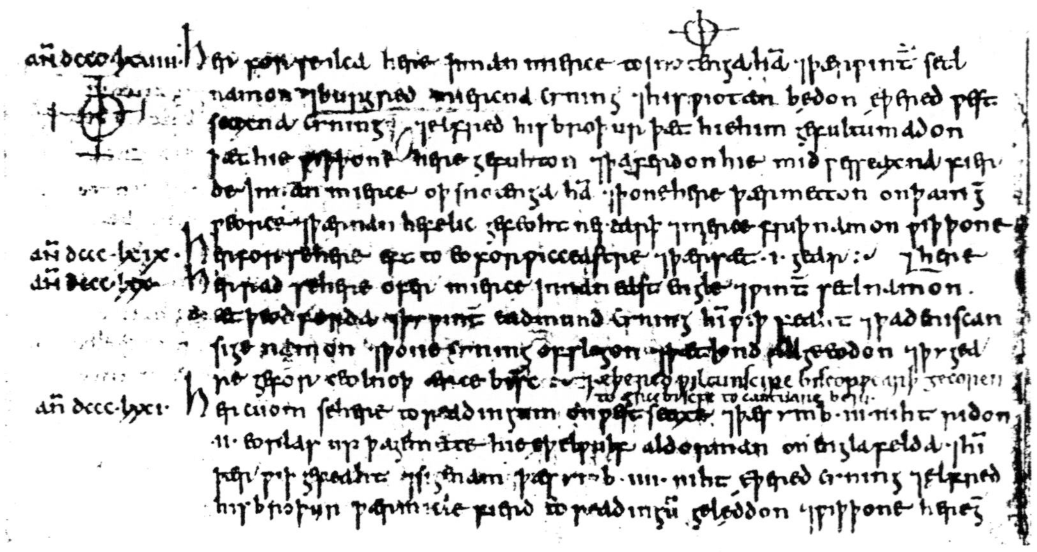

[facsimile of Anglo-Saxon manuscript text]

Figure 127. *A section of the Anglo-Saxon Chronicles (from the Parker MS, Corpus Christi College, Cambridge).*

on-Wye are other Archenfield examples. In Gwent there is Wonastow, Dingestow and Chepstow.

Bledisloe, Hagloe, Etloe and Botloe obviously derive from -*hlaw*. So does Mutloes, just east of Dean Hill, which may recall a 'moot' or meeting place. Low Cop is north west of Alvington and is closely associated with the Duncastle place-name previously cited. Baglow and Henlow are near Churcham. *Hlaw* may indicate a burial mound, or just a hill. Recent research, combined with aerial photography around Etloe has confirmed the presence of barrows there. The photographs, taken in the evening with a low sun, of ploughed fields south of Blakeney clearly showed the almost ploughed-level remains of two barrows. Subsequent research on Parish Tithe Map apportionments confirmed 'barrow' field names in the area. North of Blakeney there is Lowfield and Broadlow (324). The barrows may be Bronze Age; they could be Saxon. The general lack of major concentrations of prehistoric flint material on the surrounding ploughed fields suggests that they are more likely to belong to the Saxon period.

Plate 22. *Wonastow Church and Court and part of the 750 acres of land that changed hands in the 8th century. Traces of an early curvilinear enclosure may be discerned around the church.* Photograph by M.J.Walters.

Glimpses at Life from the Charters

Occasionally the Llandaff charters of grants of land by the wealthy to the church tell us a little about the people and the values that applied west of the Wye during the 8th century.

When the church of Wonastow changed hands along with an uncia and a half of land (about 750 acres) in the 8th century it was bought for 'a very good horse of the value of twelve cows, and a hawk of the value of twelve cows, and an useful dog which killed birds with the hawk, of the value of three cows, and another horse of the value of three cows'. The 750 acres thus equalled the value of thirty cows (325).

When the village of Breican was bought a sword changed hands to the value of twelve cows and a horn to the value of ten cows, and another horn to the value of fourteen cows (326).

Other charters list 'a trumpet worth twenty four cows',and 'clothing worth fourteen cows' (327). In Erging c.740 five hundred acres of land changed hands for 'twenty four unspecified objects, a Saxon girl, a precious sword, and a valuable horse' (328).

Fishing Rights

The fishing rights on the Severn and Wye, mentioned in numerous charters of lands that bordered these rivers, are always associated with weirs *(wera)*. These may be defined as either basket weirs *(cytweras)* or hackle weirs *(haecweras)*. The Saxon names are given here as found in a Tidenham survey of c.1050 (329). They bore no relationship to what we now call weirs, that is a solid barrier usually stretching from bank to bank. The Saxon weir represented a means to catch fish. The basket weirs were probably taper-ing baskets made from wattled hazel which were placed in groups between rows of stakes. They were probably similar to what are now called 'putts', a group of which is called a 'puttcher'.

Herrings were the principal fish taken, along with salmon. Sturgeon and porpoises were particularly valued delicacies. When the Tidenham lands were leased to archbishop Stigand in the years prior to the Norman Conquest, the abbot and community of Bath were to receive 6 porpoises and 30,000 herrings every year as part of the rent.

Water-Mills

Water-mills featured in the Saxon landscape on both sides of the Wye. Millers were held in some esteem and the flour they produced not only fed the local communities but also brought in revenue. The Domesday survey suggests that pre-Norman mills existed at Awre, Lydney, Woolaston, St.Briavels (Little Lydney), Alvington and in the Bledisloe Hundred. North of Dean, still in west Gloucestershire, two mills are recorded for Newent, one mill to the four manors of Pauntley, Kilcot, Ketford and Hayes, another at Rudford and one at Upleadon. A mill is also recorded for Longhope. By 1085 the survey was able to say of Tidenham: 'There is a mill there now'.

West of the Wye the survey recorded three mills near Chepstow, one at Caldicot and one 'between the Usk and the Wye'.

Woodland

Areas of woodland are always noted in the survey. Timber was an important asset and where it was readily available the survey frequently appended 'sufficient for the manor'.

Dr.Della Hooke has recently made some interesting observations on the Anglo-Saxon woodlands of Gloucestershire west of the Severn. She

Figure 128. *A 'Puttcher' on the Severn (from a drawing by J.W.King 1913).*

draws attention to the Old English word *haga* which refers to an enclosure and is surprisingly frequent in areas which were later declared royal forest. In such remote countryside it could often refer to land set aside for hunting and the retention of deer within an enclosure. At Oridge Ridge *'hagann rycg'* (the ridge of the haga) is the close boundary of the Norman forest. Oridge is about 1½ miles north of Hartpury and east of Upleadon in Corse parish. Dr.Hooke believes that the Norman word *haia* was used in the Domesday Book for the Anglo-Saxon *hagan* and that it implied a deer enclosure (329a).

Haia names in Dean may be perpetuated in The Haie, near Newnham, The Hayes and Hay End near Viney Hill and Hay Wood north of Gorsley. In the 1282 Regard of the Forest of Dene, Eywode (Haywood), Piriheye (Perry Hay) and Wydenhay were in the Bailiwick of Abenhall; Nywenheye in the Bailiwick of Staunton; Brerhay was Brierley in the Bailiwick of Ruardean. Pirihale in the Bailiwick of Lea may derive from *haia*. A wood called Haygrove was owned by a Richard Talebat of Eccleswalle. There was a Wydenheye in the Bailiwick of Mitcheldean. Some caution should be exercised, however, when considering the derivation of names. For example the 'Regard' also records: 'The abbot of Flaxley has cut a hay, *(hayam)* or hedge, at Newland and made it into charcoal'. This could have been a simple hedge as we understand it, or the abbot's 'crime' could have been more onerous in that he had dismantled a hedge that was part of a deer enclosure or trap in order to obtain a convenient source of wood for charcoal.

Some, or all of these names may derive from post-Conquest deer enclosures, but, as Dr.Hooke warns, 'The importance and organisation of hunting in Anglo-Saxon England has often been underestimated...... we can probably imagine these *(hagan)* as enclosures in which deer were either kept for release for the hunt or were captured during the hunt. A favourite method of capturing deer in Anglo-Saxon times was to drive them towards gaps in a hedge where archers would be waiting or nets spread.'

A search for ancient enclosure banks in these areas of woodland could prove particularly rewarding.

Iron-Working

To date no 5th to mid-11th century iron-working sites have been confirmed as such either in Dean, or west of the Wye. That is not to say that ore wasn't mined, smelted and smithed. We know it was. The key word is 'confirmed', that is

confirmed by artefactual evidence, or unquestionable association with post-Roman sites.

The problem is essentially one of lack of pottery and coin evidence. Whereas Roman and medieval iron-working sites are invariably surrounded by discarded and broken pottery, from the 5th century onwards wood was the preferred material for cups and bowls and, as such, rarely survives. Cauldrons were made from copperalloys, other vessels from pewter. These were valuable materials and when they became worn, or holed, they would logically be traded in against new ones. The damaged vessels would then be melted down and re-cycled. The metals were too valuable to be simply thrown away.

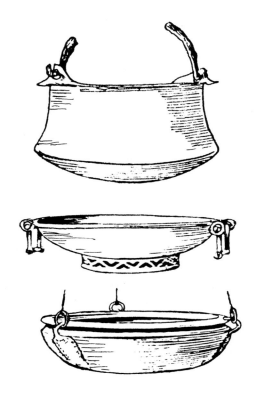

Figure 129. *A bronze cauldron with iron handles and two bronze bowls of the Saxon period.*

Many scores of iron-working sites, in the form of bloomery slag deposits, are known, both sides of the Wye, which have not yet been dated because of the absence of artefactual evidence. These may reasonably be assumed to belong to the post-Roman and Saxon periods, especially when found near to manors, monasteries or villages which are attested for those centuries. Thus negative evidence may, in fact, be positive evidence.

Some of the major 12th and 13th iron-working sites, dated by the presence of pottery from those centuries, may also have been iron-working sites in the pre-Norman period. Lower, earlier slags in the heaps (without pottery evidence) may have originated in the Saxon period. It is therefore apparent that excavators of iron-working sites, assumed to be medieval, should also record meticulously at what level the datable sequence begins, because what lies beneath could represent earlier iron-working on the site.

The evidence from Dean and the Wye Valley definitely suggests pottery was re-introduced by the Normans (330). In Monmouth, for example, where many tonnes of medieval pottery sherds and rims have been retrieved from recent rescue excavations, not a single piece need pre-date 1067 and the construction of a castle there. Much material has been retrieved from the grounds of Dean Hall, Littledean, including 11th century material, but, again, none of it can be unquestionably dated earlier than the Norman Conquest.

East of the Wye un-dated iron-working sites have been noted at: Tidenham parish, around Alvington and Plusterwine, Woolaston, Lydney, Allaston, Nursefield near Purton, Yorkley, many in the parish of Awre and within 2km of St.Briavels, Littledean, Staunton, English Bicknor, Garth Wood, Taynton parish, Newent parish, and near Upleadon, Botloe, Highnham, Churcham, Huntley and Mitcheldean; also Weston-under-Penyard and Hope Mansel (Sutton). Most of these places are known to have been in existence in pre-Norman times.

West of the Wye un-dated iron-working sites have been recorded at Llangovan, Llangattock, Trellech, Dixton, Llangarron, Rockfield and Perth-hir. All of these places are associated with recorded pre-Norman communities.

Late Pre-Norman Artefacts from Dean

Two copper-alloy artefacts have recently been discovered which, in all probability, were manufactured in the 10th or 11th centuries. The first is the upper segment of a crudely-produced cross with an inscribed simple cross. It was found on the bank of the Wye, near Lower Lydbrook, and where an ancient trackway led to the river crossing that continued up to the enclosure mentioned earlier in connection with the possible foundation site of the St.Dubricius' church, near the present Courtfield House.

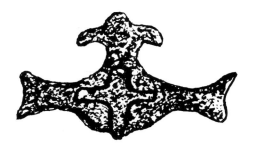

Figure 130. *Section of a bronze cross from the banks of an ancient crossing of the Wye near Lower Lydbrook. Drawn by N.Giles.* Courtesy of M.Hill.

The second artefact is a detached, enamelled late-Saxon type buckle plate with a zoomorphic design. It was found at Elton (331).

The Normans Take Control

The central woodlands of 'the Dene' became known as The Forest of Dean, a Royal Forest. The faunae of the woodlands became 'the King's beasts', and strict forest laws were applied.

William's takeover was ruthless. A new aristocracy was imposed on the peasants. The English earls and thanes were either killed or dispossessed. The new King's followers were rewarded with land and estates. As though in an instant the new landowners constructed temporary fortifications everywhere in the form of timber castles, usually elevated on a mound (motte) and surrounded by a ditched enclosure (a bayley). Many of these were to be strengthened with a central keep built of stone. Some landowners had second thoughts and re-sited them. One example of such is a suspected early timber structure at Eastbach which was re-sited at English Bicknor and later re-built in stone. Other early fortifications are still to be seen at Littledean, Stowe, Lydney, possibly Hewelsfield, Castletump, north of Newent, and in Castle Hill Wood, Taynton. The small earthwork at Great Howle may be an early medieval ringwork but there is no dating evidence from the few surface finds gathered from the adjacent field and the interior has been opencast coal mined. There are many more east, and especially west of the Wye, and there must be others which have gone unrecognised to now.

Epilogue

In 911, Charles the Simple, King of France, granted a part of northern France to Rollo, a Norse Viking, who settled there with his people. Charles' hope was that other Viking invaders would turn their attentions elsewhere. Vortigern attempted a similar strategy with the Saxons when he granted them lands at Thanet.

The Norse settlers intermarried with the native French, developed into a new aristocracy, called their leader 'Duke' and became more powerful than most other French dukedoms. They were referred to as The Normans. Their territory was called Normandy.

Ironically, what Vortigern did for the British, five centuries later, Charles the Simple did for the French. By the beginning of the second milennium AD people of Viking extraction were influential rulers in both countries.

Postscript
But for Vortigern
we might all be Welsh speakers.

Part Four

A Footpath Guide to Ancient Sites

Of the many hundreds of sites referred to in this book it must now be stated, with some sadness, that very few have visible remains. A cave, a few standing stones and a greater number of Iron Age fortifications represent the only landmarks of more than 10,000 years of occupation in Dean and the Wye Valley. Two Roman temple sites have been left uncovered following excavation and many of the Roman iron-ore extraction ditches, hollows and caverns may be viewed. No Roman villa has above-ground remains. No pre-Norman structural features can be easily discerned in ancient church buildings, although a few displaced stone carvings have been preserved.

The following walks have been selected for those who feel that, with the knowledge gained from this book, they now have a heightened awareness and sensitivity towards what it may have been like to have lived here thousands of years ago. Extensive and unexpected vistas are still here to be enjoyed. Ancient trackways may be followed by woodland streams and along elevated ridges. The eerie scowles created by those digging for iron ore can hardly fail to excite the imagination. You may even find yourself stepping aside to allow a galloping cavalry messenger to pass by on a narrow section of Roman paving. Pause by a quiet stream or bubbling spring and cast in your offering to the spirits who perhaps have not deserted it. Seek out shadowy figures in the groves of sessile oaks. Be aware: You are surrounded by the past. You only see what you see.

NB. Recommended footpaths are taken from the following Ordnance Survey Maps and were believed to be Public Rights of Way at the time of their publication. Rights of Way are subject to amendment from time to time. Rights of Way have narrow confines and usually traverse private property. These confines should be strictly adhered to. Close gates. Avoid damaging crops.

Don't deposit litter. Report any historical finds or discoveries.

Outdoor Leisure Map 14: Wye Valley & Forest of Dean; Pathfinder Series: Sheets SO 62/72; SO 41/51; SO 61/71; SO 40/50; SO 60/70; SO 40/52 and SO 49/59.

The Forest of Dean

The Wye Side Of Dean

1. OFFA'S DYKE: There is a way-marked Offa's Dyke Path. It begins just south of Sedbury, near Chepstow, but the most impressive sections are to be viewed between Dennel Hill and Madgetts Hill. Start from the footpath that leads west from the B4228 on Tidenham Chase at ST 5535 9830 and gain access to the Dyke. Follow it northwards to Devil's Pulpit. A footpath leads east from there and joins Miss Graces Lane, which is part of an ancient route from the Severn to the Wye. The Stone Row used to mark this track. Turn south past Chase Farm. There was Bronze Age settlement in this area, and the excavated Tidenham round barrow used to stand in a field to the west of the Lane. The 'hut circles' indicated on the map are in fact eroded barrows. They are on private property and there is no public access. The Chepstow road is reached just 350m from the starting point. Distance approximately 2½ miles (3.7km).

2. LANCAUT: The site of the early Christian church at Lancaut (the remains of the present church are believed to date from the post-Norman period) can be approached along the narrow lane that leaves the B4228 near Broadrock at ST 5430 9645. Follow the lane past Spital Meend hill-fort (to your right) then proceed to the hamlet of Lancaut. There is a footpath which leads in a south easterly direction to the remains of the church which stands just above the Wye. There is a footpath from here which follows the Wye downstream towards Chepstow. There are impressive cliffs below Wintours Leap. On Piercefield Cliffs, opposite, there is an Iron Age fort. Retrace steps from the church, or continue to ST 5400 9555 where the Offas's Dyke path can be picked up which will return you to Broadrock. The view from the top of the cliffs at Wintours Leap is spectacular. Short distance approximately 1¾ miles (2.7km). Extended walk 2¼ miles (3.5km).

3. SLADE BROOK: Take the footpath (an ancient route through Mork to the Wye) along the Slade Brook that leaves the St.Briavels to Coleford road (B4228) in a westerly direction just south of Bearse Farm at SO 572 051. This area was hunted in the Mesolithic period and on the fields to the north of the ravine at Slade Bottom there was a hunters' camp site. The area was also favoured for occupation during the Neolithic and Bronze Age. At Andrews Corner follow the road south for 300m then return along the footpath that leads eastwards across Dark Hill to Bearse Farm. Distance approximately 2 miles (3.2km).

4. THE BEARSE: This major Neolithic centre and trading point is easily approached from SO 572 052 opposite Bearse Farm on the B4228. Walk due east through the Forestry Commission plantation on the trackway that passes Roads House towards Bream Cross. The former site of the Longstone is in a field to the south. The whole area to north and south was heavily utilised more than 4,000 years ago. Mesolithic hunters passed through. The same fields were part of a vast Roman agricultural estate. Spring areas, sacred in earlier days, can still be seen to the south of the track. Either retrace your steps to the starting point, or take the footpath south from Roads House to The Great Hoggins and return along the footpath running north west to Little Hoggins. Distance from 1 mile (1.5km) to 1¾ miles (2.7km) depending on return route chosen.

5. CLEARWELL CAVES AND LAMBSQUAY SCOWLES: Your starting point is Clearwell Caves at SO 577 082, 3km south of Coleford. These Ancient Iron Mines are truly impressive and guided tours take about one hour. Visitor facilities are excellent. Before, or after a tour, walk downhill into Clearwell then take the footpath that leaves the road by the Post Office and goes northwards, uphill. After 350m, where footpaths cross, take the footpath that leads north east towards Lambsquay Hotel. The path runs diagonally across the first field, uphill, then crosses part of the field where the Stock Farm villa stood on level ground. Look west at the breathtaking

views, to the Brecon Beacons on a clear day. Now follow the footpath diagonally across the next field and cross a narrow bridge over a scowle (a long, sinuous ditch from which iron-ore was extracted in the Roman period). Continue along the footpath (there are poultry houses on your right) then before reaching the Lambsquay Hotel, turn right along the footpath which leads through woodlands to the entrance to Clearwell Farm. Turn right at the road and it is 400m to your starting point. There are several recommendable hostelries in Clearwell. Distance approximately 1¾ miles (2.8km). N.B. There are landscaped scowles nearby on the B4228 at 'Puzzlewood' which are usually open to the public.

6. SYMONDS YAT AND HUNTSHAM HILL: Walk downhill for 450m along the road running north from the Symonds Yat Rock viewpoint. At SO 562 163, opposite the chapel, take the footpath due north towards the summit of Huntsham Hill. The summit area was favoured by the Neolithic people but is now private property with no right of access. Just before reaching the open fields on the summit, follow the trackway downhill in an easterly direction through Elliot's Wood above the Wye. On reaching the way-marked Wye Valley Walk turn left around the northern slopes of Huntsham Hill. You are now within the great loop of the Wye. Towards the northern part of the loop the Queen Stone can be seen in the middle of a cultivated field. To the east of the road which crosses the Wye at Huntsham Bridge is the site of the Huntsham Roman villa and late Iron Age enclosures. The land is regularly ploughed and there is no right of access. Continue along the Wye Valley Walk until the road is reached. Either return to the starting point along the road, or continue along The Walk on the banks of the Wye to New Weir then turn sharp left in a north easterly direction along the Forestry footpath to Symonds Yat and its hill-fort. Shorter distance approximately 2¼ miles (3.5km). Extended walk 3¼ miles (5.3km).

7. LYDBROOK AND HANGERBURY: Start the walk at Lower Lydbrook where the B4228 (Coleford to Ross road) meets the B4234. Across the river on the hill is Courtfield House, now a monastery. Henry V spent some of his childhood there. The area is also the site of the early Christian church dedicated to St.Dubricius (Dyfrig). Walk 200m up the road towards Lydbrook village and turn right into Proberts Barn Lane by The Old Post Office. This is part of a cross-Forest prehistoric route, paved in sections during the Roman period, and now a deep hollow-way as it ascends the hill. On the rocky promontory to your left, at the top of the hill, is the site of an enclosed Roman-period building. Turn left at the end of Proberts Barn Lane. You are now on an early 18th century coach road specifically constructed for coaches plying between Coleford and Ross-on-Wye, with connections to Gloucester and London. Turn left at the tiny crossroads at the northern corner of Eastbach Court onto a footpath that passes a lovely old cottage on your left. Immediately to your left on passing through the gate are the remains of a 13th/14th century yeoman's cottage which is being excavated and part-restored by Dean Archaeological Group. Follow the gradually-rising footpath up the slopes of Hangerbury Hill until the next gate is reached. Your map shows the footpath crossing the field diagonally, however, it is recommended that the right-hand hedgerow be followed around this field as it is frequently used by light aircraft to land and take off. They cannot be seen (neither can you) until the higher ground in the centre of the field is reached. At the highest point of the field there are extensive views west into Wales. Two fields south of where you stand there was a 4th century AD Roman iron-smelting site. A band of iron-ore-bearing limestone outcrops along the summit ridge. This whole area was a favoured camping site of the late-Mesolithic hunters. On the north west edge of the field at SO 596 159 there is a choice of routes to return to your starting point at Lower Lydbrook. The first takes the direct and ancient route downhill to Central Lydbrook. The alternative is to take one of the two almost parallel footpaths which run north below Hare's Grove and gradually descend the hillside. There is a Post Office in Central Lydbrook and a general stores which is open seven days a week until late evening. The Forge Hammer Inn and the Courtfield Arms are close by your starting point at Lower Lydbrook. Distance approximately 2¾ miles (4.3km).

The Severn Side Of Dean

8. OLDCROFT: This walk encompasses splendid views, a peaceful dingle, a Mesolithic hunters' camp site, a section of paved Roman road and a Roman field boundary. Start at Oldcroft SO 650 059. Take the footpath going south that climbs to the 119m contour. At the junction of footpaths, just above a spring, turn right and loop back to Plummers Brook and Tingley Wood. Cross the Brook and turn right in a northerly direction through Tingley Wood. The surface is paved in places as it approaches the road from Oldcroft to Allaston. Turn left and follow the road uphill for 250m. Take the first turn right along Soilwell Lane. This is a section of the Lydney to Ariconium Roman military road

constructed c.AD 50 at the beginning of the campaign against Caratacus. The paving and kerbing is still visible in places. An excavation by DAG in 1991 proved that beneath the left-hand hedgerow are the remains of a later Roman dry-stone-wall field boundary. The fields to the west were therefore farmed by the Romans. The fields to the east of Soilwell Lane, above the Brook, were used by the Mesolithic hunters as a camp site. Follow the lane until, after a short rise, the road is reached at Oldcroft. Turn right to return to the starting point. Distance approximately 2 miles (3.3km).

9. SOUDLEY: An ancient earthwork, a walk along a Roman road and a primitive smithing hearth are all to be seen along this charming woodland walk. Start at Soudley Camp, SO 6615 1045, by the school. This was almost certainly a pre-Roman camp but has not been excavated. Walk south and cross the road. Proceed across Soudley Bridge and follow the footpath south into the woodlands. This is the route of the same Roman road as in 8 above. Sections of the paving and kerbing are clearly visible as the footpath rises towards Bullocks Beech. The 1920s Crown Road crosses the Roman road at the top of the rise. Follow the road south towards Blackpool Bridge. If you prefer walk to the west of the road and try to trace the route of the Roman road which runs almost parallel through the woodlands. What is thought to be part of the 'The Patten Stone', which is marked on the map, is now in the Dean Heritage Centre. 'The Drummer Boy Stone', which was used as a primitive smithing hearth is by the stream at SO 65476 08980. It has an Ordnance Survey Bench Mark cut into it. Continue to Blackpool Bridge where a well-preserved section of the Roman road is exposed. It forded the brook immediately north of the 20th century bridge, but a loop of the Roman road also crossed an earlier bridge. Most of the loop is now beneath the present road. Retrace your steps, or follow map-marked forestry trackways northwards over Broom Hill and Little Middle Ridge back to Bullocks Beech and Soudley. Distance approximately 3 miles (5km).While in Soudley visit the splendid Dean Heritage Centre and Museum.

10. WELSHBURY HILL FORT AND ST.ANTHONY'S WELL, LITTLEDEAN: Start from SO 6721 1500 which is on the Littledean to Mitcheldean road, exactly 1km (almost ⅛ of a mile) from Littledean along George Lane. Turn right along the Forestry Commission track running north east towards Welshbury Wood. It is a further ¾ mile (1km) to the path leading up to the wooded hill-fort. The ramparts are the best preserved in The Forest. Return part of the way downhill from the fort then take the footpath running near north towards Shapridge. It passes below the western ramparts, then turns eastwards to join the Flaxley to Mitcheldean road (there is a shorter, steeper forestry path marked on the map which descends directly to the road). Turn left on the road to where three roads meet (the third road is the one you set out on from Littledean). At this fork in the road take the footpath that leads west past Gunns Mill (on your right) to St.Anthony's Well. This is a very ancient sacred spring but its present name is late Medieval. The location is enchanting. Ancient hollow-ways lead up to Edge Hills and part of the nearby trackway is Roman paved towards Mitcheldean. Prehistoric flint implements have been found around here, as well as Roman and Viking-period artefacts. Follow woodland trackways south from here and you will be returned to your starting point. Distance approximately 3 miles (5km). A visit to Littledean Hall with its Roman temple, museum and spectacular views across the Severn to the Cotswolds is strongly recommended.

North of Dean In West Gloucestershire

11. TAYNTON: This is a pleasant little walk on which to share some of the extensive views enjoyed by the earliest hunters in this region. Part of the route, of necessity, is along roads.

Do choose a fine, clear day. Start the walk to the west of Taynton village at SO 7270 2175. Follow the road (B4216) towards Newent in a north westerly direction, or take the slightly further footpath route east of Ryelands House towards Taynton House. The road passes over a stream and through a copse.

Continue until a road forks sharply back towards Glasshouse. Take this road for just short of 1km (a little over ½ mile) until you reach the footpath marked on the Pathfinder Series 62/72 at SO 715 220 which leads uphill just north of Home Farm to the 95m contour. At the top of the slope take the footpath that follows the right-hand boundary of the field in a southerly direction, then turn sharply eastwards along the southern boundary of the field. On a clear day you will see the Malverns to the north; Bredon Hill to the north-east; Gloucester and the Cotswolds to the east. To the west May Hill rises above the Newent Woods. Now you can see why the Mesolithic hunters chose to camp on this area. They also hunted all the surrounding fields and stream-sides. It has to be said that it was popular with the later prehistoric people too. Follow the footpath downhill until you attain the

Glasshouse to Taynton road. It is 750m back to your starting point. Distance approximately 2½ miles (4km).

12. NEWENT: This walk takes you around a deserted 2nd century AD Roman industrial site and along Roman roads. Start at SO 739 240 and take the footpath leading north west towards Newent and past Caerwents. This is a Roman period trackway and formed the eastern boundary of the industrial settlement. Proceed along it for approximately one mile (1.6km) until the outskirts of Newent are reached. Here take the footpath that leads west towards Brook Farm. The road may be followed south to Anthony's Cross, or the footpath to Moat Lodge. Return along the Roman road that runs east to west from Anthony's Cross towards Kents Green which will bring you back to your starting point. Distance approximately 3 miles (5km). A visit to ancient Newent will be rewarding while in this area. Late Saxon carved stones in the church.

North Of Dean in south Herefordshire

13. MAY HILL: The summit stands at 971 feet (296m) and the views obtained are the finest in the region. Choose a clear day so as not to be disappointed. Prehistoric people must have stood in awe of this majestic hill for, from it sprung the many streams along which they hunted. As your map will indicate, SO 69/21, there are several tracks to the summit. The shortest (and steepest) begins by May Hill Farm at SO 6910 2115. This route is also to be preferred if you like to stop and look back from time to time, for the views west into Wales are remarkably extensive. One cannot help but speculate on the possibility that the Roman commander, Ostorius Scapula, stood on the summit of this hill when he was planning his strategy against Caratacus, for the Silurian territories, west of the Wye, stretched as far as the eye can see. There was no better viewpoint from which to plan an initial Roman road network through the hills and mountains.

14. HENTLAND: This encompasses the lands granted to Saint Dubricius (Dyfrig). Start south of Hoarwithy at SO 545 291. Take the footpath that leads south west between Gwatkin's Grove and Llanfrother. Llanfrother (The Church of the Brothers) is believed by some to be the site of the seminary founded by Dubricius in the 5th/6th century. Follow the footpath through Grandoo's Coppice and Woodlands Farm to Harewood End. Turn left here along the footpath running east through Harewood End Wood. Turn left when you come to the narrow road and follow it to Kynaston Farm. At this T-junction turn left to Hentland House then keep straight on along the footpath until you reach the spinney. Here take the footpath that follows the spinney towards the Wye. It is a Roman road which now has an iron-slag surface in places. There was probably a ford over the river at this point, linking it to King's Caple. Red Rail is from Rhyd-yr-Heol (Ford of the Road). Follow the riverside road north for 800m back to your starting point. Distance approximately 5½ miles (9km). A short route taking in Llanfrother and the Roman road can be obtained by turning south at Llanfrother along the track to the spinney north of Hentland House. Distance 1¾ miles (3km).

15. KINGS CAPLE: While near Hoarwithy, inspect the church, then cross the bridge and take the first footpath on the right which runs by the riverside for a while and then turns up south east through Mayfields towards Kings Caple church. This is a most interesting and ancient church. The Roman road from the Red Rail ford passes it in an easterly direction as Caple Street. Across the road from the church is the motte of Caple Tump. Take the footpath north from the church and join the road from Pen-allt to Hoarwithy Bridge. Distance just over 2 miles (3.5km).

16. THE WELSH BICKNOR PENINSULA AND COPPET HILL: This is a splendid long-distance walk of around 6½ miles (10.5km) through the lands that were granted to St.Dubricius by King Peibio, the son of King Erb, in the 5th/6th century AD. Start from the inn at Goodrich SO 575 194. Take the lane to the south of the inn that crosses the bridge under which passes the road to Kerne Bridge. 300m south of the bridge strike up to the 188m OS Trig Point summit of Coppet Hill along the trackway indicated on the map. This is the steepest part of the whole route but the summit views are worth it. Your route is now southwards along the ridge of Coppet Hill with splendid views ahead to Huntsham Hill, Symonds Yat, the Coldwell Rocks, and for many miles on a clear day west into Wales. At Jelemy Tump a footpath should be taken that runs north east through The Green. At the beginning of Park Wood take the lower footpath that descends to a disused railway viaduct where the Wye Valley Walk is picked up to pass Welsh Bicknor church. You are now in the area where one of the earliest churches dedicated to St.Dubricius was established. Continue upstream along the Wye Valley Walk past Courtfield House in the loop of the Wye opposite Lower Lydbrook. There is a choice of return routes here. You may either follow the riverside walk back to Kerne Bridge, or take the footpath uphill past the monastery and follow it past Courtfield Farm until it picks up the road. The road, which is a pleasant walk,

may then be followed back to the inn at Goodrich through woodland above the Wye. Make sure you arrive in Goodrich at opening time.

17. 'KING ARTHUR'S CAVE': You can drive up to a small Forestry Commission car park at SO 5485 1585. Access is from Crocker's Ash just south of the Ross to Monmouth dual-carriageway. If travelling south on the dual carriageway turn off left at Whitchurch or Daff-y-Nant. If travelling north turn off left at Ganarew and double back over the bridge. Follow the lanes past Doward Farm to the above grid reference. From the car park take the footpath that runs a few metres east of the open fields in a south west direction. The Cave is about 400m from the car park along a well-walked track. The spoil heap in front of the cave resulted from excavations in the 1920s. It makes a useful elevated point from which to take photographs. Ancient hunters, and animals long extinct, like the mammoth, woolly rhino and cave bear, inhabited these caves during, and to the end of the last ice age. Those wishing to spend the day walking could descend along the same footpath to the Wye, follow the Wye Valley Walk upstream, then return along the footpath to the north of Lord's Wood. Those with a head for heights could take the short route from 'King Arthur's Cave' to the top of the sheer 'Seven Sisters Rocks', but take care, there is no safety fencing or warning of approach to the cliff edge. There are ancient churches worth a visit at Ganarew and Whitchurch. Inns at Symonds Yat west by the river, and at Whitchurch.

West of the Wye in Gwent

18. MONMOUTH AND THE KYMIN: NB Monmouth is west of the Wye, The Kymin is east of it. There are some delightful views west from the summit of the Kymin which has evidence of prehistoric occupation. It is an excellent place to view the Roman and medieval town of Monmouth (Blestium). Leave Monmouth by the Wye Bridge and take the road towards Staunton. There is a footpath that leaves the road on a bend at SO 515 126. Follow this until it joins the Kymin Road. This may be followed to the summit. To return take one of the footpaths running north towards Garth Wood then turn left downhill through the wood on the footpath that follows the cross-Forest Roman road westwards to the Kymin Road. Retrace your steps to the Wye Bridge. Distance approximately 2¾ miles (4.5km). There is nothing of Roman Monmouth to be seen above ground at the moment but watch out for a rescue excavation by the Monmouth Archaeological Society. There is usually public access and helpful explanation, and Roman levels may be discerned beneath the rich medieval levels in their excavated sections. Two fine churches in Monmouth, and Dixton church is just north of the town by the roundabout on the dual carriageway.

19. TRELLECH: SO 500 055 is a most ancient village on the Roman road from Chepstow to Monmouth. The area was inhabited during the Neolithic period and the 'Harold's Stones' may be seen alongside the road to the south of the village. There was a late Iron Age settlement at the Gaer, south west of the village, with iron-working evidence for the Roman period. An early Christian church was established here c.755. There is a Saxon font in the present church and the one in use, octagonal in shape, is reputedly early English. There is also an early preaching cross in the churchyard. Take a walk to Forestry Commission land on Beacon Hill 1km east of the village. Follow the road towards Llandogo and Tintern past Crosshands Farm. The waters of the well in the field to the left are strongly impregnated from the natural iron deposits of bog ore which occur in this area and were much sought in the past for medicinal benefits. Turn north, after 1km, along Beacon Road to the viewpoint which is just over 1,000 feet (306m) high. Return via the old Greenway Lane, or follow the footpath past Upper Barn to the village. Distance 2¾ miles (4.5km).

20. CHEPSTOW AND PIERCEFIELD: Chepstow is best known as a medieval town, however it has a very important Roman and prehistoric past that is largely unrecognised. There was a Roman bridge which carried the Newnham to Caerleon military road across the Wye. First century AD Roman pottery has recently been found in the town and Roman tiles were incorporated into the castle walls. There was an early Christian church established in Chepstow c.625. Take the Wye Valley Walk north from the Castle through Alcove Wood to Piercefield Cliffs. Trackways may be followed east to the promontory fort which faces the Spital Meend fort and the Lancaut peninsula on the other side of the Wye. Retrace your steps to Chepstow. Distance approximately 2½ miles (4km).

Local Information

Museums and Heritage Centres Open to the Public
Chepstow Town Museum.
Clearwell Caves (Ancient Iron Mines), near Coleford.
Dean Heritage Centre and Museum, Soudley, Cinderford.
Gloucester City Museum.
Hereford City Museum.
Littledean Hall (Roman Temple & Museum).
Lydney Park (Roman Temple Complex & Museum).
Monmouth Museum.
Newport (Gwent) Museum.
Puzzlewood (Landscaped Scowles), near Coleford.

Note: All of these museums display archaeological material relevant to this region. There is limited opening at Lydney Park and at some of the other visitor centres. Contact one of the local Tourist Information Centres.

The magnificent Newland Church has changing exhibitions arranged by Dean Archaeological Group and the Dean Heritage Museum (open all year).

There are Tourist Information Centres at: 27, Market Place, Coleford, Forest of Dean, Glos.(open all year).
12, Belle Vue Road, Cinderford, Forest of Dean.
Newent Library, Glos.
Church Street, Monmouth, Gwent.
20, Broad Street, Ross-on-Wye, Herefs.
and at Chepstow, Gwent.

Independent Archaeological Groups and History Societies covering this region with regular publications.
Dean Archaeological Group
Forest of Dean Local History Society
Gloucester & District Archaeological Research Group
Monmouth Archaeological Society
Woolhope Field Club: Archaeology Section (Herefs.)

For current contact person consult a local or County library.

There is a very active Ramblers Association in Dean and a Rights of Way Association.

Wyedean Archaeology and History Tours
Extended, drive/walk conducted tours of local archaeological and historical sites for large or small parties can be arranged through Wyedean Archaeology and History Tours who have several experienced guides including the author. For further information send a SAE to: Wyedean Archaeology and History Tours, c/o Thornhill Press, Unit 3, Fountain Way, Parkend, Nr.Lydney, Glos. GL15 4HJ.

References

The first reference to all authorities is shown in bold type for easy location. All subsequent references are shown as an ibid. or an op.cit.

1. **Earp JR & Hains BA, 1971,** *British Regional Geology: The Welsh Borderland,* pp.61,99-100. HMSO.
2. **Evans JG, 1975,** *The Environment of Early Man in the British Isles,* pp.71-90. Paul Elek, London.
3. **Taylor H, 1927,** *'King Arthur's' Cave,* 2nd Report. Excavations in 1926-27. Proc. of the Speleological Soc. of Bristol, Vol.3 No.2, pp.59-83.
4. **Campbell JB, 1977,** *The Upper Palaeolithic of Britain,* Vol.1, pp.44-45,146,167-169 & Vol.II, p.18. Clarendon Press, Oxford.
5. **Saville A, 1986,** Trans. BGAS, pp.229-230. Alan Saville has since reported on most of the Mesolithic material from Dean (Pers. Comm. with author 13.1.92). See also DA 2, 1989 & No.4, 1991.
6. **Hart CE, 1966,** *Royal Forest,* p.1. Clarendon Press, Oxford.6a. **Longworth IH, 1985,** *Prehistoric Britain,* p.9. British Museum Publication.
7. Saville A, 1986, op.cit. p.228-229.
8. **Clarke S, 1984,** *The Stone Age Around Monmouth,* MA 15, pp.4-5 & MA 14, p3.
9. **Stanford SC, 1980,** *The Archaeology of the Welsh Marches,* pp.42-43, Collins.
10. **George TN, 1970,** *British Regional Geology, South Wales,* 3rd Ed, pp.67-68, HMSO.
11. **Scott-Garrett C, 1955,** *Tidenham Chase Barrow,* Trans.BGAS, Vol.74, pp.15-35.
12. **Hart CE, 1967,** *Archaeology in Dean,* pp.4-5. Bellows, Gloucester.
13. **Case HJ, 1969,** *Neolithic Explanations,* Antiquity 43, pp. 176-186.
14. **Pullinger J.** Pers. Comm. with author, 20.11.1991.
15. **Walters M, 1989,** DAG Aerial Survey, 15/14, 5.9.89.
16. **Grundy GB, 1935-36,** *Saxon Charters and Field Names of Gloucestershire.* Trans.BGAS, p.241.
17. **Hart CE, 1991,** *Notes on Medieval Gloucestershire South of St.Briavels,* NR 7, FoD LHS, pp.11-12.
18. Hart CE, 1967, op.cit. p.8.
19. Clarke S, 1984, op.cit.
20. Clarke S, ibid. p.7.
21. Clarke S, ibid. p.10-11. See also MA 10, Oct.1982, p.1 for a report on the axe from English Newton.
22. **Saville A, 1987,** Glevensis 21, p.51 (Gadarg).
23. **Leach PA, 1969,** *Hereford Museum Arch. Report,* Trans.WNFC, pp.479-480.
24. **Cummins WA, 1988,** *Stone Axes as a Guide to Neolithic Communications and Boundaries in England and Wales.* Proc. Prehistoric Soc. 46, pp.45-60.
25. **Briggs CS, 1989,** *Axe-Making Traditions in Cumbrian Stone.* Arch.J. 146, pp.1-43.
26. Scott-Garrett C, 1955, op.cit.
27. **Darvill T,** *Neolithic Gloucestershire,* in Saville A (Ed), 1984, Archaeology in Gloucestershire, p.91. BGAS & Cheltenham Museum.
28. Scott-Garrett C, 1955, op.cit.
29. **Ellison A,** *Bronze Age Gloucestershire,* in Saville A (Ed) 1984, op.cit. p.117.
29a. Found by N.Webley in the 1980s.
30. **Barnett C, 1964,** *A Beaker Cist at Beachley.* The Monmouth Antiquary 1(IV), pp.112-116.
31. **Johns B, 1991,** *A Suspected Burial Mound,* NR 7, FoD LHS, pp.4-7.
32. Herefs. & Worcs. SMR Site Nos. 07133-07137.
32a. CADW SMR File No. ANC/1370 Monmouth, Gwent.
33. Tintern. CADW SMR 191, Gwent.
34. **Savory HN, 1940,** *Crick Barrow,* Archaeologia Cambrensis, pp.169-191.
35. **Hadingham E, 1974,** *Ancient Carvings in Britain,* Garnstone Press, London.
36. **Johns B, 1990,** *Cup Stones and Arrow Stones,* NR 6, FoD LHS, pp.19-25.
37. Walters B, 1985, NR 1, FoD LHS, p.31.
38. **Saville A & Roe F, 1984,** *Trans.BGAS, pp.18-19.*
39. Walters B, 1985, op.cit. p.21.
40. **Rowlands NJ, 1976,** *The Organisation of Middle Bronze Age Metalworking in Southern Britain.* BAR 31, Oxford (2 vols.)
41. **Timberlake S, 1989,** *Parys Mountain & Nantyreira, C14 Dates.* Arch. in Wales, Vol.29, pp.41-42.
42. **Lewis CA, 1989,** *Great Orme Copper Mines, Llandudno.* Arch. in Wales, Vol.29, pp.42-43.
43. **Lewis CA, 1990,** *Great Orme Copper Mines, Llandudno.* Arch. in Wales, Vol.30, p.43.
44. **Tylecote RF, 1986,** *The Prehistory of Metallurgy in the British Isles,* pp.5-42. Inst. of Metals, London.
45. Antiquaries J. 1935, Vol.15 (2), pp.196-197.
46. Hart CE, 1967, op.cit. pp.11-12.
47. Stanford SC, 1980, op.cit. p.66.
48. ibid.
49. **Evans, Sir John, 1881,** *Ancient Bronze Implements of Great Britain.* London.
50. Hart CE, 1967, op.cit. p.11.
51. **Smith C, Feb.1989,** *The Searcher,* No.42, p.35.
52. Stanford SC 1980, op.cit. p.66 & Cohen I, 1954, Trans.WNFC No. 34, pp.296-301.

53. **Walters B, 1989,** *A Survey of Prehistory in Dean.* DA 2, DAG, pp.13,27.
54. Stanford SC, 1980, op.cit. pp.62,66.
55. Saville A, 1986, Trans.BGAS, Vol.104, pp.226-228.
56. Hart CE, 1967, op.cit. p.11.
57. Hart CE, 1967, ibid. & Glos.SMR No.5140 for the urn.
58. Ellison A in Saville A, 1984, op.cit. p.119.
59. Trans. Cotteswold Naturalists Field Club, 1891 (X) p.121.
59a. Herefs. & Worcs. SMR. Site No. 06629.
60. Stanford SC, 1980, op.cit. p.64.
61. **Parry SJ & Parkhouse J, 1989,** Arch. in Wales, pp.47-48.
62. Parry SJ & Parkhouse J, 1990, ibid. pp.48-49.
63. Archaeologia Cambrensis, 1946, p.114.
64. Hart CE, 1967, op.cit. p.12.
65. **Grimes WF, 1951,** *The Prehistory of Wales,* Cardiff.
66. **Chitty LF, 1952,** *A Late Bronze Age Spear-head from the Great Doward.* Trans.WNFC (34), pp.21-23.
67. Proc. of Bristol Univ. Speleological Soc. IV, p.23 and II (1924), p.147.
68. Chitty LF, 1952, op.cit.
69. Walters B, 1989, DA 2, DAG, pp.15,28-29.
70. Walters B, 1991, DA 4, DAG.
71. Ellison A in Saville A, 1984, op.cit. pp.122-124.
72. **Evans JG, 1975,** *The Environment of Early Man in the British Isles,* pp.147-150. Paul Elek, London.
73. **Darvill T, 1987,** *Prehistoric Gloucestershire,* pp.124-125. Alan Sutton, Gloucester and Glos. County Library.
74. **Bradley R, 1979,** *The Interpretation of Later Bronze Age Metalwork from British Rivers,* pp.3-6, The International J. of Nautical Arch. and Underwater Exploration, 8.1.
75. **Hutton R, 1991,** *The Pagan Religions of the Ancient British Isles,* pp.184-192. Blackwell. See also **Merrifield R, 1987,** *The Archaeology of Ritual and Magic,* Batsford.
76. Darvill T, 1987, op.cit. pp.119-120.
77. Heighway C, *Anglo-Saxon Gloucestershire* in Saville A, 1984, op.cit. p.235.
77a. Pers. Comm. with Dr.H.Cleere, 1.11.91.
78. Tylecote RF, 1986, op.cit. pp.136-142.
79. **Megaw & Simpson (Ed.), 1981,** *Introduction to British Prehistory,* pp.337,412-413. Leics. Univ. Press.
80. **Stanford SC, 1981,** *Midsummer Hill-An Iron Age Hill Fort on the Malverns,* p.132. Leominster.
81. **Wheeler REM & TV, 1932,** *Report on the Excavation of the Prehistoric, Roman and Post-Roman Site in Lydney Park, Glos..* Report of the Research Committee of the Soc. of Antiquaries IX.
82. ibid. p.11.
83. ibid. pp.4-7,12-13,68-74.
84. **Walters B, 1992,** *Ariconium* (Monograph), DAG Occ. Pub.
85. Walters B, 1987, NR 3, pp.77-78. FoD LHS.
86. Walters B & M, 1989, DA 2, p.39. DAG.
87. Walters B, 1990, DA 3, pp.49-50. DAG.
87a. I am most grateful to Mike Hill of Cinderford who found the coin and allowed me to record and photograph it.
88. **Walters B, 1992,** *The Forest of Dean Iron Industry, 1st to 4th Centuries AD* (M.Phil thesis). DAG Occ. Pub.
89. **Parry C & Sims M, 1991,** Trans.BGAS, p.227.
90. **Leach PJ, 1969,** Trans.WNFC, pp.479-480.
91. Walters B, 1987, NR 3, p.78, Fod LHS.
92. Hart CE, 1967, op.cit. p.53.
93. Saville A, 1984, op.cit. p.165.
94. Clarke S, MA for 1981, 1983 & 1984. MAS.
95. **Nash-Williams VE, 1939,** *An Early Iron Age Coastal Camp at Sudbrook, Monmouthshire.* Archaeologia Cambrensis 94, pp.42-79.
96. **Fox C, 1931,** Archaeologia Cambrensis, p.53 & GRO, D726,III, p.38.
97. **Ormerod G, 1842.** Sketch plan in GRO, D726, p.250.
98. **Witts GB, 1883,** *Archaeological Handbook of the County of Gloucestershire,* p.14.
99. **Burrow EJ, 1919,** *The Ancient Entrenchments and Camps of Gloucestershire,* p.53.
100. **Ormerod G, 1861,** *Strigulensia,* p.4.
101. **Ormerod G. 1840.** Sketch in GRO, D726 III, p.38.
102. Hart CE, 1967, op.cit. p.21 and Plate Xb.
103. Hart CE, 1967, op.cit. p.14 and Plate IXa.
104. Pengaer is the name given to the summit of Orcop Hill on a 15th century deed. A war-time RAF photograph shows earthworks there. My thanks are due to Elizabeth Taylor of WNFC for this information which derived from her field and documentary researches (pers. comm. 7.7.90).
105. Walters B, 1989, DA 2, pp.43-44. DAG.
106. Walters B, 1985, NR 1, p.24. FoD LHS.
107. Walters B, 1992, M.Phil. thesis, op.cit.
108. Walters B, 1992, ibid. & MA for the years 1964, 1965, 1966 and 1981. MAS.
109. Walters B, 1989, DAG Newsletter for May, p.8. The site was discovered by T.James of DAG.
110. Walters M, 1990, DA 3, pp.40-44 & DA 4. DAG.
111. Walters B, 1988, DA 1, pp.3-38. DAG.
112. Walters B, 1992, M.Phil. thesis, op.cit.
113. **Walters B and Clarke S,** *Castlefield Roman Fort Excavation (forthcoming).* DAG/MAS.
114. Leach PJ, 1969, op.cit. p.480.
115. Walters B, 1987, NR 3, pp.59-60.
116. Walters B, ibid. pp.60,63.
117. Walters B, 1989, DA 2, pp.15,25 & 1990, DA 3, pp.49-50. Brooches found by D.Allen, K.Burge and M.Sterry.
118. Clarke S, 1982, MA 9, pp.1-2 plus illus. facing p.6.
119. **Ross A, 1986,** *The Pagan Celts,* pp.7-8,12. Batsford.
120. Hutton R, 1991, op.cit. p.139.
121. **Champion T, 1985,** *The Myth of Iron Age Invasions in Ireland,* in Scott BGS (Ed), Studies of Early Ireland, pp.39-44, Belfast.
122. **Jones S, 1991,** *The Reith Lectures,* from extract pub. in The Independent (5.12.91), p.18.
123. **Webster G, 1986,** *The British Celts and Their Gods Under Rome,* pp.39-40. Batsford.
124. Diodorus Siculus: History, v.29.
125. I Samuel 17:50-57.
126. **Price DJ, 1990,** NR 6, p.50, FoD LHS.
127. **Jones B & Mattingly D, 1990,** *An Atlas of Roman Britain,* pp.194-196,292-294. Blackwell, Oxford.
128. Ross A, 1986, op.cit. p.146.
129. DA 3, 1990, pp.49-50. Found by M.Hill.
130. **Webster G, 1990,** *Britannia,* Vol.XXI, pp.294-295.
131. Piggott S, 1968, *The Druids.* Thames & Hudson.
132. **Suetonius:** *The Twelve Caesars,* v.25. Trans. by Robert Graves.
133. **Tacitus:** *The Annals of Imperial Rome,* XIV. Trans. by M.Grant.
134. Ross A, 1986, op.cit. pp.25-26.
135. Strabo: IV.5,2.
136. **Cunliffe B, 1978,** *Hengistbury Head,* pp.67-75. Paul Elek.

137. Strabo: III,147 & Diodorus Siculus: *History*, v.22. See also: *Cross Channel Trade Between Gaul and Britain in the Pre-Roman Iron Age*, **1984, Ed. by Macready S & Thompson FH**, Soc. of Antiquaries, London.
138. Julius Caesar: *The Battle for Gaul*, v.20-21.
139. Cunliffe B, 1978, op.cit. p.79.
140. Stanford SC, 1980, op.cit. pp.117-122.
141. ibid. p.122 and **Stanford SC, 1970**, *Credenhill Camp*, Arch.J. (127), pp.82-129. **1974**, *Croft Ambrey*, Leominster. **1981**, *Midsummer Hill*, Leominster.
142. Darvill T, 1987, op.cit. pp.139,159-169.
142a. **Webster G, 1981,***Rome Against Caratacus*, p.14-15. Batsford.
142b. **Webster G, 1980**, *The Roman Invasion of Britain*, Batsford & **Peddie J, 1987**, *Invasion: The Roman Conquest of Britain*. Alan Sutton.
143. **Dio Cassius:** LX,19.
144. ibid. LX,20.
145. **Hart CE, 1987**, *The Regard of the FoD in 1282*. Translation, Comments & Notes, p.33. FoD LHS.
146. **Wright R, 1980**, *Secret Forest*, pp.26-27. McLean, Coleford.
147. **Ryder TA, 1950**, *Gloucestershire Through The Ages*, pp.20-21. The Worcester Press.
148. Tacitus: XII, 29-33.
149. ibid.
150. **Brayley & Britton, 1805**, *The Beauties of England and Wales*.
151. Walters B, 1992, Ariconium. DAG.
152. Walters B, 1992, FoD Iron Industry 1st to 4th Centuries AD. DAG.
153. **Webster G, 1981**, *Rome Against Caratacus*, p.116. Batsford.
154. **Garrod AP & Moss PA, 1967**, Glevensis 1, pp.6-7 (Gadarg) and 1968, Trans.WNFC, p.363.
155. Tacitus: Annals XII,33-37.
155a. Webster G, 1981, op.cit. p.55. & Manning WH, 1981, pp.40-43.
156. ibid.
157. **Margary ID, 1967**, *Roman Roads in Britain*. Constable, London. The Glos. to Mitcheldean road is listed as Route No.61.
157a. Trans.BGAS, 1978, p.84.
157b. **Kenyon R & Reece R, 1985, in Hurst HR,** *Kingsholm*, pp.22-26, Glos. Arch. Pubs.
158. FoD Newspapers for Feb.6th 1987, p.1 under *'Dean Road Dating Shock'* and Standing IJ, 1988, NR 4, pp.35-43. FoD LHS.
159. Extensive correspondence and reports, along with lab. samples and original species report now in archives of DAG.
160. Walters B, 1989, Forest & Wye Valley Review, editions of: 3.11.89; 10.11.89; 1.12.89; 29.12.89. Walters B&M, 1989, Ariconium Military Site Excavation, DA 2, p.32. DAG. Walters B, 1991, *The Forester* (FoD Newspapers) of 27.12.91. Garrod AP, 1984, *Roman Road at Mitcheldean*, p.69 (photo.), *Garrod's Gloucester*, Western Arch. Trust. Walters B, 1992, *Ariconium*, DAG.
160a Walters M, 1991, *A New Roman Coin Hoard From The Forest Of Dean: Oldcroft 2,* Dean Archaeology No.4, pp.4-15. DAG.
161. Webster G, 1981, op.cit. p.116.
161a. **Manning WH, 1981,** *Usk: The Fortress Excavations 1968-71.*Univ. of Wales Press.
162. Walters B&M, 1989, DA 2, pp.33-46. DAG.
163. Walters B, 1992, M.Phil. thesis.
163a. Pers. Comm. with Prof.P.Salway and Dr.H.Cleere.
164. Tacitus: Annals XII,33-37.
165. Webster G, 1981, op.cit. p.29.
166. **Jones GDB, 1990,** in *Trivium 25*, St.David's Univ. Coll. Lampeter.
167. Tacitus: op.cit.
168. Tacitus: op.cit. XII,38.
169. Tacitus: ibid.
170. Walters B, 1992, M.Phil. thesis.
171. **Tacitus:** *Agricola*, XIV. Trans. by H.Mattingly.
172. ibid.
173. **Webster G, 1978,** *Boudica*, pp.96-99,111-112. Batsford.
174. Walters B, 1987, NR 3, p.76 & 1988, DA 1. p.40.
175. **Bagnall-Oakley ME, 1881-82**, Trans.BGAS, pp.107-108.
176. Tacitus: Agricola, XVII.
177. **Cleere H & Crossley D, 1985,** *The Iron Industry of the Weald*, p.66. Leics. Univ. Press.
178. Suetonius: The Twelve Caesars, Vespasian XVI.
179. Walters M, 1990, DA 3, pp.40-44. DAG.
180. **Nash-Williams VE, 1939,** *Archaeologia Cambrensis* (94), pp.108-110.
181. **Walters B, 1988,** *Excavation at Glendower St. School, Monmouth*, pp.3-28. DA 1 DAG; Monmouthshire Beacon for 10.8.73 and Clarke S, 1981, MA p.2 MAS.
182. Clarke S, 1991 (March), MA pp.1-5 MAS.
182a. Pers. Comm. from S. Clarke.
183. Walters B, 1992. M.Phil. thesis; Clarke S, 1984, MA pp.2-4; 1981, p.10; 1983 (May), pp.3,7,14,17; and 1984 (Feb.) pp.2-9.
183a. **Shoesmith R, 1991,** *Excavations at Chepstow 1973-74.* Cambrian Arch. Monographs No.4. The Cambrian Arch. Association.
184. Tacitus: Agricola, 22-24.
185. ibid. 21.
186. ibid. 23-24.
187. ibid. 25.
188. **Manning WH, 1985.** Published by the British Museum.
189. **Bridgewater NP, 1965,** Trans.WNFC, pp.124-135.
190. **Tomlin R, 1990,** DA 3, p.30. DAG.
191. **Bridgewater NP, 1968,** Trans.WNFC, p.30.
192. **Wyrral G, 1877-78,** Trans.BGAS Vol.2, pp.225-226.193.
193. **Watkin WT, 1877,** *Roman Herefordshire*, p.234. Arch.J. Vol.XXXIV. and Bridgewater NP, Trans.WNFC, 1969, p.447; 1968, pp.9,30; 1970, p.75.
194. Walters B, 1990, DA 3, pp.26-29. The site was discovered by N & E Webley.
195. Walters B, 1992, M.Phil. thesis.
195a. **Gethyn-Jones E, 1991,** *Roman Dymock: A Personal Record.* Trans.BGAS, Vol. 109, pp.91-98.
196. **Walters B, 1992,** *Coleford, High Nash: Rescue Excavation.* DAG Occ. Pub.; **Hart CE, 1983,** *Coleford,* p.50. Alan Sutton; Standing IJ, 1985, NR 1 pp.37-38; 1987, NR 3 p.85.
197. Walters B, 1985, NR 1 p.36; Atkinson H, 1986, NR 2 pp.28-35.
198. **Fitchett M, 1986,** NR 2 pp.24-27. FoD LHS. Dr.C.E.Hart donated the excavation notes etc. to the GRO.
199. **Scott-Garrett C & Harris F, 1938,** Archaeolgia Cambrensis pp. 93-125; DAG Aerial Survey: 12/17-20, 18.7.89.
200. **Pullinger J, 1990,** DA 3 pp.12-25. DAG.
200a. Shoesmith R, 1991, op.cit. p.159.

201. **Bridgewater NP, 1962,** Trans.WNFC pp.179-191 and 1965, p.96; DAG Aerial Survey: 1/26, 18.6.89; 7/15-18, 2.7.89; 10/4-10, 2.7.89.
202. Clarke S, 1981, MA, p.4.
203. Walters B, 1985, NR 1, p.24 and Bagnall-Oakley ME, 1881-82, Trans.BGAS, pp.108-109.
204. Scott-Garrett C, 1956, Trans.BGAS, pp.199-202.
205. **Jack GH, 1923,** Trans.WNFC, pp.1-47.
206. **Lewis & Reinhold, 1966(Ed),** *Roman Civilisation, Sourcebook II: The Empire,* pp.178-179,188. Harper & Row, New York.
207. See Distribution Map of High Status Buildings.
208. Walters B, 1992, Thesis.
209. ibid. p.148.
210. ibid. p.143-145.
211. **Wildgoose P, 1988,** NR 4, pp.4-9. DAG.
212. Walters B, 1992, Thesis.
213. Bagnall-Oakley ME, 1881-82, op.cit. p.109.
214. **Peddie J, 1987,** *Invasion: The Roman Conquest of Britain,* pp.154-156. Alan Sutton.
215. **Webster G, 1986,** *The British Celts and their Gods Under Rome,* pp.55-56,70-71,134. Batsford.
216. **Boon G, 1987,** *The Legionary Fortress at Caerleon: Isca,* pp.35-40. Roman Legionary Museum, Caerleon.
217. Wheeler REM & TV, 1932, op.cit. pp.18-22.
218. **Fulford MG, 1991,** *Woolaston Excavation and the Chesters Villa,* Glos., Royal Arch. Inst. Newsletter & BGAS Newsletter No.28, Feb.1991: Summary Report. Also Trans.BGAS, p.236.
219. Scott-Garrett C, 1956, Trans.BGAS, pp.199-202.
220. Walters B, 1992, High Nash etc. op.cit. DAG.
221. Scott-Garrett C & Harris F, 1938, op.cit.
222. Walters B&M, 1987, NR 3 pp. 50-53.
223. Walters B, 1992, Thesis.
224. **Ammianus Marcellinus:** *The Later Roman Empire (354-378),* Book 14.5. Trans. by W.Hamilton.
225. Wheeler & Wheeler, 1932, op.cit. pp.60-61 & Walters B, 1992, Thesis.
226. **Frere S, 1978,** *Britannia,* p.404. Routledge & Kegan Paul.
227. **Birley A, 1979,** *The People of Roman Britain,* p.130. Batsford.
228. **Richardson L, 1964,** *The River Severn Between Upper Arley and Gloucester,* pp.3-4. Worcester.
229. **Atkins M, 1989,** *Excavations on Quay St. Gloucester,* pp.9-11. Glos. Exc. Unit.
230. **Stevens BJ, 1965,** *Navigation on the Wye.* Memorials of Monmouth No.5.
231. **Rev. Bathurst WMH, 1879,** Ed. by King CW, *Roman Antiquities at Lydney Park,* p.1. Longman, Green & Co. London.
232. Calendar. State Papers Domestic 29/94,100. See also Harris FH, 1945, Lydney Ships, Trans.BGAS.
233. **Fulford MG & Allen JRL, 1987,** *Romano-British Settlement & Industry on the Wetlands of the Severn.* The Antiquaries J.
234. ibid. pp.279-281. See also **Tylecote RF in Branigan K, 1977,** *Gatcombe: The Excavation and Study of a Romano-British Villa Estate,* pp.125-126. BAR 44, Oxford and **Price E.** *Excavations at Frocester* (forthcoming).
235. Hart CE, 1987, op.cit. p.52.
236. Hart CE, 1966, op.cit. pp.1-3.
237. **Nicholls HG, 1858,** *The FoD: An Historical & Decriptive Account,* p.5. John Murray,London.
238. Hart CE, 1987, op.cit. pp.27-28.
239. **Fastidius:** *de Vita Christiana,* 11 & 14.
240. **Gildas:** 21.4. Trans. by M.Winterbottom.

241. **Procopius:** *de Bello Vandalico,* i,2,38.
242. Gildas: 30.1.
243. **Sicilian Briton:** *de Divitiis:* 5 and 8.1-3.
244. **Morris J, 1973,** *The Age of Arthur,* p.46. Weidenfeld & Nicholson. Also published in 3 vols. by Phillimore & Co. of London and Chichester in 1977.
245. ibid. pp.35-36.
246. **Nennius:** 49. Trans. by J.Morris.
247. ibid. 44 and Morris J. op.cit. p.74.
248. Gildas: 19.1-4.
249. Nennius: 31.
250. Gildas: 25.3.
251. Nennius: 31. Dating the event: Readers consulting the 9th century Saxon Chronicles will note that the arrival of Hengest and Horsa is usually given as 449. The Chroniclers made use of Bede's 'History' written in 731. Bede's dating for the 5th century was based on Gildas who wrote his 'Ruin of Britain' c.540. Gildas wrongly placed the arrival of the Saxons as c.449 and his error was perpetuated. Thus, all Saxon Chronicle dates for the 5th and early 6th centuries are around 20 years too late. For a full discussion see Morris J, 1973, pp.39-41.
252. Nennius: 36,37.
253. ibid.
254. Nennius: 66.
255. Gildas: 23.5 to 25.1.
256. Gildas: 25.2,3.
257. **Sidonius:** *Epistles,* 3,9; **Jordanes:** *Getica* 45; **Mansi:** 7.941. In Gaul, Mansuetus is termed Bishop of the British in 461.
258. Nennius: 43,44.
259. ibid. 45,46.
260. ibid. 47.
261. ibid. 48.
262. **Thorpe L,** (Ed). Introduction to 1966 edition of *The History of the Kings of Britain,* p.15.Penguin.
263. **Roberts, Brynley F, 1991** in *The Arthur of the Welsh,* p.101. Ed. by Rachel Bromwich, AOH Jarman & Brynley F.Roberts. Univ. of Wales Press, Cardiff.
264. **Geoffrey of Monmouth,** *The History of the Kings of Britain,* viii, 1,2 & 8.
265. Gildas: 25.2,3 & 26.1.
266. Nennius: 56.
267. ibid.
268. Geoffrey of Monmouth, op.cit. viii, 8.
269. ibid. viii, 18.
270. Gildas: 26.2,3.
271. Nennius: 56.
272. The Mabinogion: *'Geraint, The Son of Erbin',* from 'The Red Book of Hergest'. Trans. by Lady Charlotte Guest, 1877.
273. Nennius: 68.
274. ibid. 70.
275. ibid. 72.
276. ibid. 73.
277. Wheeler & Wheeler, 1932, op.cit. pp.63-64,79-81.
278. Morris J, 1973, op.cit. p.99.
279. For a more detailed discussion see Morris J, 1973 op.cit. pp.126-132.
280. **Applebaum S, 1972,** *Roman Britain,* in HPR Finberg (Ed) *The Agrarian History of England and Wales,* vol.I,ii AD 43-1042 (Cambridge).
281. **Fenn RWD, 1968,** *Early Christianity in Herefordshire,* pp.333-347. Trans.WNFC.
281a. **Davies W, 1992,** *The Myth of the Celtic Church,* in Edwards & Lane (Ed.), *The Early Church in Wales and the West,* pp.12-21. Oxbow Monograph 16, Oxford.

282. See **Davies W, 1978,** *An Early Welsh Microcosm: Studies in the Llandaff Charters*, London, and: Davies W, 1979, *The Llandaff Charters*, Aberystwyth. Compare with Morris J, 1973, op.cit. pp.356-370; Fenn RWD, 1968, op.cit. pp.333-347, and many others.

283. **Gregory of Tours:** *Historia Francorum I.*

284. Geoffrey of Monmouth op.cit. IX.1.

285. **Liber Landavensis** trans. **Rees WJ, 1840,** Sec.2 Ch.2:2. *The Life of Dubricius.*

286. ibid.

287. Davies W, 1978, op.cit. pp.17,62,63,93,134.

288. *Liber Landavensis* 6:4.

288a. Davies W, 1978, p.166.289. ibid. *Life of Teilo* 3:1.

289a. See Morris J, 1973, op.cit. pp.458-459 & 363 plus footnote 458.5 *Life of Winwaloe*, died c.583.

289b. **Bowen EG, 1977 Edn.,** *Saints, Seaways and Settlements in the Celtic Lands*, pp. 69-72, 169-171. Univ. of Wales Press. See also **De la Borderie, 1887,** *Histoire de Bretagne*, Paris.

289c. **Edwards N & Lane A, 1992,** *The Archaeology of the Early Church in Wales: An Introduction, in The Early Church in Wales and the West*, p.2. Oxbow Monograph 16, Oxford.

290. *Anglo-Saxon Chronicles* for the year 577. Trans. by A.Savage.

291. ibid. for year 597, and *Liber Landavensis*, Ch.4 Sec.3.

292. Illustrated in Hart CE, 1967, op.cit. Plate XXc. See also p.49.

293. *Liber Landavensis*, 4:11.

293a. **Parry C, 1990,** *A Survey of St.James's Church, Lancaut, Gloucestershire.* Trans.BGAS, Vol.108, pp.53-103.

294. See Davies W, 1978, pp.29,47,124,135.

295. *Anglo-Saxon Chronicles* for 628.

295a. British Museum Add. MS 34,633. British Museum Harley MS 3271 f6v. Birch, 297. Transcript by R.H.Hodgkin, 1952, *History of the Anglo-Saxons*, II. HPR Finberg, 1961, *Early Charters of the West Midlands*, p.234. See also Hillaby J, 1978, *Origins of the Diocese of Hereford*, Trans.WNFC Part 1, pp.16-52.

296. Heighway C, 1987, *Anglo-Saxon Gloucestershire*, p.39. Alan Sutton & Glos. County Library.

297. Fenn RWD, 1968, op.cit. p.339.

298. GRO D6177/1/2.

299. **Copley G, 1986,** *Archaeology and Place-Names in the Fifth and Sixth Centuries*, pp.120,125. BAR 147, Oxford. An alternative is the OE 'dune', down, i.e. the 'down-river' people.

299a. See Davies W, 1978. Cadoc: **Gale D,** *Monasticon IV*, p.595. See also **Kissack K, 1974,** *Medieval Monmouth*, p.12. Monmouth Historical & Educational Trust.

300. **Noble F, 1983,** *Offa's Dyke Reviewed*, (Ed) M. Gelling. BAR 114, Oxford.

301. Hart CE, 1967, op.cit. p.49.

302. **Finberg HPR, 1957,** *Gloucestershire Studies*, pp.2-3.

303. *Anglo-Saxon Chronicles* for the year 914.

304. Heighway C, 1987, op.cit. p.72.

305. *The Chronicles of Florence of Worcester*, p.75 (year 915). Translation by Joseph Stephenson, 1853. Facsimile edition published by Llanerch Enterprises, Felinfach, Lampeter.

306. Found by D.Allen of DAG in the 1980s.

307. Found by M.Hill of DAG in the 1980s.

308. Found by M.Hill of DAG, and submitted to the British Museum for identification.

309. See **Whitelock D, 1952,** *The Beginnings of English History*, p.238. Pelican. Also: **Richards JD, 1991,** *Viking Age England*, pp.81-82. Batsford.

309a. My thanks to Brian Johns for sharing with me the results of his research which re-discovered this spear which is not labelled with its find location in the Gloucester City Museum. I wish to acknowledge further information from Malcolm J.Watkins, the Archaeology Director of the Museum. My thanks to W.J.Laughlin (Archaeological Illustrator) and to Gloucester City Council Museum, Archaeology Unit, for permission to reproduce the illustration of the spear.

310. Davies W, 1978, op.cit. pp.136-137. Llangynfyl: David Hancocks of DAG and MAS is currently carrying out documentary and archaeological field work in order to determine the sitings of early Lower Monnow Valley churches. I am most grateful to him for allowing me to study his interim papers, and for generously sharing with me his accumulated knowledge. St.Arvans stone illustration from Nash-Williams VE, 1939, Antiq. J. xix, pp.150-152.

310a. **Thomas C, 1971,** *The Early Christian of North Britain, Oxford.* **Brook DL, 1981,** *Early Ecclesiastical Sites in South-East Wales.* MA thesis, Cardiff. Brook DL, 1985-1988, *The Early Christian Church in Gwent*, Proc. Monmouthshire Antiquarian Association, Vol.V Part 3, pp. 67-84. **Brook D, 1992,** *The Early Christian Church East and West of Offa's Dyke*, in *The Archaeology of the Early Church in Wales*,pp.77-89. Oxbow Monograph 16, Oxford.

311. MSS 383 in Corpus Christi, Cambridge. Translation of text in Noble, op.cit. pp.103-109. I am also most grateful to Elizabeth Taylor for allowing me access to a translation she had personally commissioned, and for her observations on it.

312. Elizabeth Taylor suggests that 'established' would be better translated as 'imposed'.

313. Elizabeth Taylor felt that 'belonged to the Dunsaete' might make more sense if translated as 'with the Dunsaete'.

314. Noble F, op.cit. p.11.

315. ibid. p.17.

316. From an earlier paper of F.Noble dated 17.2.69 and kindly facilitated by E.Taylor.

316a. **Clark A, 1962,** *The Story of Monmouthshire*, Vol.1, p.45. Christopher Davies.

317. **Grundy GB, 1935-36,** *Saxon Charters and Field Names of Gloucestershire*, p.241. Trans.BGAS.

318. See **CE Hart, 1991:** *Notes on Medieval Gloucestershire South of St.Briavels, part 1: Ancient Tidenham and its Neighbours*, pp.11-15 for a list of original MS sources and more detailed information. NR 7, FoD LHS.

319. The coins, in private hands, have been viewed by members of MAS and DAG, but, up to the time of writing of this book, this very important coin group had not been made available for official identification and cataloguing.

320. Florence of Worcester, op.cit. p.115 (year 1041).

320a. ibid. for year 1049. See also Clark A, 1962, op. cit. p.47.

320b. **Dobson DP,** *Anglo-Saxon Buildings and Sculptures*, Trans.BGAS, Vol.53., and **Zarnecki G,** *The Newent Funerary Tablet*, Trans.BGAS, Vol.72.

321. **Hart CE, 1989,** *Aluredstone of Domesday*, pp.18-23. NR 5, FoD LHS.

322. All these people are confirmed as holding land in Dean and west Gloucestershire during the years leading up to 1066. They are as recorded in the *Domesday Book for Gloucestershire,* edited and translated by **John S.Moore** and published by Phillimore in 1982.

323. *Thorn F&C,* Translators: *Herefordshire Domesday Survey.* Phillimore.

324. I am very grateful to Jill David of DAG who researched the parish of Awre from the Tithe Maps and Apportionments of 1840 and provided a considerable number of field names that have proved to have archaeological associations.

325. *Liber Landavensis* VII.7 (201). Translation by **J.Gwenogvryn Evans and J.Rhys,** 1893.

326. ibid. VII.8 (Evans 202).

327. Evans JG, ibid. 204b and 203a.

328. ibid. 185.

329. Hart CE, 1991, pp.12-13. NR 7, FoD LHS.

329a. **Hooke D, 1990,** *The Anglo-Saxon Landscape in North Gloucestershire.* The Seventh Deerhurst Lecture, 8th Sept.1990.

330. **Clarke S, 1992** (forthcoming). I am grateful to Stephen Clarke for allowing me to read his paper: *'The Origins of Medieval Pottery in South-East Wales',* and for confirming my own feelings that this area was probably aceramic until after the Norman Conquest.

331. I am grateful to Keith Burge of DAG who found these artefacts and allowed me to record them; also to Neil Giles of Littledean who drew them and gave permission for publication.

Index